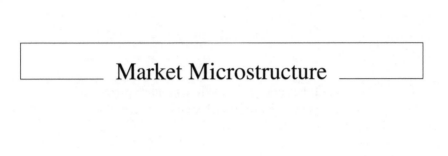

Market Microstructure

For other titles in the Wiley Finance series
please see www.wiley.com/finance

Market Microstructure

Confronting Many Viewpoints

Edited by

Frédéric Abergel
Jean-Philippe Bouchaud
Thierry Foucault
Charles-Albert Lehalle
Mathieu Rosenbaum

A John Wiley & Sons, Ltd., Publication

Library of Congress Cataloging-in-Publication Data:

Market microstructure : confronting many viewpoints / edited by Frédéric Abergel ... [et al.].
    p. cm. – (The Wiley finance series)
  Includes bibliographical references and index.
  ISBN 978-1-119-95277-0 (cloth)
  1. Securities.   2. Securities – Prices.   3. Stock exchanges.   4. Microfinance.   I. Abergel,
Frédéric.
  HG4521.M319 2012
  332.64′2 – dc23   2012002916

A catalogue record for this book is available from the British Library.

ISBN 978-1-119-95241-1 (hardback) ISBN 978-1-119-95277-0 (ebk)
ISBN 978-1-119-95278-7 (ebk)   ISBN 978-1-119-95279-4 (ebk)

Cover images reproduced by permission of Shutterstock.com
Set in 11/13pt Times by Aptara Inc., New Delhi, India
Printed and bound by TJ International Ltd, Padstow, Cornwall, UK

Contents

Introduction

The accumulation of high frequency market data in recent years has revealed many surprising results. These results are interesting both from theoretical and practical standpoints. The mechanism of price formation is at the very heart of economics; it is also of paramount importance to understand the origin of the well-known anomalous 'stylized facts' in financial price series (heavy tails, volatility clustering, etc.). These issues are of obvious importance for practical purposes (organisation of markets, execution costs, price impact, etc.). This activity is also crucial to help the regulators, concerned with the organisation of liquidity in electronic markets and the issues raised by 'high frequency trading'.

Correspondingly, this problem has been vigorously investigated by at least five different communities (economics, financial mathematics, econometrics, computer science and econo-physics), scattered in academic institutions, banks and hedge funds, with at present limited overlap and sometimes lack of visibility. On the other hand, due to the gigantic amount of available data, precise quantitative theories can now be accurately tested.

At the time where this conference series started in 2010, the interest for market microstructure had finally reached a stage where the interest for the theoretical breakthroughs of the pioneers in the field had become comparable to its practical importance for market practitioners. Thanks to the development of high frequency trading, market microstructure is now, not only a subject of theoretical modelling and simulation but, more interestingly maybe, a real practical field where a better model can make a big difference.

The organisers of the conference thought that it would be extremely fruitful to confront the ideas that have blossomed in those different communities in the past decade. In order to foster this confrontation and ease communication, we have gathered researchers from these different communities, including professionals, and ask them to give introductory tutorials, reviewing both their recent activity and the problems that, in their eyes, are most relevant to address in the near future.

Our aim in setting up this friendly, knowledge-oriented confrontation has been to examine and compare possibly very different views on the nature of the mechanisms relevant to describe and understand what one can actually observe when scrutinising the tick-by-tick behaviour of markets. Such important questions as the interplay between liquidity taking and providing, the existence and characterisation of various types of market impact, the statistical tools designed to handle well the 'tick' effect, the 'best-execution' and other algorithmic trading strategies, or the question of market design and organisation ... have been studied in-depth by the speakers at the conference, and their contributions to this present volume will help shed a new light, or, rather, new lights, on the market microstructure viewed as an object for scientific study as well as a wealth of information for price discovery and trading.

Frédéric Abergel
Jean-Philippe Bouchaud
Thierry Foucault
Charles-Albert Lehalle and
Mathieu Rosenbaum

About the Editors

Frédéric Abergel
After graduating from École Normale Supérieure in 1985 and completing a PhD in Mathematics in 1986, Frédéric Abergel started an academic career as a researcher with the CNRS. He spent ten years in the Mathematics Department of the University of Orsay Paris XI, where he obtained his habilitation degree in 1992. He then switched to the capital markets industry and became a 'quant' (quantitative analyst). During the second part of his career, Frédéric Abergel has worked for trading floors in various financial institutions, mainly in the derivatives sector, developing pricing and hedging models. In July 2007, he decided to return to Academia, where he now holds the BNP Paribas Chair of Quantitative Finance at École Centrale Paris. His research focuses on the study of empirical properties and mathematical model of market microstructure, high frequency data and algorithmic trading.

Jean-Philippe Bouchaud
Jean-Philippe Bouchaud graduated from the École Normale Supérieure in Paris, where he also obtained his PhD in physics. He was then appointed by the CNRS until 1992. After a year spent in the Cavendish Laboratory (Cambridge), he joined the Service de Physique de l'État Condensé (CEA-Saclay), where he worked on the dynamics of glassy systems and on granular media. He became interested in economics and theoretical finance in 1991. His work in finance includes extreme risk models, agent based simulations, market microstructure and price formation. He has been very critical about the standard concepts and models used in economics and in the financial industry (market efficiency, Black-Scholes models, etc.) He founded the company Science &

Finance in 1994 that merged with Capital Fund Management (CFM) in 2000. He is now the President and Head of Research at CFM and professor at Ecole Polytechnique since 2008. He was awarded the IBM young scientist prize in 1990 and the C.N.R.S. Silver Medal in 1996. He has published over 250 scientific papers and several books in physics and in finance.

Thierry Foucault

Thierry Foucault is Professor of Finance at HEC, Paris, where he received his PhD in Finance in 1994. He is a research fellow of the Centre for Economic Policy (CEPR). He has taught in various institutions such as Carnegie Mellon University, the École Polytechnique Fédérale de Lausanne, Oxford (Said Business School), Pompeu Fabra University (Spain), the Tinbergen Institute and the School of Banking and Finance at UNSW. His research focuses on the determinants of financial markets liquidity and the industrial organisation of the securities industry. His work has been published in top-tier scientific journals, including *The Journal of Finance*, *The Journal of Financial Economics* and *The Review of Financial Studies*. He serves on the scientific committees of the Autorité des Marchés Financiers, the Research Foundation of the Banque de France, the Group of Economic Advisors of the Committee of Economic and Markets Analysis of the European Securities and Markets Authority (ESMA) and on the executive committee of the European Finance Association (EFA). He acts as co-editor of the Review of Finance since 2009 and is an Associate Editor of *The Review of Asset Pricing Studies*. For his research, he received awards from the Europlace Institute of Finance in 2005 and 2009, the annual research prize of the HEC Foundation in 2006 and 2009, and the Analysis Group award for the best paper on Financial Markets and Institutions presented at the 2009 Western Finance Association meetings.

Charles-Albert Lehalle

Currently Head of Quantitative Research at CA Cheuvreux, Charles-Albert Lehalle is an international expert in optimal trading. He published papers in international journals about the use of stochastic control and stochastic algorithms to optimise a trading flow with respect to flexible contraints. He also authored papers on post-trade analysis, market impact estimates and modelling the dynamics of limit order books. Charles-Albert Lehalle lectures at 'Paris 6 (El Karoui) Master of Finance' (École Polytechnique, ESSEC, École Normale Supérieure) and

MASEF/ENSAE, and gives master classes in the Certificate in Quantitative Finance in London. With a PhD in applied mathematics, his core fields are stochastic processes, information theory and nonlinear control.

Mathieu Rosenbaum

Mathieu Rosenbaum obtained his PhD from Université Paris-Est in 2007. He is now Professor at Université Pierre et Marie Curie (Paris 6) and École Polytechnique and is a member of the CREST (Center of Research in Economics and Statistics). His research mainly focuses on statistical finance problems, such as market microstructure modeling or designing statistical procedures for high frequency data. Also, he has research collaborations with several financial institutions, in particular BNP-Paribas since 2004.

Part I
Economic Microstructure
Theory

1

Algorithmic Trading: Issues and Preliminary Evidence

Thierry Foucault

1.1 INTRODUCTION

In 1971, while the organization of trading on the NYSE had not changed much since its creation in 1792, Fischer Black (1971) was asking whether trading could be automated and whether the specialist's judgement could be replaced by that of a computer (the specialist is a market-maker designated to post bid and ask quotes for stocks listed on the NYSE). Forty years later, market forces have given a positive reponse to these questions.

Computerization of trading in financial markets began in the early 1970s with the introduction of the NYSE's "designated order turnaround" (DOT) system that routed orders electronically to the floor of the NYSE. It was then followed with the development of program trading, the automation of index arbitrage in the 1980s, and the introduction of fully computerized matching engines (e.g., the CAC trading system in France in 1986 or the Electronic Communication Networks in the US in the 1990s). In recent years, this evolution accelerated with traders using computers to implement a wide variety of trading strategies, e.g., market-making, at a very fine time scale (the millisecond).

The growing importance of these "high frequency traders" (HFTs) has raised various questions about the effects of algorithmic trading on financial markets. These questions are hotly debated among practitioners, regulators, and in the media. There is no agreement on the

Market Microstructure: Confronting Many Viewpoints. Edited by F. Abergel, J.-P. Bouchaud,
T. Foucault, C.-A. Lehalle and M. Rosenbaum.
© 2012 John Wiley & Sons, Ltd.

effects of HFTs.[1] As an example consider these rather opposite views of the HFTs' role by two Princeton economists, Paul Krugman and Burton Malkiel. Krugman has a rather dim view of HFTs:

> High-frequency trading probably degrades the stock market's function, because it's a kind of tax on investors who lack access to those superfast computers – which means that the money Goldman spends on those computers has a negative effect on national wealth. As the great Stanford economist Kenneth Arrow put it in 1973, speculation based on private information imposes a "double social loss": it uses up resources and undermines markets. (Paul Krugman, "Rewarding Bad Actors", *New York Times*, 2 August 2009).

In contrast, for Malkiel, high frequency traders have a more positive function:

> In their quest to find trading profits, competition among high-frequency traders also serves to tighten bid-offer spreads, reducing transactions costs for all market participants, both institutional and retail. Rather than harming long-term investors, high-frequency trading reduces spreads, provides price discovery, increases liquidity and makes the market a fairer place to do business. (Burton Malkiel, "High Frequency Trading is a Natural Part of Trading Evolution", *Financial Times*, 14 December 2010).

Concerns have also been voiced that HFTs could manipulate markets to their advantage, exacerbate market volatility and that high frequency trading could be a new source of fragility and systemic risk for the financial system. In particular, some have suggested that HFTs may have been responsible for the flash crash of 6 May 2010.

Not surprisingly, given these concerns and lack of consensus on the exact role of algorithmic traders, debates are now raging about whether actions should be taken to regulate algorithmic trading. A (certainly incomplete) list of questions raised in these debates is as follows (see SEC, 2010, Section IV, or CESR, 2010a and 2010b):

1. *Liquidity.* What is the effect of algorithmic trading on market liquidity? Is liquidity more likely to evaporate in turbulent times when it is provided by HFTs?

---

[1] Although algorithmic trading is not a new phenomenon, algorithmic trading, especially high frequency trading, went to the forefront of policy debates in recent years. A search on articles from newspapers, magazines, academic journals, trade publications, etc., containing the words "algorithmic trading" on EBSCO yields 2502 hits over the period 2005–2011 and only 329 over the period 1999–2004.

2. *Volatility*. Do algorithmic traders dampen or exacerbate price volatility?
3. *Price discovery*. Does algorithmic trading make prices closer to fundamental values?
4. *Distributional issues*. Do "fast traders" (HFTs) make profits at the expense of "slow" traders (long-term investors, traditional market-makers, etc.)? Or can fast trading benefit all investors?
5. *Systemic risk*. Does algorithmic trading increase the risk of market crashes and contagion? Does it make securities markets more fragile? Does it increase the risk of evaporation of liquidity in periods of crisis?
6. *Manipulation*. Are securities markets more prone to price manipulation with the advent of algorithmic trading?
7. *Market organization*. What are the effects of differentiating trading fees between fast and slow traders or between investors submitting limit orders and those submitting market orders?[2] Should exchanges be allowed to sell ticker tape information? Should there be "speed limits" in electronic trading platforms? etc.

The goal of this report is to discuss some of these issues in the light of recent empirical findings. In Section 1.2, I first define more precisely what algorithmic trading is while in Section 1.3, I describe the close relationships between changes in market structures and the evolution of algorithmic trading. Section 1.4 describes possible costs and benefits of algorithmic trading while Section 1.5 reviews recent empirical findings regarding the effects of algorithmic trading.

Throughout this report I use results from various empirical studies. There are as yet relatively few empirical studies on algorithmic trading (especially high frequency trading) as it is a relatively new phenomenon and data identifying trades by algorithmic traders are very scarce. Consequently, one must be careful not to generalize the results of these studies too hastily: they may be specific to the sample period, the asset class, the identification method used for the trades of algorithmic traders, and the type of algorithmic trading strategy considered in these studies. For this reason, in Table 1.1 (in the Appendix), I give, for each empirical study mentioned in this article, the sample period, the type

---

[2] A limit order is an order to buy or sell a given number of shares at a pre-specified price. Typically, these orders cannot be executed upon submission as their price usually does not match the price requested by other traders in the market. In this case, limit orders are stored in a limit order book, waiting for future execution. A market order is an order to buy or sell a given number of shares at any price. It is therefore immediately executed against posted limit orders, if any.

of asset considered in the study, and whether the study uses direct data on trades by algorithmic traders or has to infer these trades from more aggregated data.

1.2   WHAT IS ALGORITHMIC TRADING?

1.2.1   Definition and typology

Algorithmic trading consists in using computer programs to implement investment and trading strategies.[3] The effects of algorithmic trading on market quality are likely to depend on the nature of the trading strategies coded by algorithms rather than the automation of these strategies in itself. It is therefore important to describe in more detail the trading strategies used by algorithmic traders, with the caveat that such a description is difficult since these strategies are not yet well known and understood (see SEC, 2010).

Hasbrouck and Saar (2010) offer a useful classification of algorithmic traders based on the distinction between Agency Algorithms (AA) and Proprietary Algorithms (PA).

Agency Algorithms are used by brokers or investors to rebalance their portfolios at the lowest possible trading costs. Consider, for instance, a mutual fund that wishes to sell a large position in a stock. To mitigate its impact on market prices, the fund's trading desk will typically split the order in "space" (i.e., across trading platforms where the stock is traded) and over time, in which case the trading desk has to specify the speed at which it will execute the order. The fund can also choose to submit a combination of limit orders and market orders, access "lit" markets or dark pools, etc. The fund manager's objective is to minimize its impact on prices relative to a pre-specified benchmark (e.g., the price when the manager made his portfolio rebalancing decision). The optimal trading strategy depends on market conditions (e.g., the prices standing in the different markets, the volatility of the stock, the persistence of price impact, etc.), and the manager's horizon (the deadline by which its order must be executed).[4]

---

[3] As mentioned in the introduction, algorithmic trading is not a new phenomenon. "Program trading" was developed in the 1980s as an automated strategy to hedge a large basket of stocks. Some hedge funds (e.g., "stat arbs") have also been using highly automated strategies for a long time. What is novel is the frequency at which computers are used for trading decisions. As explained below, some investors now use computers to place orders at the super high frequency (e.g., the millisecond).

[4] See Bertsimas and Lo (1998) and Huberman and Stanzl (2005) for formulations and analyses of this optimization problem.

The implementation of this strategy is increasingly automated: that is, computers solve in real-time for the optimal trading strategy and take the actions that this strategy dictates. The software and algorithms solving these optimization problems are developed by Quants and sold by brokers or software developers to the buy-side.

Proprietary Algorithms are used by banks' proprietary trading desks, hedge funds (e.g., Citadel, Renaissance, D.E. Shaw, SAC, etc.), proprietary trading firms (GETCO, Tradebot, IMC, Optiver, Sun Trading, QuantLab, Tibra, etc.), or even individual traders for roughly two types of activities: (i) electronic market-making and (ii) arbitrage or statistical arbitrage trading.

As traditional dealers, electronic market-makers post bid and ask prices at which they are willing to buy and sell a security and they accommodate transient imbalances due to temporary mismatches in the arrival rates of buy and sell orders from other investors. They make profits by earning the bid-ask spread while limiting their exposure to fluctuations in the value of their positions ("inventory risk").

In contrast to traditional dealers, electronic market-makers use highly computerized trading strategies to post quotes and to enter or exit their positions in multiple securities at the same time. They also hold relatively small positions that they keep for a very short period of time (e.g., Kirilenko *et al.*, 2010, find that high frequency traders in their study reduce half of their net holdings in about two minutes on average). Moreover, they typically do not carry inventory positions overnight (see Menkveld, 2011). In this way, electronic market-makers achieve smaller intermediation costs and can therefore post more competitive bid-ask spreads than "bricks and mortar" market-makers. For instance, they considerably reduce their exposure to inventory risk by keeping positions for a very short period of time and by acting in multiple securities (which better diversify inventory risk over multiple securities). Moreover, as explained in Section 1.5.2, by reacting more quickly to market events, electronic market-makers better manage their exposure to the risk of being picked off, thereby decreasing the adverse selection cost inherent to the market-making activity (Glosten and Milgrom, 1985).

Arbitrageurs use algorithms to analyze market data (past prices, current quotes, news, etc.) to identify price discrepancies or trading patterns that can be exploited at a profit. For instance, when a security trades in multiple platforms, its ask price on one platform may be smaller than its bid price on another platform (market participants call such an occurrence a "crossed market"). Such an arbitrage opportunity never lasts long and the corresponding arbitrage strategy can be easily automated.[5] Triangular arbitrage in currency markets and index arbitrage are other types of trading strategies that can be coded with algorithms.[6]

Statistical arbitrageurs ("stat arbs") use trading strategies whose payoffs are more uncertain. For instance, a large buyer may leave footprints in order flow data (trades and price movements). Traders with the computational power to detect these footprints can then forecast short-term future price movements and take speculative positions based on these forecasts. Similarly, imbalances between the arrival rates of buy and sell orders can create transient deviations from fundamental values in illiquid markets. For instance, a streak of buy market orders in a security will tend to push its price up relative to its fundamental value. When this buying pressure stops, the price eventually reverts to its long run value. Hence, one strategy consists in selling securities that experience large price increases and buying securities that experience large price decreases, betting on a reversal of these price movements.[7] This type of strategy is automated as it is typically implemented for a large number of securities simultaneously. Moreover, if implemented at the high frequency, it requires acting very quickly on recent price evolutions. The SEC (2010) refers to these strategies as "directional strategies" as they consist in taking a speculative position based on the perception that prices differ from the fundamental value and will tend to revert toward this value.[8]

Investors using Agency Algorithms and those using Proprietary Algorithms do not operate at the same speed. A very quick reaction to changes in market conditions (for instance a change in the limit order book or a trade in one security) is critical for electronic market-makers and arbitrageurs, as they often attempt to exploit fleeting profit

---

[5] Sorkenmaier and Wagener (2011) report the duration of crossed quotes for stock constituents of the FTSE 100 and traded on the LSE, Chi-X, BATS, and Turquoise. They found that this duration was 16 minutes in April/May 2009 but only 19.8 seconds in April/May 2010. This dramatic decline is most likely due to an intensification of automated arbitrage between these markets.

[6] Triangular arbitrage consists in buying and selling simultaneously the same currency against another currency in two different ways (directly and indirectly through a third currency) so as to capture any price discrepancy between the purchase price and the sale price. Kozhan and Tham (2010) found occurrences of triangular arbitrage opportunities but they are very short lived (on average they lasted 1.37 seconds in their sample).

[7] This contrarian strategy is well known and can be implemented at various frequencies (see Khandani and Lo, 2011).

[8] Another strategy consists in using newsreader algorithms, which use statistical analysis and text analysis methods to process news and take positions based on the news.

opportunities with a "winner takes it all" flavor. For instance, a brochure from IBM describes algorithmic trading as

> The ability to reduce latency (the time it takes to react to changes in the market [. . .] to an absolute minimum. Speed is an advantage [. . .] because usually the first mover gets the best price) (see "Tackling Latency: The Algorithmic Arms Race", IBM, 2008).

As an example, consider, for instance, an electronic market-maker in a stock and suppose that a large market order arrives, consuming the liquidity available in the limit order book for this stock. As a result the bid-ask spread for the stock widens momentarily (see Biais *et al.*, 1995, for evidence on this type of pattern). This increase creates a profit opportunity for market-makers who can then post new limit orders within the bid-ask spread. First-movers have an advantage as their orders (if aggressively priced) will have time priority for the execution of the next incoming market order.[9]

As computers can be much quicker than humans in reacting to market events or news, the interval of time between orders submitted by Proprietary Algorithms can be extremely short (e.g., one millisecond). For this reason traders using Proprietary Algorithms (electronic market-makers or statistical arbitrageurs) are often referred to as high frequency traders (HFTs). In contrast, buy-side investors using Agency Algorithms make their decisions at a lower frequency. Hence, HFTs can enter more than thousands of orders per second while traders using Agency Algorithms will enter only a few orders per minute.[10]

Another difference between electronic market-makers and Agency Algorithms is that the latter are used by brokers who need to execute orders from their clients by a fixed deadline. Hence, traders using

---

[9] Similarly, they can be a first mover advantage for traders who can quickly submit market orders when bid-ask spreads are tight. Garvey and Wu (2010) found that traders who get quicker access to the NYSE because of their geographical proximity to the NYSE pay smaller average effective spreads.

[10] There is not yet a well-accepted definition of high frequency traders. A report by the SEC defines them as proprietary trading firms characterized by

> (1) the use of extraordinarily high-speed and sophisticated computer programs for generating, routing, and executing orders; (2) use of co-location services and individual data feeds offered by exchanges and others to minimize network and other types of latencies; (3) very short time-frames for establishing and liquidating positions; (4) the submission of numerous orders that are cancelled shortly after submission; and (5) ending the trading day in as close to a flat position as possible (that is, not carrying significant, unhedged positions over-night) (see SEC, 2010, p. 45).

Agency Algorithms are more "impatient" and more likely to use market orders (demand market liquidity) than limit orders (provide liquidity). In contrast, electronic market-makers are more likely to use limit orders. For instance, Kirilenko *et al.* (2010) find that 78 % of HFTs orders in their sample (trades in the E-mini futures S&P500) provide liquidity through limit orders while Broogard (2010) finds that HFTs' in his sample provide (respectively demand) liquidity in 48.65 % (43.64 %) of the trades in which they participate. Jovanovic and Menkveld (2011) study one electronic market-maker in Dutch stock constituents of the Dutch stock index. They find that this market-maker is on the passive side of the transaction in about 78 % (respectively 74 %) of the transactions on which he is involved on Chi-X (respectively Euronext).[11]

As speed is of paramount importance for HFTs, they seek to reduce *latency*, i.e., the time it takes for them to (i) receive information from trading venues (on execution of their orders, change in quotes in these markets, etc.), (ii) process this information and make a trading decision, and (iii) send the resulting order to a platform (a new quote, a cancellation, etc.). Latency is in part determined by the HFTs computing power (which explains the massive investment of HFTs in computing technologies) and trading platform technologies.[12] Trading platforms have struggled to reduce latencies to a minimum and they now offer *co-location* services; i.e., they rent rack space so that HFTs can position their servers in close proximity to platform matching engines.

As mentioned in the introduction, there is a concern that some HFTs may use their fast access to the market to engage in market manipulation. For instance, the SEC (2010) describes two types of strategies that could be seen as manipulative (see SEC, 2010, Section IV-B). The first, called by the SEC "order anticipation", consists for a proprietary trading firm to (i) infer the existence of a large buy or sell order, (ii) trade ahead this order, and (iii) provide liquidity at an advantageous price to the large order. This strategy (a form of front-running) can potentially raise the trading cost for long-term investors seeking to trade large quantities.

---

[11] Trading platforms distinguish two sides in each transaction: the active side that initiates the transaction by submitting a market order and the passive side that acts as the counterparty to the active side (with a limit order).

[12] Trading platforms define latency as the communication time between a trader's server and the platform (e.g., the time for the platform to acknowledge reception of an order submitted by the trader). This delay is just one component of the relevant latency for traders, which are also concerned by the speed at which they can process and react to information received from trading platforms.

The second strategy, called by the SEC "momentum ignition strategy" consists in submitting aggressive orders to spark a price movement in the hope that other algorithms will wrongly jump on the bandwagon and amplify the movement.

1.2.2   Scope and profitability

It is difficult to obtain measures of algorithmic traders' share of trading activity. Existing figures are provided mainly for high frequency traders.[13] HFTs are present globally and in various asset classes (equities, derivatives, currencies, commodities). There are about 15 major HFTs in US equities markets, including GETCO, Automated Trading Desk (ATD), Tradebot, Optiver, SunTrading, QuantLab, Wolverine, etc. Many of these firms are also active in Europe. Overall the total number of high frequency trading firms seems quite small relative to their share of total trading activity (see below), which suggests that these firms may, for the moment, enjoy significant market power.

A few academic studies have direct data on the trades of high frequency traders in various markets over various periods of time (see Table 1.1 in the Appendix). They confirm the importance of high frequency trading. For instance, using Nasdaq data for 120 stocks, Brogaard (2010) found that 26 HFTs participate in 68.5 % of the dollar volume traded on average and accounted for a larger fraction of the trading volume in large capitalization stocks than in small capitalization stocks. Jovanovic and Menkveld (2011) studied one electronic market-maker in Dutch stock constituents of the Dutch stock index. They found that this market-maker is active in about 35 % (7 %) of all trades on Chi-X (Euronext). Kirilenko *et al.* (2011) used data on trades in the e-mini S&P500 index (a futures contract on the S&P500 index) and found that HFTs account for 34.22 % of the daily trading volume in this asset (for four days in May 2010). Chaboud *et al.* (2009) considered the foreign exchange market (euro–dollar, yen–dollar, and euro–yen cross rates) and found that algorithmic trading in this market grew steadily from about zero in 2003 to about 60 % (80 %) of the trading volume for euro–dollar and dollar–yen (euro–yen) in 2007.

---

[13] See, for instance, the estimates of the contribution of high frequency traders to their trading volume provided by trading platforms in response to the "Call for Evidence on Micro-structural Issues of the European Equity Markets" by CESR. This contribution varies between 13 % (Nasdaq OMX) and 40 % (Chi-X).

There are also very few reliable estimates of the profitability of high frequency traders. Indeed, such estimates require relatively long time series on HFTs' holdings and data on prices at which HFTs enter and exit their position. Few studies have such detailed data (see Table 1.1 on page 38). Brogaard (2010) estimated the average annual gross aggregate profits of the 26 HFTs in his sample at $2.8 billions and their annualized Sharpe ratio at 4.5. Kirilenko *et al.* (2010) found that HFTs' daily aggregate gross profits vary between $700 000 and $5 000 000 in their sample (which covers four days in May 2010). Menkveld (2011) computed the gross profit of one electronic market-maker active on Chi-X and Euronext in Dutch stock. He estimated the gross profit per trade of this trader to be €0.88 and its annualized Sharpe ratio to be 9.35. Interestingly, he also shows that this Sharpe ratio is much higher in large stocks than in small stocks, which is consistent with the more active presence of HFTs in large capitalization stocks.

1.3 MARKET STRUCTURE AND ALGORITHMIC TRADING

The growth of algorithmic trading in the last twenty years is closely related to technological and regulatory changes in the organization of securities markets. On the one hand, it is a consequence of market fragmentation due to the entry of new electronic trading platforms in the market for trading services. On the other hand, algorithmic trading has induced changes in the business models used by these platforms.

Technological advances have considerably reduced the cost of developing and operating trading platforms in securities markets. This cost reduction triggered the entry of new, fully computerized, trading platforms (Island, Archipelago, etc.), known as Electronic Communication Networks (ECNs), in the early 1990s in US equities. This evolution accelerated in recent years with a new wave of entry (with the arrivals of platforms such as BATS or Direct Edge), resulting in a high fragmentation of trading so that, in 2009, NYSE and Nasdaq had only a 27.9 % and 22.7 % market share in their listed stocks (see Figure 1.1).[14]

This proliferation of new trading platforms was facilitated by the implementation of a new set of regulations, known as RegNMS, in 2006 for US equity markets. Indeed, RegNMS leveled the playing field between new trading platforms and incumbent exchanges by providing

---

[14] Archipelago and Nasdaq OMX are part of NYSE and Nasdaq, respectively.

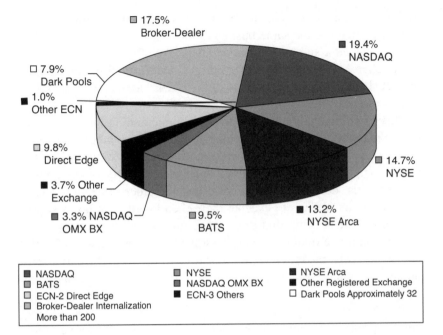

Figure 1.1 Market Shares of Exchanges, ECNs, Dark Pools, and Broker-Dealers (internalization) circa 2010 in US equity markets.

Source: (SEC, 2010)

a common regulatory framework for trade execution. In particular, the so-called "order protection rule" (also known as the "no trade-through rule") requires market orders to be directed to the platform posting the best price at any point in time. Hence limit order traders in a platform know that they will have price priority if they post aggressive orders. This makes entry of new trading platforms easier, as liquidity suppliers in this platform have a high execution probability if they undercut the quotes posted in more established markets (see Foucault and Menkveld, 2008).

The same evolution has been observed in European equities markets after the implementation of MiFID in 2007. By suppressing the so-called "order concentration rule", MiFID removed a key barrier to the entry of new trading platforms.[15] These platforms (called multilateral

---

[15] The order concentration rule allowed a member state to require concentration of trading on its national stock exchange for the stocks listed on this exchange.

trading facilities, MTFs) include Chi-X, BATS Europe, Turquoise, etc., and they often use the same business model as ECNs in the US. They quickly gained a significant market share. As of May 2011, the three most active MTFs, Chi-X, BATS Europe, and Turquoise, have a daily market share in stock constituents of the FTSE index of 27.5 %, 7.4 %, and 5.2 %, respectively.[16]

This environment is favorable to algorithmic trading for several reasons. Firstly, it is easier for computers to interact with other computers. Hence, it is a natural step for investors to start generating their orders using computers when the market itself is a network of computers. Secondly, the duty of best execution and the order protection rule in the US require brokers to execute their clients' orders at the best possible price. Identifying this price takes time when the same security trades in multiple trading venues. To solve this problem and economize on search costs, brokers have an incentive to use "smart routing technologies", which are part of algorithmic trading suites provided by brokers to their clients.

Thirdly, the multiplicity of trading venues for the same security creates profit opportunities for traders who can swiftly move across trading venues. Indeed, as explained previously, this situation creates the possibility of arbitrage opportunities. Moreover, it raises the possibility of transient mismatches in the direction of order flows across platforms (especially if some investors operating on these platforms are locked in one platform).[17] For instance, suppose that a sell order imbalance on Euronext pushes the price downward on this platform while at the same time a buy order imbalance pushes the price upward on Chi-X. A dealer operating on both platforms can take advantage of these opposite price pressures by buying the stock on Euronext and reselling it at a higher price on Chi-X. Instead of solving transient mismatches between buy and sell orders over time, the dealer does it in across trading venues at a given point in time.

Algorithmic trading is therefore a natural consequence of changes in the organization of securities markets and it is fair to say that "algorithmic markets" pre-date algorithmic traders. However, in turn the need

---

[16] See http://www.ft.com/trading-room.

[17] For instance, in Europe, some French investors might perceive the cost of trading French stocks on MTFs highly prohibitive compared to Euronext because they do not have the technology to view the quotes posted on these MTFs easily and because they may face higher clearing and settlement costs on MTFs.

to attract algorithmic traders has served as a catalyst for changes in the organization of trading platforms. New electronic markets are often organized as limit order markets. Attracting limit orders is a prerequisite to generate trades on these platforms since trades happen when a market order hits a limit order. As explained previously, electronic market-makers can often achieve smaller cost of liquidity provision than traditional liquidity providers. Thus, attracting these traders is a way to display tighter bid-ask spreads for trading platforms and therefore a way for them to build up their market share. Menkveld (2011) offers an interesting case study illustrating this point. He finds that the entry of a new electronic market-maker on Chi-X in August 2007 coincides with a sharp drop in bid-ask spreads on this platform and a large jump (from 1–2 % to more than 10 %) in its market share.

As a result, trading platforms have strived to attract electronic market-makers and more generally high frequency traders by reducing their latency (as HFTs have a high demand for low latencies; see previous section) and by offering so-called "liquidity rebates" to limit order traders; i.e., each time a limit order executes, trading platforms often rebate, to the investor holding this limit order, a fraction of the fee charged to the market order triggering the transaction. This rebate contributes to the P&L of electronic market-makers and incentivizes them to post more aggressive limit orders to earn the rebate (see Foucault *et al.*, 2011, and Colliard and Foucault, 2011, for theoretical analyses of these rebates).[18]

Algorithmic trading has also increased the demand for very quick access to market data. For instance, smart routers need real time access to quotes posted in various trading venues to allocate orders optimally among platforms. Moreover, data on last trade prices and volume (the "ticker tape") are a useful input to reassess in real time asset values. For instance, an increase in the price of a futures index signals an increase in the value of some or all stock constituents of the index. This information can then be used by HFTs to buy these stocks before other market participants notice the change in the futures index price (see Cespa and Foucault, 2011a and 2011b for a theoretical analysis of the value of ticker tape information). The informational value of the ticker tape creates a demand for ultra quick access to market data to which

---

[18] Menkveld (2011) finds that the liquidity rebate paid by Chi-X constitutes a significant fraction of the gross profit for the electronic market-maker analyzed in his study.

exchanges have responded by supplying direct access to their individual datafeed and co-location services (see previous section).[19]

Another consequence of algorithmic trading is the huge increase in messages traffic (i.e., various types of orders) on trading platforms (see Angel *et al.*, 2010, Hasbrouck and Saar, 2010, or Hendershott *et al.*, 2011). Indeed, some algorithmic trading strategies require making a decision (a quote update, a trade, a cancellation, etc.) each time an event happens in the market (e.g., an option market-maker may want to update his bid and ask prices each time there is an update in the price of the asset underlying the option). For instance, Hasbrouck and Saar (2010) document periods with very intense activity in terms of submission of orders and cancellations (e.g., more than one thousand messages in a couple of seconds). This evolution has obliged trading platforms to increase their capacity to process a large number of orders in a very short period of time and raises the possibility of bottleneck effects ("quote stuffing") induced simply by the sheer amount of messages generated by traders reacting to the same event.

1.4 COSTS AND BENEFITS OF ALGORITHMIC TRADING

1.4.1 Algorithmic trading reduces search costs

Trading in financial markets is in part a search problem (Angel *et al.*, 2010): buyers and sellers search for each other and the market is liquid if they can complete their trades quickly at small cost. The nature of this search problem depends on market structure. For instance, in "over the counter" (OTC) markets, quotes and trades are not centralized in a single market place (a trading floor or a computer memory). Brokers search for good execution prices by contacting dealers sequentially until they find an acceptable price. The search cost in this case involves the opportunity cost of time for the broker. Brokers face a trade-off between this cost and taking more time to obtain a better price.

---

[19] For instance, US trading platforms must also transmit their data to plan processors (the Consolidated Tape Association and Consolidated Quote Association) who then consolidate the data and distribute them to the public (the proceeds are then redistributed among contributors). As this process takes time, market participants with a direct access to trading platforms' individual data feed can obtain market data faster than participants who obtain the data from plan sponsors. See the SEC concept release on equity market structure, Section IV.B.2, for a discussion.

In many other markets, quotes are posted in limit order books displayed on-line to market participants. Yet, even in this case, traders face a search problem. For instance, as mentioned previously, when the same security trades in multiple limit order books, traders must consolidate the quotes posted in the different trading platforms to identify the best routing strategy. The search cost in this case comprises the cost of collecting and processing the information on the quotes posted in different trading venues. Traders can also expedite the search process by trading at standing quotes, but in this case their trade will move prices by a large amount if the limit order book is thin. To reduce this cost of immediacy, traders can split their order in space or over time, which is another way to search for a counterpart.

Algorithmic trading helps to reduce search costs for investors. For instance, as explained previously, smart routing technologies automatically consolidate quotes posted in different markets and determine the optimal routing decision given these quotes. In addition, these technologies can automatically determine how to split a large market order optimally over time. As a result, total trading costs borne by long-term investors (institutional investors and retail investors) should decrease as brokers increasingly use algorithmic trading. This proposition is difficult to test as it requires data on both brokerage fees and the total cost associated with the execution of a single order. As orders are increasingly split, measures of trading costs based on trade and quote data (e.g., time-weighted average bid-ask spreads) may overestimate or underestimate the true cost of trading, especially for institutional investors.

There is also an indirect effect. As the cost of searching for the best price decreases, competition among trading platforms and liquidity suppliers operating on these platforms increases as it becomes easier for traders to compare prices across platforms. This effect should also contribute to a decline in both explicit and implicit trading costs for long-term investors. Foucault and Menkveld (2008) provide direct evidence on this point. They consider the entry of a new trading platform for Dutch stocks, EuroSETS, in 2004. This trading platform was owned by the London Stock Exchange and its goal was to make inroads into the market share of the then incumbent market, Euronext-Amsterdam. At this time, the European market was not yet very fragmented and accordingly smart routing technologies were not very developed. Foucault and Menkveld (2008) use their data to build a proxy for the fraction of Dutch brokers using smart routing technologies (or behaving as smart routers would do) at the time of their study. They then analyze the effect of this fraction on the competitiveness of the quotes posted in EuroSETS and the contribution of its limit order book to consolidated market liquidity (i.e., the consolidated limit order book for each stock). In line with the hypothesis that smart routing technologies foster competition among liquidity providers, they find that quotes in EuroSETS were relatively more competitive in stocks for which the fraction of smart routers was higher.[20]

Duffie (2010) demonstrates that the price impact of supply and demand shocks is more persistent when new capital responds slowly to these shocks. He notes that this effect manifests itself at various time scales, including the high frequency. For instance, Duffie (2010, p. 1237) observes that:

> The arrival of new capital to an investment opportunity can be delayed by fractions of a second in some markets, for example an electronic limit-order-book market for equities, or by months in other markets [. . .].

Traders do not instantaneously react to a change in the state of the market because obtaining, processing, and acting upon new information takes time. As explained previously, algorithmic traders refer to this delay as "latency" (see Hasbrouck and Saar, 2010). For human traders, reducing latency (i.e., monitoring the market more intensively) is costly as it requires attention, and traders must allocate their limited attention among multiple tasks (e.g., trading in multiple securities). As argued by Biais *et al.* (2010), algorithmic trading considerably relaxes the cost of attention and expands traders' cognitive capacities.

Hence, one benefit of algorithmic trading is to enable liquidity suppliers (e.g., electronic market-makers) to respond more quickly to price pressures due to sudden order imbalances between the flows of buy and sell market orders. Foucault *et al.* (2011) show that this feature can considerably accelerate the rate at which trading takes place in line with the explosion in trading frequency that has been observed in recent years (see Chordia *et al.*, 2010).

One implication is that high frequency traders should frequently set the best bid and ask quotes as they reinject liquidity more quickly than other investors after a transient decrease in liquidity. Empirical findings

---

[20] They also note that the entry of EuroSETS induced Euronext to cut its trading fees. Competition for order flow has put considerable pressures on trading fees charged by trading platforms in Europe since the implementation of MiFID.

indicate that this is the case. For instance, Brogaard (2010) found that the high frequency traders in his sample are active at the best quotes 65 % of the time (tied with other investors or alone).

1.4.2 Algorithmic trading has an ambiguous effect on adverse selection costs

As explained in the previous section, algorithmic trading enables traders to increase their monitoring capacity and to react quickly to market events that create profit opportunities. In particular, investors can better monitor the flow of information relevant to value a security. For instance, for listed firms, this information includes news about the firm's prospects (macroeconomic information, firm-specific information, information on the firm's competitors, etc.). It also includes trade-related information such as transaction prices and quote updates in securities with payoffs correlated with the stock (e.g., stock prices of competitors, index futures prices, prices of derivatives written on the stock, etc.).

Traders with quick access to information can exploit it by "picking off" stale limit orders, i.e., limit orders whose prices do not yet reflect the new information regarding a security. This behavior exposes those submitting limit orders to a picking off risk (a form of adverse selection).[21] In anticipation of this risk, traders posting limit orders bid more conservatively, which reduces market liquidity (see Copeland and Galai, 1983, Foucault, 1999, or Foucault et al., 2003, for theoretical analyses of this effect). Thus, if algorithmic trading is mainly used to pick off stale limit orders, it should have a negative effect on market liquidity.

However, traders submitting limit orders (e.g., electronic market-makers) can also use monitoring technologies to react fast to new information, by cancelling their stale limit orders and submitting new limit orders posted at prices that reflect the new information. In this case, algorithmic trading reduces liquidity suppliers' exposure to the risk of being picked off and should therefore contribute to tighter bid-ask spreads.

---

[21] This problem is not new. For instance, in the 1990s, Nasdaq dealers complained that the possibility given to investors to execute small orders automatically against their quotes (at this time, execution was not yet automatic on Nasdaq, except for small quotes) was used by some investors (dubbed "SOES bandits" by the dealers) to pick off dealers who were slow to adjust their quotes in case of news arrival. See Foucault et al. (2003).

This is another reason for which, as mentioned in the previous section, algorithmic traders may frequently set the best bid and ask quotes.

Note, however, that if some limit order traders become faster in canceling their limit orders when news arrive then the exposure of the limit orders submitted by slow traders to the risk of being picked off becomes higher. Indeed, the slow traders are more likely to be first in line to sell an asset when its value is moving up and to buy it when its value is moving down. This form of winner's curse can lead slow limit order traders to supply liquidity at less attractive terms in the first place (see Cespa and Foucault, 2011b).

The net effect of algorithmic trading on limit orders' exposure to the risk of being picked off is therefore unclear. Ultimately, it depends on specialization choices of algorithmic traders (market-making versus event-based trading strategies) and their investment in monitoring technologies (see Foucault *et al.*, 2003, for a model in which the investment in monitoring is endogenous). As we shall see in more detail in Section 1.6, the jury is still out on whether algorithmic trading enhances or alleviates adverse selection.[22]

1.4.3   Algorithmic trading and price discovery

A key function of securities markets is to discover asset fundamental values. Price discovery is more efficient if asset prices deviate less from fundamental values. Measuring the quality of price discovery is difficult as fundamental values are not observed. However, one can consider the speed at which arbitrage opportunities disappear, the speed at which asset prices reflect new information, or the speed at which price pressures induced by transient order imbalances disappear as measures of the quality of the price discovery process.

As explained previously, algorithmic trading accelerates the speed at which traders can detect and exploit price discrepancies between related

---

[22] For instance, the electronic market-maker studied in Menkveld (2011) makes "positioning losses"; i.e., if one assumes that all his trades execute at the mid-quote then the market-maker loses money. This finding implies that, on average, when the market-maker buys (respectively sells) an asset, the value of this asset tends to fall (increase) afterwards. This does not support the view that he systematically picks off stale limit orders and is a source of adverse selection. The market-maker makes money because he does not buy (sell) at the mid-quote but at its bid (ask) price and thereby earns the bid-ask spread. Chaboud *et al.* (2009) also suggest that algorithmic traders mainly use algorithms to protect themselves against the risk of being picked off. Yet the empirical literature also finds that market orders placed by algo traders contain information that suggests that they may sometimes be submitted to pick off stale limit orders.

securities. Moreover, it considerably leverages traders' ability to scan the market for public information and trade on this information if it is not yet incorporated into prices. These observations suggest a positive effect of algorithmic trading on price discovery.

Another benefit of algorithmic trading, untested to my knowledge, is that the duration of price pressures induced by transient order imbalances should be smaller with the advent of algorithmic trading. Chordia *et al.* (2005) show that, conditional on order imbalance, returns are negatively correlated over intervals of up to thirty minutes for stocks listed on the NYSE, using data from 1996, 1999, and 2002. The reason is that an excess of, say, buy orders pushes prices up relative to fundamental values. This increase attracts sell orders from liquidity suppliers (market-makers, arbitrageurs, etc.) as the latter become aware of the price pressure. These sell orders offset the initial price pressure and contribute to a reversal of prices to their initial value.

Chordia *et al.* (2005) show that the predictability of stock returns (using past returns as predictors) disappears after no more than 30 minutes. They interpret this as evidence that traders become aware of order imbalances and undertake countervailing trades in no more than 30 minutes. Algorithmic trading should increase the speed at which investors can become aware of price pressures and offset these pressures, bringing back prices to their fundamental levels. It would be interesting to test this conjecture by replicating the Chordia *et al.* (2005) study with more recent data and check whether the negative autocorrelation of stock returns vanishes more quickly in recent years.

One can also develop a case for high frequency trading hindering price discovery. As high frequency traders take a position for very short periods of time, they may focus on forecasting very short-term price movements rather than long-term price movements. Froot *et al.* (1992) demonstrate that short-term traders may acquire information unrelated to asset true values. Moreover, Vives (1995) found that short-term investors can impair informational efficiency.[23]

Another problem is that high frequency traders often use *trade-related* information; i.e., they trade on data generated by the trading process itself: order flow, prices, volume, duration between trades, etc. There is no doubt that these data can be useful to forecast asset values, as implied

---

[23] In Vives (1995), informational efficiency is measured by the precision of investors' forecasts of an asset liquidation value conditional on the asset price. This precision is higher when the asset price is closer to the asset fundamental value.

by the literature on trading in the presence of asymmetric information (e.g., Grossman and Stiglitz, 1980). However, ultimately, these data are informative because they reflect more primitive signals acquired by other investors (portfolio managers, hedge funds, etc.). High frequency traders free ride on the acquisition of information by these investors, which may reduce investors' incentives to acquire information in the first place.[24] If this is the case, the overall informativeness of securities markets may have decreased with the proliferation of high frequency traders.

Last, by trading quickly on news, high frequency traders take the risk of trading on inaccurate information. In this case, their trades could inject noise in the price system rather than making it more efficient, at least at very high frequency. The following anecdote illustrates this point, in a rather extreme way. On Monday 8, 2008, the stock price of United Airlines dropped to $3 a share from nearly $12.80 in about fifteen minutes. Then the price bounced back at $10.60 at the end of the Tuesday session. The cause of these swings was an old article about United Airlines' 2002 bankruptcy court filing that mistakenly appeared on 8 September 2008 as a seemingly new headline on Google's news service. Many commentators pointed out that high frequency trading could be responsible for the wave of sell orders triggering the price decline.[25]

1.4.4 Welfare effects

Trading is often portrayed as a zero sum gain where trading profits by informed participants just offset trading losses for uninformed market participants. The reality is probably more complex as market participants can also achieve a better allocation of risk by trading together. Hence there are gains from trade. One can then ask two questions: (i) the gains from trade being fixed, is algorithmic trading a way to appropriate a larger fraction of these gains and (ii) does algorithmic trading reduce or increase total gains from trade? For instance, Stoll (2000, p. 1482) points out that liquidity provision, like other business activities, consumes

> real economic resources – labor and capital – to route orders, to execute trades, and to clear and settle trades.

---

[24] This problem is just another manifestation of the well-known Grossman and Stiglitz (1980) paradox.

[25] See "UAL Story Blame Is Placed on Computer", *Wall Street Journal*, European Edition, 10 September 2008.

If algorithmic trading results in a more efficient use of these resources, it reduces the cost of liquidity provision and thereby it increases gains from trade. Biais *et al.* (2010) also show that algorithmic trading helps to reallocate the asset faster from investors with relatively low valuations for holding the security to investors with relatively high valuations.

Jovanovic and Menkveld (2011) argue that another way in which high frequency trading could increase realized gains from trade is by reducing adverse selection. It is well known that asymmetric information between trading partners lowers the likelihood that mutually profitable deals will take place. An extreme case occurs when informational asymmetries are so large that the market breaks down and no one trades. As discussed previously, algorithmic trading can reduce traders' exposure to adverse selection by enabling them to update their quotes more quickly in case of information events. Thus, it can alleviate informational asymmetries and increase the chance that mutually profitable trades will happen. In this case, Jovanovic and Menkveld (2011) show that algorithmic trading can increase the size of expected gains from trade.

They also uncover a darker side of high frequency trading. Indeed, it might be used by traders to pick off stale quotes by slow traders, as explained in Section 1.4.2. In this case, instead of alleviating informational asymmetries, high frequency trading exacerbates them. If this scenario holds true then high frequency trading has a negative effect on investors' welfare. Testing this proposition is difficult as measuring investors' welfare is difficult.

Biais *et al.* (2011) point to another problem: investment in high frequency trading technologies might be excessive from a welfare point of view. In their model, algorithmic trading brings both benefits and costs in terms of welfare. On the one hand, it increases the likelihood that investors can complete their trades, other things being equal. On the other hand, it increases the exposure of 'slow traders' to adverse selection. Hence, algorithmic trading raises trading costs for slow traders and, as a result, they may exit the market. This decline in market participation impairs welfare since it implies that some investors are unable to carry out trades that are mutually profitable (e.g., hedging trades). The socially optimal level of algorithmic trading balances this benefit and this cost of algorithmic trading.

Biais *et al.* (2011) show that an individual investor's investment decision in algorithmic trading leads to a level of high frequency trading that is in general too high relative to the socially optimal level. Indeed, in making their investment decision in fast trading technologies, investors have no incentive to internalize the negative externality they exert on slow investors. Moreover, in the fear of being sidelined if they remain slow, investors may all decide to be fast, even though they would be better off all staying slow (a form of destructive arms race). These two effects lead in general to an overinvestment in high frequency trading technologies, relative to what would be socially optimal, in the Biais *et al.* (2011) model.[26]

1.4.5   Algorithmic trading as a source of risk

As explained previously, HFTs carry their inventory positions for a very short period of time. Hence, the absorption of large persistent order imbalances between buy and sell orders of long-term investors arriving at different points in time requires either the intervention of a "chain" of high frequency traders or, at some point, the intervention of more traditional market-makers willing to carry a risky position for a sufficiently long time (e.g., overnight). However, these intermediaries now make less profit in normal times as they face competition from faster intermediaries and are more exposed to adverse selection (see Section 1.4.2). Hence, they are less able to recoup the losses they experience in highly volatile periods with profits in normal times. This reasoning suggests that some traditional market-makers (or providers of liquidity) may have been crowded out of the market. This "crowding out effect" could be a source of fragility as it reduces the overall risk bearing capacity of the market-making sector. This is especially true if one assumes that traditional market-makers are more willing or able than HFTs to "lean against the winds" by providing liquidity even when markets are highly volatile.[27]

Speed of trading also means that human errors (e.g., "fat finger errors" that consist in pressing the wrong key on a keyboard) or ill-conceived algorithms are more difficult to identify and correct before they affect

---

[26] One way to alleviate this problem would be to tax fast traders and to redistribute the proceeds from this tax to slow traders (a form of Pigouvian tax). As usual, however, the problem with this solution is to find the optimal level for the tax (a too large tax can be more suboptimal than no tax) and also to target the right kind of algorithmic traders (i.e., those who mainly use algorithms for speculative purposes).

[27] It is unclear whether this is the case. During the market crash of October 1987, NYSE specialists stopped executing orders, which suggests that traditional market-makers may also stop providing liquidity when markets become highly volatile.

the market.[28] The flash crash of May 6, 2010 provides a vivid illustration of this risk. According to CFTC–SEC (2010), this crash finds its origin in one very large sell order in the E-mini S&P500 index. Specifically, one fund decided to sell 75 000 E-mini futures contracts on the S&P500 index traded on the CME (the largest change in a trader's position since January 2010 according to CFTC–SEC, 2010). The trader in charge of executing this order decided to split the order to mitigate his impact on prices, using a "constant participation rate" strategy. This strategy consists in splitting an order in such a way that the "child orders" represent a fixed fraction of the total trading volume over a given period of time, say a minute.[29] Hence, it calls for larger trades when volume increases. This strategy becomes problematic when the parent order is relatively large (as the 75 000 contracts order was) since child orders themselves can give a false impression of large volume, leading to an acceleration of the speed at which the order gets executed. In such a situation, a large sell order can potentially trigger a large price drop as it quickly exhausts the liquidity available in the market (by hitting lower and lower quotes), unless traders make their strategy contingent on the execution price they receive (by trading less as the price impact increases). This snowballing effect is apparently what triggered the flash crash (although the exact cause is still much discussed), proving a sharp illustration of how a badly conceived algorithm can destabilize the market.[30]

Algorithmic trading also makes trading platforms and market participants more exposed to a failure of their trading systems. In recent years, several trading platforms have experienced outages, as the huge amount of traffic generated by algorithmic trading often pushes trading systems to their limits in terms of absorption of the flow of orders. For instance, on 24 May 2011, Chi-X stopped for half an hour while in February 2011 the London Stock Exchange stopped for four hours. Such outages are problematic since they create uncertainty for traders operating on multiple platforms about whether they will be able

---

[28] Examples of human errors abound. For instance, in September 2006, a rugby ball (!) landed on a Bank of America trader's keyboard, triggering the execution of a $50 million trade ahead of schedule.

[29] When a large sell or buy order is split, each piece is called a child order while the original order itself is called the "parent order".

[30] There exist other, less dramatic, examples of ill-conceived algorithms. In 2010, the NYSE fined Credit Suisse $150 000 for poorly supervising the development and execution of an algorithm that severely disrupted the speed at which trading could take place on the NYSE.

to carry out the various legs of their hedging or arbitrage strategies. They also suppress one or multiple sources of ticker tape information for market participants since prices on platforms that are shut down are no longer visible.

Algorithmic trading also amplifies the risk that such market disruptions propagate very quickly to other asset classes. Indeed, an electronic market-maker's strategy in one security often relies on the information conveyed by the prices of other securities, especially those, such as index futures, that contain information for a wide array of securities. Per se, quick access to ticker tape information is beneficial to liquidity as it reduces uncertainty and inventory risk for liquidity providers. However, it also makes markets more interconnected, which is a source of fragility. Indeed, a drop in liquidity in one security makes its price less accurate. Thus, it raises the uncertainty for traders relying on this price to provide liquidity in other securities, which can induce them to curtail or even stop their provision of liquidity (see Cespa and Foucault, 2011b, for a theoretical analysis of this propagation mechanism and its implications for market liquidity).

In line with this propagation mechanism, the CFTC–SEC report on the flash crash has emphasized the role that uncertainty on the cause (transient price pressures or changes in fundamentals) of the large price movements in the E-mini futures on the S&P500 played in the evaporation of liquidity during the flash crash. The authors of this report write (on page 39):

> Market makers that track the prices of securities that are underlying components of an ETF are more likely to pause their trading if there are price-driven or data-driven integrity questions about those prices. Moreover extreme volatility in component stocks makes it very difficult to accurately value an ETF in real-time. When this happens, market participants who would otherwise provide liquidity for such ETFs may widen their quotes or stop providing liquidity [. . .].

1.5   EMPIRICAL EVIDENCE

As discussed in the previous section, algorithmic trading can have both positive and negative effects on market quality (price discovery, market liquidity, participants' welfare, etc.). Ultimately, which effects dominate is an empirical question. In this section, we describe and discuss some empirical findings regarding the effects of algorithmic trading. As algo trading is a relatively recent phenomenon, empirical studies are still scarce and many are still "work in progress". Consequently, conclusions from these studies should certainly not be seen as definitive but rather as a starting point for future investigations.

1.5.1   Algorithmic trading and market liquidity

The causal effect of algorithmic trading on various measures of market quality is at the heart of many controversies on this practice. However, identifying this causal effect is difficult as the amount of algorithmic trading and measures of market quality (e.g., bid-ask spreads and price impact measures) are likely to be jointly determined by a myriad of variables. As a result, algorithmic trading and measures of market quality may appear correlated (positively or negatively) even though there is no direct effect of algo trading on market quality.

To appreciate this difficulty, consider the evolution of liquidity in European equity markets since the advent of MiFID in 2007. Liquidity declined in 2008 and it is tempting to attribute this decline to the increasing fragmentation of equity trading in Europe and the increase in algorithmic trading over the same period. Yet, there are other first order factors that may have played a role, the credit crunch of 2008 not being the least of course. Hence, a major obstacle in assessing the impact of algorithmic trading is to isolate the contribution of this practice to measures of market quality (e.g., bid-ask spreads), holding other factors constant. This caveat must be kept in mind in interpreting empirical findings regarding algorithmic trading.

To overcome this problem, Hendershott *et al.* (2011) consider a technological change in the organization of the NYSE that made algorithmic trading easier. As of 2003, the NYSE started disseminating automatically, with a software called "Autoquote", any change in the best quotes in its listed stocks (before this date, specialists had to update manually new inside quotes in the limit order book). The implementation of Autoquote considerably accelerated the speed at which algorithmic traders receive information on the state of the NYSE limit order book and for this reason it increased the amount of algorithmic trading in the stocks in which Autoquote was introduced.[31]

---

[31] Hendershott *et al.* (2011) use the daily message traffic of each stock (i.e., the number of orders submitted and cancelled for that stock) normalized by trading volume in dollars as a proxy for algo trading.

Autoquote was phased in gradually. The NYSE first introduced Autoquote for six stocks in January 2003 and then progressively expanded this system to 200 stocks. Eventually Autoquote was implemented for all stocks by May 2003. This staggered introduction of Autoquote enabled Hendershott *et al.* (2011) to study how liquidity changes for stocks in which Autoquote is introduced while controlling for market-wide factors affecting liquidity using stocks for which Autoquote was not yet implemented. The change in liquidity for the stocks affected by Autoquote could then be confidently ascribed to the increase in algorithmic trading associated with Autoquote.

Hendershott *et al.* (2011) found that standard measures of market liquidity (the quoted bid-ask spread and the effective bid-ask spread) had improved after the introduction of Autoquote for large capitalization stocks. One exception is the quoted depth (i.e., the number of shares offered at the best quotes), which has decreased for these stocks. However, this decline seems too small to offset the decline in bid-ask spreads and Hendershott *et al.* (2011) argue that the net effect of algorithmic trading on trading costs is negative for large capitalization stocks. In contrast, they do not find any significant effect of algorithmic trading on market liquidity for stocks with small capitalizations, maybe because algorithmic traders were mainly active in large caps at the time of the Hendershott *et al.* study or because their tests did not have enough statistical power to detect an effect.

In addition, Hendershott *et al.* (2011) found that the reduction in bid-ask spread measures is driven by a reduction in the adverse selection component of the spread.[32] This result is consistent with the view that algorithmic trading helps traders reduce their exposure to the risk of being picked off (see the previous section). In line with this interpretation, Hendershott *et al.* (2011) show that the permanent price impact of trades measured using Hasbrouck's (1991) methodology is *smaller* after the implementation of Autoquote. Moreover, they found that the contribution of trades to the volatility of innovations in stock returns (a measure of the informational content of trades) becomes smaller *relative* to nontrade related sources of volatility. This finding suggests that after the implementation of Autoquote, liquidity providers more quickly reset their quotes after news arrivals. As a result, quotes better track fundamental values.

---

[32] The adverse selection component of the bid-ask spread is measured by the extent to which prices move against the submitter of a limit order after execution of the order.

They also show that the decrease in the adverse selection component of the bid-ask spread is larger than the reduction in the bid-ask spread itself. Hence liquidity suppliers' expected profit increases after the implementation of Autoquote. This finding may reflect the ability of algorithmic traders to earn superior profits (by managing their exposure better to the risk of being picked off), at least in the short run (i.e., before new algo traders enter to compete away firstly movers' rents).[33]

It is worth stressing some limitations of Hendershott et al. (2011). Firstly, they note that the technological change considered in their analysis chiefly benefits algorithmic traders submitting limit orders (algorithmic liquidity suppliers). Hence, a conservative interpretation of their findings is that algorithmic liquidity supply (in particular, electronic market-making) has a beneficial effect on market liquidity. However, as discussed in Section 1.2.1, electronic market-making is only one type of strategy used by algorithmic traders and one may wonder whether an increase in, say, automated arbitrage has also a positive effect on liquidity. Secondly, their metrics for liquidity capture trading costs for investors submitting aggressive orders (market orders). They do not study the effect of algorithmic trading on human traders submitting limit orders. As discussed in Section 1.4.4, these traders may have suffered from more intense competition from algorithmic liquidity suppliers (e.g., their execution probabilities could have declined).

Broogaard (2010) also provides evidence that HFTs contribute to market liquidity. He shows that HFTs in his sample follow a price reversal (or "contrarian") strategy: i.e., they buy stocks whose prices have been declining in the last 10 to 100 seconds and they sell stocks whose prices have been increasing in the last 10 to 100 seconds. Interestingly, they implement this strategy by submitting both limit orders and by hitting limit orders resting in the limit order book. Kirilenko et al. (2010) reach a similar conclusion. HFTs in their sample tend to accumulate positions when prices are dropping and decumulate positions when prices are increasing.

1.5.2   Algorithmic trading and volatility

Identifying the causal effect of algorithmic trading on volatility is challenging as well. Indeed, a positive correlation between these two

---

[33] This finding suggests that HFTs have some market power, maybe because the concentration of HFT firms is relatively high, as mentioned in Section 1.2.2.

variables does not mean that algorithmic traders are responsible for higher volatility. Instead, this correlation may simply reflect the fact that the algorithmic traders' participation rate is higher in more volatile stocks (maybe because profit opportunities in these stocks are more frequent). Hence, as for liquidity, empiricists need to devise careful experiments to isolate and measure the effect of algorithmic trading on volatility.

Chaboud et al. (2009) offer an interesting approach to this problem. They consider algorithmic trades and human trades in three currencies: euro–dollar, yen–dollar, and euro–yen, all traded on EBS (an electronic limit order book). Chaboud et al. (2009) find a positive correlation between the daily realized volatility of the currencies analyzed in their study (euro–dollar, dollar–yen, and euro–yen) and the daily amount of algorithmic trading activity in these currencies. However, this correlation may simply reflect the fact that algorithmic trading is more prominent when volatility is high. One factor that determines the volume of algorithmic trading on EBS is the number of trading floors (relative to all trading floors) equipped to trade algorithmically on EBS. This number is unlikely to be affected by the realized volatility of the currencies traded on this platform in a given day since setting up a trading floor for algorithmic trading takes time (more than one day). Hence, variations in this variable over time can be used to identify the causal effect of algorithmic trading on volatility since it affects the volume of algorithmic trading on EBS without being directly affected by volatility.

Interestingly, a regression of the daily realized volatility of these currencies on the fraction of trading floors equipped for algorithmic trading (and other control variables) shows that this fraction has a (weak) negative effect. Hence, "exogenous" variations in algorithmic trading dampen volatility instead of increasing it, as the simple correlation analysis would suggest at first glance.

Other empirical studies reach a similar conclusion with different methods and for different markets. Hasbrouck and Saar (2010) address the simultaneity problem by running a system of regressions in which volatility can influence algorithmic trading and vice versa. They measure volatility over 10 minute intervals for Nasdaq stocks and they use a proxy for the amount of algorithmic trading over the same time intervals as they do not directly observe algorithmic traders' orders. They find a negative effect of algorithmic trading on short-run volatility.

These studies do not describe in detail the mechanisms by which algorithmic traders influence volatility. One possibility is that an increase in short-run volatility in a security signals a transient lack of liquidity in this security (e.g., an increase in the bid-ask spread). Traders' computers interpret this signal as a profit opportunity (prices are temporarily out of line with fundamental values due to a buying or selling pressure) and inject liquidity with limit orders where it is needed. Alternatively, algorithmic traders could act as positive feedback traders: they buy securities after price increases and sell them after price decreases. In this case, they exacerbate price volatility. Hendershott and Riordan (2009) find no evidence in favor of this second scenario. In their data, market orders from algorithmic trading are statistically unrelated to lagged volatility (measured over a fifteen minute interval prior to the algorithmic trader's order arrival).[34]

1.5.3   Algorithmic trading and price discovery

As explained in Section 1.4.3, HFTs can make prices more informationally efficient. Indeed, their technology gives them the possibility to react more quickly to news or ticker tape information. Consequently, one expects prices to impound new information more quickly in the presence of HFTs. Testing for this possibility requires "pricing errors" to be measured, i.e., the distance between an asset fundamental value and the price at which it trades. As asset fundamental values are unobserved, this test is difficult.

One basic question is whether trades and/or quotes posted by algorithmic traders contain information on asset values. This is a prerequisite for algorithmic traders to have a positive effect on price discovery.

Hendershott and Riordan (2009) are the first to address this question, using data from Deutsche Börse. One interesting feature of their data is

---

[34] Kirilenko et al. (2010) find weak evidence in favor of positive feedback trading for high frequency traders. Indeed, changes in the holdings of these traders are positively correlated with very recent price changes (from 1 second up to 4 seconds). This suggests that they buy when prices are just moving up and sell when prices are just moving down. In contrast, changes in their holdings are negatively correlated with price changes at further lags (11 seconds, etc.). The positive correlation between HFT changes in holdings and very recent price changes may simply reflect HFTs reacting to the same information and taking advantage of this information with market orders. In line with this hypothesis, Kirilenko et al. (2010) found that the positive correlation between HFT holdings changes, and recent changes in prices are positive only when HFTs change their positions with market orders.

that they have information on orders submitted by algorithmic traders and orders submitted by human traders. They can therefore measure the informational content of orders submitted by each category of traders. To this end, they use the Vector Autoregression Approach advocated by Hasbrouck (1991) to measure the permanent impact of aggressive orders (i.e., market orders) submitted by algorithmic traders, on the one hand, and human traders, on the other hand. This approach measures the average change in price after a buy or a sell market order (a trade) over a given period of time after the trade (e.g., 10 trades after the initial trade). This average change is called the permanent impact of trades, which is deemed to capture the change in the evaluation of the asset by market participants. This permanent impact is therefore often used as one measure of the information content of trades. Hendershott and Riordan (2009) find that algorithmic traders' market orders have on average a larger permanent impact than human traders' market orders in their sample (53 bps against 44 bps). Other studies (Hendershott et al., 2011, or Brogaard, 2010) obtain similar findings. Hence, according to these studies, trades by algorithmic traders contain more information than trades by human traders.

Chaboud et al. (2009) consider a different asset class (currencies) and interestingly they obtain quite different results. Using the same methodology as Hendershott and Riordan (2009), they find that a one standard deviation shock for the order size of a trade initiated by a computer has a smaller long-run (30 minutes) impact than the same shock for a trade initiated by a human trader. Hence, in contrast to the results obtained for equity markets, trades initiated by human traders in the currencies considered in Chaboud et al. (2009) seem to contain more information than trades initiated by computers. This finding suggests that the purpose of algorithmic trading in these currencies is not mainly to exploit superior information at the expense of slower traders (e.g., by picking off stale limit orders).

Instead, Chaboud et al. (2009) find evidence consistent with the view that algo trading is used to reduce traders' exposure to the risk of being picked off. Indeed, they find that market orders from human traders move prices much less when their counterpart is a computer than when it is a human. Hence, computers are better than humans at avoiding trades with better informed agents.

Hendershott and Riordan (2009) also study whether quotes (i.e., limit orders) posted by algorithmic traders contain information. To address this question, they build two separate time series: the time series of best bid and ask prices using only the quotes posted by algorithmic traders and the time series of best bid and ask prices using only the quotes posted by human traders. Then they measure the relative contributions of changes in the mid-quotes of each series to the variance of the changes in the (unobserved) fundamental value of the security (using a methodology developed by Hasbrouck, 1995). This contribution can be interpreted as a measure of the contribution of the quotes of each type of trader (computers/humans) to price discovery.[35] They find that the contribution of algorithmic traders' quotes (their "information share") to price discovery is higher than that of human traders. Brogaard (2010) obtained a similar finding for a different sample.

To sum up, empirical findings suggest that algorithmic trading contributes to price discovery in two ways: (i) algorithmic traders' quotes contain information and (ii) algorithmic traders' market orders contain information. Hence, algorithmic traders contribute to price discovery and sometimes more than humans (Hendershott and Riordan, 2009, or Brogaard, 2010).[36] Note, however, that if algorithmic traders' market orders contain information, their trades are a source of adverse selection for traders posting limit orders. Hence, although informed market orders contribute to price discovery, they may have a deleterious effect on market liquidity by increasing the cost of trading against better informed investors for liquidity providers.[37]

There are still many questions that are unanswered. In particular, what is the source of the informational advantage for algorithmic traders? Do

---

[35] For instance, if quotes posted by human traders do not contain information, these quotes will not move estimates of the fundamental value of the security when they are updated. In this case, changes in quotes posted by human traders will have a zero contribution to the variance of the fundamental value of the security.

[36] Zhang (2010) offers a dissenting view. Using a proxy for HFTs' trading volume, he considers the effect of HFTs on price movements after an earnings announcement. He shows that the prices of stocks that attract more trading from HFTs overshoot their fundamental value after earnings announcements. This suggests that HFTs have a negative effect on price discovery. In contrast to other studies mentioned in this section, however, Zhang (2010) cannot directly measure HFTs' trading volume. He infers this volume from data on institutional holdings, which raises the possibility that his proxy for HFTs capture the activity of individual investors rather than HFTs.

[37] This is a standard effect in models of trading with asymmetric information: trades by informed investors accelerate the price discovery process but tend to make the market illiquid (see Glosten and Milgrom, 1985).

they trade on publicly available news not yet impounded into prices or do they simply use ticker tape information, etc.? Moreover, as mentioned at the outset of this section, the effect of algorithmic traders on pricing errors is still an open empirical question.

More efficient prices lead to a better capital allocation in the economy (Hayek, 1945; Dow and Gorton, 1997). However, do we need prices to be right as fast as possible given that capital allocation decisions are made at low frequencies (certainly not at the millisecond)? Moreover, better price discovery has a cost: HFTs' investment in information acquisition and technology consume resources. Does the gain for society of better price discovery due to algorithmic trading offset the cost incurred by market participants to achieve this gain? There are not yet any well-articulated answers to these questions.

1.5.4   Algorithmic trading and market stability

As explained previously, one concern is that algorithmic trading may fragilize financial markets. A first source of fragility is that high frequency traders could stop providing liquidity when markets become excessively turbulent. One way to study this question consists in studying whether algorithmic traders behave differently in periods in which volatility is low ("normal times") and periods in which volatility is high ("turbulent times").

Hasbrouck and Saar (2010) and Brogaard (2010) follow this approach to see whether volatility has a negative effect on liquidity provision by algorithmic traders. Hasbrouck and Saar (2010) measure the impact of high frequency trading on measures of market quality (volatility and liquidity) for Nasdaq stocks in October 2007 and June 2008, respectively. Volatility and uncertainty were much higher in June 2008 than in June 2007 due to the subprime crisis. They do not find that high frequency traders curtailed their provision of liquidity in the second period.

Brogaard (2010) consider the effect of earnings announcements on the demand and supply of liquidity by high frequency traders. Earnings announcements are associated with an increase in volatility. Brogaard (2010) find that high frequency traders tend to increase their supply of liquidity (submit more limit orders) and decrease their demand of liquidity (submit fewer market orders) in periods of earnings announcements (periods of high volatility) relative to periods without earnings announcements (periods of low volatility). As also found by Hasbrouck and Saar (2010), this result does not support the view that HFTs stop providing liquidity when volatility increases.

Kirilenko *et al.* (2010) provide an in-depth empirical analysis of high frequency traders' behavior in the E-mini S&P500 index during the flash crash of 6 May 2010. This is interesting since the crash finds its origin in this market (see Section 1.4.5). Moreover, the flash crash is an event of extreme volatility and instability (e.g., from 1:30 p.m. to 1:45 p.m., the S&P500 E-mini lost about 5 % before bouncing back by the same amount almost as quickly). They compare the behavior of high frequency traders in their sample during the period of the flash crash with their behavior in the two days before the flash crash. These two days serve as a benchmark, representative of "normal times".

Kirilenko *et al.* (2010) do not find significant differences in the behavior of high frequency traders on the day of the flash crash and their behavior in the days immediately preceding the crash. High frequency traders' trading strategy depends on past prices. They use a combination of market orders and limit orders. They trade in the direction of recent price changes with market orders and opposite to this direction with limit orders. When they trade with limit orders, HFTs provide liquidity to other market participants and they do not seem to have reduced their supply of liquidity on the day of the flash crash relative to the other days.

However, it is noteworthy that HFTs keep their positions for a very short period of time and they never accumulate large positions (their net aggregate position fluctuates in a band of ±3000 contracts). As a result, although they initially absorbed part of the large sell orders triggering the downward price pressure in the S&P500 E-mini, they also quickly (in a matter of minutes) unwound their positions, passing them to more traditional intermediaries.[38] Thus, they did not keep their positions long enough for the selling price pressure not to aggravate. In this sense, although HFTs do not seem to have caused the flash crash or amplified it, Kirilenko *et al.* (2010) conclude that they did not help to prevent it.

---

[38] Kirilenko *et al.* (2010) show, over the period 1:30 p.m. to 1:45 p.m., that the excess of sell orders over buy orders by fundamental traders (those that they do not classify as intermediaries or HFTs) was 30000 contracts.

Interestingly, Kirilenko *et al.* (2010) find that HFTs did not lose money during the flash crash (in fact they seem to have made more profits than on the previous days). In contrast, other intermediaries incurred significant losses. If, in addition, the presence of HFTs makes it more difficult for traditional intermediaries to earn profits in normal time (a conjecture that has not been studied empirically to my knowledge), then some traditional intermediaries could be crowded out of the market, as explained in Section 1.4.5.

One question that has not yet been investigated empirically is whether algorithmic traders played a role in the propagation of the drop in prices and the shortage of liquidity in the E-mini S&P500 index futures to other asset classes, in particular US equities. There are at least two reasons for which one may think that HFTs could have played a role. Firstly, when the price of an index futures becomes low relative to the value of its constituent stocks, arbitrageurs start selling the constituent stocks and buying the index futures. Through this arbitrage activity, the selling pressure in the index futures propagates to the cash market. This propagation is faster when arbitrage is faster, which is the case with algorithmic trading. Note, however, that in this case arbitrage activities should have dampened the selling pressure in the futures market. Secondly, as explained in Section 1.4.5, electronic market-makers rely heavily on prices of other securities to provide liquidity in other securities. A sharp drop in liquidity in a security like an index futures, which is a key source of information, significantly raises the uncertainty on the value of all securities and thereby accelerates the evaporation of liquidity in other securities.

1.6 CONCLUSIONS

As mentioned in the introduction, many have voiced concerns that algorithmic trading could impair market quality. It is fair to say that the early empirical evidence on the effects of algorithmic trading does not offer much support for this view. Indeed, to date, empirical findings suggest that:

1. Algorithmic trading improves liquidity.
2. Algorithmic trading does not increase volatility and may even dampen it.
3. Algorithmic trading improves price discovery.

Hence, initial evidence supports the view that algorithmic trading makes the market more efficient and more liquid. This should help investors to make better portfolio decisions at lower costs. However, it is not clear whether the conclusions from existing empirical studies are robust since empirical studies regarding the effects of algorithmic trading are still scarce. Hence, one must be careful in not generalizing too quickly the current results about the effects of algorithmic trading: much more research is needed.

Furthermore, there are still many important questions that remain to be investigated. Firstly, we do not know whether algorithmic trading has decreased transaction costs for institutional investors (mutual funds, pension funds, etc.). There are good reasons to believe that this could be the case since algorithms enable buy-side investors to optimize their routing decisions and because electronic market-making seems to have improved liquidity. Yet, there is no systematic empirical study about the impact of algorithmic trading on institutional investors' transaction costs.[39]

Secondly, we do not know whether algorithmic trading makes markets more fragile or more robust. As explained in Section 1.5.4, Kirilenko *et al.* (2010) do not find evidence that HFTs contributed to the flash crash but they do point out that HFTs did not help to prevent the crash. More work should be done to evaluate whether algorithmic trading increases or decreases systematic risk.

Lastly, algorithmic trading involves large investments in new technologies. These technologies have some benefits if they reduce transaction costs and if they foster price discovery. However, can we trust the invisible hand to strike the right balance between these benefits and the costs of algorithmic trading technologies? Answering this question requires, among other things, a better understanding of the real effects of having more efficient price discovery at high frequency. Economic theory does not yet provide much guidance on this question.

---

[39] Some brokers monitor the evolution of execution costs for their clients taking into account the fact that a single order may be "chopped" in small pieces. Reports of these brokers provide information on the evolution of trading costs. For instance, ITG reports that, for the US, execution costs for orders executed by ITG have declined in US equities from 68 bps to 40 bps (brokerage fees included) from 2004 to 2007, but have increased again in 2008 to reach a high of 80 bps at the end of 2008, maybe because of the subprime crisis. See ITG Global, "Trading Cost Review, Q4 2008", available at http://www.itg.com/news_events/papers/ITGGlobalTradingCostReview_2008Q4.pdf.

APPENDIX

Table 1.1

Author(s)	Asset class	Sample	Sample period	Direct data on AT's orders
Chaboud, Chiquoine, Hjalmarsson, and Vega (2009)	Currencies	Euro–dollar, dollar–yen, euro–yen	01/01/2006–31/12/2007	Yes
Brogaard (2010)	US stocks	120 stocks listed on Nasdaq and NYSE	22/02/2010–26/02/2010 for quote data, 2009 and 2009 for trade data	Yes
Foucault and Menveld (2008)	Dutch stocks	25 stocks constituents of the AEX index	April–May 2004–August 2004 and January 2005	No
Hasbrouck and Saar (2010)	US stocks	345 and 394 stocks listed on Nasdaq	10/2007 and 06/2008	No
Hendershott, Jones, and Menkveld (2011)	US stocks	NYSE	2001–2005	No
Hendershott and Riordan (2009)	Dax stocks	30 stocks listed on Deustche Börse	01/1/2008–18/01/2008	Yes
Jovanovic and Menkveld (2011)	Dutch stocks	14 stocks constituents of the AEX index	01/1/2008–23/04/2008	No[a]
Kirilenko, Kyle, Samadi, and Tuzun (2010)	Futures	E-mini futures on the S&P500	03/05/2010–08/05/2010	No[b]
Menkveld (2011)	Dutch stocks	14 stocks constituents of the AEX index	01/01/2007–17/06/2008	No[c]
Zhang (2010)	US stocks covered by CRSP and Thomson Reuters	All stocks covered by CRSP and Thomson Reuters	Q1/1985–Q2/2009	No

[a] Jovanovic and Menkveld (2011) infer trades by one HFT matching trades in Euronext and Chi-X.
[b] They have data on trades by all market participants in the E-mini futures on the S&P500. Participants who account for a large fraction of total trading volume but who hold small positions at the end of the day and whose inventories vary little relative to the end of the day position are classified as high frequency traders.
[c] Menkveld (2011) infers trades by one HFT matching trades in Euronext and Chi-X.

ACKNOWLEDGMENT

The author acknowledges the support of the Europeans Savings Institute (OEE) for this research.

REFERENCES

Angel, J.J., L.E. Harris and C.S. Spatt (2010) Equity Trading in the 21st Century, Working Paper, Carnegie Mellon.
Bertsimas, D. and A.W. Lo (1998) Optimal Control of Execution Costs, *Journal of Financial Markets* **1**, 1–50.
Biais, B., T. Foucault and S. Moinas (2011) Equilibrium High Frequency Trading, Working Paper, Université de Toulouse.
Biais, B., P. Hillion and C. Spatt (1995) An Empirical Analysis of the Limit Order Book and the Order Flow in the Paris Bourse, *Journal of Finance* **50**, 1655–1689.
Biais, B., J. Hombert and P.O. Weill (2010) Trading and Liquidity with Limited Cognition, Working Paper, Toulouse University, IDEI.
Black, F. (1971) Towards an Automated Exchange, *Financial Analysts Journal*, July–August.
Brogaard, J.A. (2010) High Frequency Trading and Its Impact on Market Quality, Working Paper, Northwestern University.
Cespa, G. and T. Foucault (2011a) Sale of Price Information by Exchanges: Does It Promote Price Discovery?, Working Paper, HEC.
Cespa, G. and T. Foucault (2011b) Learning from Prices, Liquidity Spillovers, and Endogenous Market Segmentation, CEPR Working Paper 8350.
CESR (2010a) Trends, Risks and Vulnerabilities in Financial Markets, Report.
CESR (2010b) Call for Evidence: Micro-Structural Issues of the European Equity Markets.
CFTC & SEC (2010) Commodity and Futures Trading Commission and Securities and Exchange Commission, Findings Regarding the Market Events of May 6, 2010, Report of the Staffs of the CFTC and SEC to the Joint Advisory Committee on Emerging Regulatory Issues (September 30, 2010).
Chaboud, A., B. Chiquoine, E. Hjalmarsson and C. Vega (2009) Rise of the Machines: Algorithmic Trading in the Foreign Exchange Market, Working Paper, FED, New York.
Chordia, T., R. Roll and A. Subrahmanyam (2005) Evidence on the Speed of Convergence to Market Efficiency, *Journal of Financial Economics* **76**, 271–292.
Chordia, T., R. Roll and A. Subrahmanyam (2010) Recent Trends in Trading Activity, Working Paper, Anderson School, UCLA.
Colliard, J.-E. and T. Foucault (2011) Trading Fees and Efficiency in Limit Order Markets, CEPR Discussion Paper Series 8395.
Copeland, T. and D. Galai (1983) Information Effects on the Bid-Ask Spread, *Journal of Finance* **38**, 1457–1469.
Dow, J. and G. Gorton (1997) Stock Market Efficiency and Economic Efficiency: Is There a Connection?, *Journal of Finance* **52**, 1087–1129.
Duffie, D. (2010) Presidential Address: Asset Price Dynamics with Slow Moving Capital, *Journal of Finance*, 1237–1267.
Foucault, T. (1999) Order Flow Composition and Trading Costs in a Dynamic Limit Order Market, *Journal of Financial Markets* **2**, 99–134.
Foucault, T. and A.J. Menkveld (2008) Competition for Order Flow and Smart Order Routing Systems, *Journal of Finance* **63**, 119–158.

Foucault, T., O. Kadan and E. Kandel (2011) Liquidity Cycles, and Make/Take Fees in Electronic Markets, forthcoming in *Journal of Finance*.

Foucault, T., A. Roëll and P. Sandas (2003) Market Making with Costly Monitoring: an Analysis of SOES Trading, *Review of Financial Studies* **16**, 345–384.

Froot, K., D.S. Scharfstein and J. Stein (1992) Herd on the Street: Informational Inefficiencies in a Market with Short-Term Speculation, *Journal of Finance* **47**, 1461–1484.

Garvey, R. and F. Wu (2010) Speed, Distance, and Electronic Trading: New Evidence on Why Location Matters, *Journal of Financial Markets* **13**, 367–396.

Glosten, L.R. and P. Milgrom (1985) Bid, Ask, and Transaction Prices in a Specialist Market with Heterogeneously Informed Traders, *Journal of Financial Economics* **14**, 71–100.

Grossman, S. and J. Stiglitz (1980) On the Impossibility of Informationally Efficient Markets, *American Economic Review* **70**, 393–408.

Hasbrouck, J. (1991) Measuring the Information Content of Stock Trades, *Journal of Finance* **46**, 179–207.

Hasbrouck, J. (1995) One Security, Many Markets: Determining the Contribution to Price Discovery, *Journal of Finance* **50**, 1175–1199.

Hasbrouck, J. and G. Saar (2010) Low-Latency Trading, Working Paper, New York University.

Hayek, F. (1945) The Use of Knowledge in Society, *American Economic Review* **35**, 519–530.

Hendershott, T. and R. Riordan (2009) Algorithmic Trading and Information, Working Paper, University of Berkeley.

Hendershott, T., C.M. Jones and A.J. Menkveld (2011) Does Algorithmic Trading Improve Liquidity? *Journal of Finance* **66**, 1–33.

Huberman, G. and W. Stanzl (2005) Optimal Liquidity Trading, *Review of Finance* **9**, 165–200.

Jovanovic, B. and A. Menkveld (2011) Middlemen in Limit Order Markets, Working Paper, VU University Amsterdam.

Khandani, A. and A.W. Lo (2011) What Happened to the Quants in August 2007? Evidence from Factors and Transactions Data, *Journal of Financial Markets* **14**(1), 1–46.

Kirilenko, A.A., A.S. Kyle, M. Samadi and T. Tuzun (2011) The Flash Crash: the Impact of High Frequency Trading on an Electronic Market, Working Paper, University of Maryland.

Kozhan, R. and W.W. Tham (2010) Arbitrage Opportunities: a Blessing or a Curse?, Working Paper, University of Warwick.

Menkveld, A. (2011) High Frequency Trading and the New-Market Makers, Working Paper, VU University, Amsterdam.

SEC (2010) Concept Release on Equity Market Structure, Release 34-61358; File S7-02-10.

Sorkenmaier, A. and M. Wagener (2011) Do We Need a European "National Market System"? Competition, Arbitrage, and Suboptimal Executions, Working Paper, Karlsruhe Institute of Technology.

Stoll, H.R. (2000) Friction, *Journal of Finance* **55**, 1479–1514.

Vives, X. (1995) Short-Term Investment and the Informational Efficiency of the Market, *Review of Financial Studies* **8**, 125–160.

Zhang, F. (2010) High Frequency Trading, Stock Volatility, and Price Discovery, Working Paper, Yale University.

2

Order Choice and Information
in Limit Order Markets

Ioanid Roşu

2.1 INTRODUCTION

In recent years, trading via limit orders and market orders has become the dominant form of trading in most exchanges around the world, whether these are pure electronic limit order markets or hybrid markets in which limit order traders are in competition with floor traders, specialists, or dealers.

A pure limit order market is defined as a market in which there are essentially only limit orders and market orders. A market order demands immediate execution, irrespective of the price. A limit order is an instruction to buy or sell only at a pre-specified price, and is placed in a queue based on price/time priority. A limit order is usually executed only after a market order clears it from the queue. A limit order that gets immediate execution because the price is already met is called a marketable order and is not differentiated from a market order. A sell limit order is also called an ask (or offer), while a buy limit order is also called a bid. The *limit order book*, or simply the *book*, is the collection of all outstanding limit orders. The lowest ask in the book is called the ask price, or simply ask, and the highest bid is called the bid price, or simply bid.[1] This chapter does not discuss *hidden* limit orders, which are limit orders for which some of the quantity is not visible to the market.

---

[1] One can think of limit orders as supplying liquidity (i.e., immediacy) to the market, and market orders as demanding liquidity. In reality, the distinction between the supply and demand of liquidity is not as clear cut. For example, an aggressive limit order, e.g., a limit order submitted close to the ask or the bid, is likely to be executed, and can be thought as demanding liquidity, at least relative to the limit orders that are submitted further away from the market.

Market Microstructure: Confronting Many Viewpoints. Edited by F. Abergel, J.-P. Bouchaud,
T. Foucault, C.-A. Lehalle and M. Rosenbaum.
© 2012 John Wiley & Sons, Ltd.

Given the importance of limit order markets, there have been relatively few models that describe price formation and order choice in these markets. The main reason for this scarcity is the difficulty of the problem. In dealer or specialist markets, liquidity provision is restricted to one or several individuals, who are easier to model, especially if they are assumed to be uninformed.[2] In contrast, in limit order markets, liquidity provision is open to everyone via limit orders. Therefore, in order to achieve the tractability of previous models, one may assume, as in Glosten (1994), Rock (1996), Seppi (1997), or Biais *et al.* (2000), that limit order traders are uninformed. If instead informed traders are allowed to choose how to trade, the problem becomes significantly more difficult, especially in dynamic models. This chapter focuses on the order choice; therefore we do not discuss the literature in which traders cannot choose between market orders and limit orders.

The author has benefited from some excellent surveys on the market microstructure literature, e.g., O'Hara (1995), Madhavan (2000), Biais *et al.* (2005), and especially Parlour and Seppi (2008), which focuses on limit order markets.

This survey begins by an analysis of order choice in the presence of symmetric information (Section 2.2) and then discusses the same choice under asymmetric information (Section 2.3). The next section discusses the empirical literature on order choice, as well as on the information content and price impact of various types of orders (Section 2.4). The survey ends with some questions for future research (Section 2.5).

2.2   ORDER CHOICE WITH SYMMETRIC INFORMATION

In the absence of asymmetric information, the choice between market orders and limit orders is decided by comparing the certain execution of market orders at possibly disadvantageous prices with the uncertain execution of limit orders at more advantageous prices. If, moreover, limit orders cannot be freely canceled or modified, one additional cost of limit orders is that they can be picked off by the new traders.

The intuition for the trade-off between price and time goes back to Demsetz (1968), but it was first modeled explicitly in Cohen *et al.*

---

[2] Dealer and specialist markets are modeled, for example, in Amihud and Mendelson (1980), Kyle (1985), and Glosten and Milgrom (1985). See also the equivalence result of Back and Baruch (2007).

(1981). This paper assumes an exogenous price process that determines whether a limit order becomes executed by the next period or not, in which case the limit order is canceled. The model produces a nonzero bid-ask spread. Moreover, if the market has a smaller trading intensity (it is thinner), the equilibrium bid-ask spread is larger. To understand these results, consider an investor who contemplates placing a limit buy order below the ask. Due to the frictions in the model, the probability of execution is always significantly less than one, while the price improvement converges to zero as the limit buy order approaches the ask. This "gravitational pull" makes it certain that above a certain price below the ask it is always more advantageous to buy with a market order than with a limit order. Thus, there is a minimum distance between the bid and the ask, i.e., a minimum bid-ask spread. One can see also that this minimum spread must be larger when the probability of execution of the limit order gets smaller, which happens when the market is thinner.

Parlour (1998) presents a model of a limit order book in which there are only two prices: the bid, B, and the ask, A. The buy limit orders a queue at B and the limit orders a queue at A. The trading day is divided into $T + 1$ subperiods, $t = 0, 1, \ldots, T$. On each trading subperiod, one trader arrives, that is either a seller (with probability π_S), a buyer (with probability π_B), or neither. A buyer can make one of three choices: submit a market buy order, submit a limit buy order, or stay out of the market. Each trader is characterized by a parameter $\beta \in [\underline{\beta}, \overline{\beta}]$ (with $0 \leq \underline{\beta} \leq 1 \leq \overline{\beta}$), which determines the trade-off between consumption on the trading day and on the next day, when the asset value is realized. The parameter β can be interpreted as an impatience coefficient, or alternatively as a private valuation for the asset. Traders with extreme values of β prefer to trade immediately, and use market orders. Traders with intermediate values of β prefer to wait, and use limit orders. A low β indicates that the trader prefers consumption today to consumption tomorrow, which means that, given the choice, he or she prefers to sell the asset to get cash today. Similarly, high β characterizes a propensity to buy. A trader arriving at t has only one opportunity to submit an order. Once submitted, orders cannot be modified or canceled.

The model leads to a stochastic sequential game and has a cutoff equilibrium. For example, buyers with high β submit a market buy order; with intermediate β submit a limit buy order; and with low β stay out of the market. The model produces interesting liquidity dynamics, and in particular it provides an explanation for the diagonal effect of Biais *et al.* (1995), who find that, for example, buy market orders (BMOs) are more likely after a BMO than after sell market orders (SMOs). To see this, consider the arrival of a BMO at t. This reduces the liquidity available at the ask by one unit, and, if the next trader is a seller, the trader is more likely to submit a sell limit order (SLO) than a sell market order (SMO). This in turn makes future buyers prefer a BMO to a BLO. Note that this type of dynamics also involve a correlation between a BMO and an SLO, which provides an additional empirical prediction.

Foucault *et al.* (2005) explicitly model waiting costs as linear in the expected waiting time. Limit orders cannot be canceled and must be submitted inside the existing bid-ask spread. Prices are constrained in a fundamental band $[B, A]$: a competitive fringe of traders stands ready to buy at B and sell at A an unlimited number of shares. Traders arrive according to a Poisson process with parameter λ, and can trade only *one* unit. Traders can be either patient, by incurring a waiting cost of δ_P per unit of time, or impatient, with a waiting cost of $\delta_I \geq \delta_P$. The fraction of impatient traders out of the total population is θ_P.

The assumption that limit orders must always improve the spread implies that the only relevant state variable is the bid-ask spread, which is an integer multiple of the minimum tick size, Δ. This in turn means that a limit order can be characterized simply by the bid-ask spread that it creates after being submitted: a j-limit order is a limit order that results in a bid-ask spread of size $j\Delta$. The resulting Markov perfect equilibrium depends on the current spread: if the spread is below a cutoff, both patient and impatient traders submit market orders; if the spread is above a cutoff, both types of traders submit limit orders and if the spread is of intermediate size, the patient traders submit limit orders and impatient traders submit market orders.

Foucault *et al.* (2005) focus on the case when it is never optimal for impatient traders to submit limit orders. Not all spreads can exist in equilibrium, but only a subset: $n_1 < n_2 < \cdots < n_q$. Then a patient trader facing a spread between $n_h + 1$ and n_{h+1} is to submit an n_h-limit order. The expected time to execution of such a limit order has a closed-form expression: $T(n_h) = (1/\lambda)(1 + 2\sum_{k=1}^{h-1} \rho^k)$, where $\rho = \theta_P/\theta_I$ is the ratio of the proportions of patient and impatient traders. Relatively more patient traders (higher ρ) induce more competition for providing liquidity, and hence a higher expected waiting time for limit orders. Aware of this, each patient trader submits more aggressive orders and consequently reduces the spread more quickly.

The paper discusses the notion of resiliency: e.g., the propensity for the bid-ask spread to revert to its lower level after a market order has consumed liquidity in the book. Note that in the context of the model there is no *pressure* to revert to the former level, which would be due, for example, to the arrival of more liquidity providers when the bid-ask spread becomes wider. Here resilience is due to the ergodicity of the Markov equilibrium: any possible equilibrium spread is attainable after a while. Intuitively, more patient traders make the book more resilient. Surprisingly, a higher arrival rate λ *decreases* the resiliency of the book; i.e., fast markets are less resilient than slow markets. The intuition is that, in a faster market, limit traders become less aggressive in improving the spread, and the spread reverts more slowly to smaller levels.

Goettler *et al.* (2005) propose a model in which traders have private valuations about the value of an asset. Each period, the common value v_t stays the same; or moves up by one tick, with probability $\lambda/2$; or moves down by one tick with probability $\lambda/2$. Each trader can trade up to $\bar{z}$ units of the asset. Limit orders can be submitted on a discrete price grid, $p^{-N}, \ldots, p^{-1}, p^{1}, \ldots, p^{N}$. The common value of the asset is at the midpoint between p^{-1} and p^{1}. A competitive crowd of traders provides an infinite depth of buy orders at p^{-N} and sell orders at p^{N}. The limit order book is described by a vector $L_t = \{l_t^i\}_{i=-(N-1)}^{N-1}$, where l_t^i represents the number of units of limit orders on level i at time t. Limit orders cannot be modified, but can be canceled according to an exogenously specified cancellation function, which may depend on whether the common value moves in an adverse direction. Indeed, the payoff of a trader with private valuation β_t who submits at t an order of one share with price p^i is: $(p^i + v_t) - (\beta_t + v_\tau)$ if the share will be sold at $\tau \geq t$; $(\beta_t + v_\tau) - (p^i + v_t)$ if the share will be bought at $\tau \geq t$; or 0 if the share is canceled before it is executed.

The state space is too large to be able to find the Markov perfect equilibrium in closed form, so the authors find a numerical solution, using an algorithm by Pakes and McGuire (2001). The initial parameter choices are: $N = 4$ (8 ticks); maximum trading volume per trader $\bar{z} = 2$; and the trading day has $M = 250$ transactions. Since the common value moves over time and traders cannot modify their limit orders, there are picking-off risks, and this creates patterns in the book. For example, a BMO is more likely after a BMO than after an SLO: following an increase in v_t, sell orders in the book become stale and the incoming traders are more likely to submit a BMO until the book fully adjusts.

Interestingly, the common value is often shown in simulations to be outside of the bid-ask spread, and this is not due only to stale orders. Indeed, consider the case when a trader with a very high private valuation encounters a book with a deep buy side but a thin sell side. Then it is often optimal for this trader to submit a BLO above the common value v_t (which places the common value outside the spread) in order to attract more future SMOs and hence potentially execute at a better price than from a BMO.

Large (2009) analyzes the choice between market orders and limit orders based on indirect waiting costs. The model assumes that limit orders are always submitted inside the spread. The slippage of an order is defined as $sign \times (p - m_t)$, where $sign$ is $+1$ or -1 if the order is to buy or sell, respectively; p is the trade price; and m_t is the bid-ask midpoint. A market order has positive slippage while a limit order has negative slippage. Negative slippage is preferable, because it means trading at a more advantageous price. The payoff from trading is given by $sign \times \beta - slippage$, where β is the trader type. Given a time discount $\rho < 1$, an extreme β implies a bigger loss from waiting; i.e., extreme β is essentially equivalent to high waiting costs. Therefore, extreme β types tend to place market orders, while moderate β types tend to place limit orders. This is a cutoff strategy similar to that in Parlour (1998) or to the strategy of the informed trader in Roşu (2010), except that in Large (2009) there is no asymmetric information. The rest of the model relies on the idea that limit orders and market orders have to be in equilibrium: the volume of market orders and uncanceled limit orders must be mechanically equal.

Roşu (2009) presents the first dynamic model in which agents are allowed to freely modify or cancel their limit orders. The model is similar to that of Foucault et al. (2005), except that prices are continuous rather than discrete and there are no restrictions on order submissions. Surprisingly, allowing traders to be fully strategic turns out to simplify the problem. This is because, with waiting costs, all traders on the same side of the book have the same expected utility – even if they are on different levels. For example, a seller with a higher limit price gets a better expected execution price, but also waits longer. The seller with the lower limit price cannot move above the price at which the two expected utilities are equal; otherwise, he will instantly be undercut by the other trader.

Since all traders on the same side of the book have the same expected utility, there exists a Markov perfect equilibrium in which the state variable is (m, n), with m the number of sellers and n the number of buyers in the book. Their expected utility follows a recursive system of difference equations. The recursive system can be solved numerically, in many cases in closed form. In equilibrium, impatient agents submit market orders, while patient agents submit limit orders and wait, except for the states in which the limit order book is full. When the book is full, some patient agent either places a market order or submits a quick (fleeting) limit order, which some trader from the other side of the book immediately accepts.[3] This result provides one explanation for the very short-lived limit orders documented by Hasbrouck and Saar (2009). In states in which the book is not full, new limit orders are always placed inside the bid-ask spread, thus endogenizing one assumption of Foucault *et al.* (2005).

In Roşu (2009) orders have a price impact, even if the information is symmetric. To study price impact, one has to go beyond one-unit orders and allow impatient traders to use multi-unit market orders. There is a *temporary* (or instantaneous) price impact function, which is the actual price impact suffered by the market order trader, and also a *permanent* (or subsequent) price impact, which reflects the fact that traders modify their orders in the book to account for the new reality. This permanent price impact is the difference between the new ask price and the ask price before the market order was submitted. In this setup, the temporary price impact is larger than the permanent price impact, which is equivalent to price overshooting. The intuition is that, before a multi-unit market order comes, the traders who expect their limit orders to be executed do not know the exact order size, so they stay higher in the book. Once the size becomes known, the sellers regroup lower in the book.

Also, if multi-unit market orders arrive with probabilities that do not decrease too fast with order size, then the price impact function is typically first concave and then convex. This is the same as saying that the limit orders cluster away from the bid and the ask or that the book exhibits a "hump" shape. Empirically, this is documented by Bouchaud *et al.* (2002) and Biais *et al.* (1995). In the model, the hump shape arises because patient traders cluster away from the bid-ask spread when they expect to take advantage of large market orders that are not too unlikely.

---

[3] This comes theoretically as a result of a game of attrition among the buyers and sellers. The game is set in continuous time and there is instant undercutting.

The general, two-sided case is more difficult and the solution is found numerically. An empirical implication is the *comovement* effect between bid and ask prices, documented by Biais *et al.* (1995). For example, a market sell order not only decreases the bid price – due to the mechanical execution of limit orders on the buy side – but also subsequently decreases the ask price. Moreover, the decrease in the bid price is larger than the subsequent decrease in the ask price, which leads to a wider bid-ask spread. The comovement effect is stronger when there are more limit traders on the side of the subsequent price move and the competition among them is stronger.

2.3   ORDER CHOICE WITH ASYMMETRIC INFORMATION

Models of the limit order book with asymmetric information provide further insights into the choice between market and limit orders. Handa and Schwartz (1996) note two risks of limit orders: (1) an adverse information event can trigger an undesirable execution; i.e., limit orders can be "picked off" either by traders with superior information or simply by traders who react more quickly to the public news (this is also called a *winner's curse* problem); and (2) favorable news can result in desirable execution not being obtained (this is also called the *execution risk* problem).[4] Furthermore, there is a balance between liquidity demand and supply: a relative scarcity of limit orders makes prices more volatile, and thus increases the benefits of a limit order.

Chakravarty and Holden (1995) present a static model of order choice with asymmetric information. In this model, limit order traders compete with market-makers in a hybrid market (e.g., NYSE). The market-makers set quotes first, and then market orders and limit orders are set simultaneously by one informed trader, and two or more uninformed traders. Since this is a one-period model, limit orders must be quote improving in order to be executed. The presence of uninformed limit orders inside the spread creates an additional reason for informed market orders, even if the true asset value is within the spread. (Normally, informed market orders should not be submitted when the true value is within the spread.) Furthermore, Chakravarty and Holden (1995) show that a combination of a BMO and an SLO is sometimes better for the

---

[4] For example, if a trader has a BLO in the book, good news about the asset raises the price and makes it less likely that the BLO will be executed; i.e., its execution costs increase.

informed trader than a BMO alone. This is because an SLO provides insurance against the uncertainty about whether uninformed traders will supply liquidity on the sell side; a BMO-only might execute at a disadvantageous price.

Foucault (1999) studies the mix between market and limit orders in a model with a moving fundamental value. For tractability, limit orders have a one-period life. They are subject to both the winner's curse problem and the execution risk problem. Similar to Goettler et al. (2005), Foucault's (1999) model is technically not an asymmetric information model, but the presence of trading frictions makes it resemble such a model. The fundamental value is assumed to move by $\pm\sigma$ according to a binomial tree with the same up and down probabilities. Each trader's private valuation is either L or $-L$, and this determines whether the trader is a buyer or a seller, and whether it uses a market order or a limit order. This decision also depends on whether the limit order book is empty or has already one limit order (it cannot have more than one).

The mix between market and limit orders depends essentially on the volatility of the asset, σ. When σ is higher, the picking off risks are larger, and the limit order therefore incorporates a larger compensation. This increases the cost of market orders and makes them less frequent. In turn, this decreases the execution probability of a limit order. This analysis leads to two empirical implications: (1) the fraction of limit orders in the order flow increases with volatility and (2) the fill rate (ratio of filled limit orders to the number of submitted limit orders) is negatively related to volatility.

Handa et al. (2003) extend Foucault (1999) by introducing privately informed traders, whose information becomes public after one trade. Additionally, the proportion of traders with high and low valuations is allowed to be unbalanced. One implication of their model is that spreads should be higher in the balanced case, compared with the unbalanced case. This is because, in unbalanced markets, the relatively scarce category of traders can extract better terms of trade from the other side, and this translates into tighter spreads.

Goettler et al. (2009) numerically solve the first dynamic model of limit order markets with asymmetric information. The model is similar to that of Goettler et al. (2005), with the main difference being that traders can acquire information about the fundamental value. Traders arrive according to a Poisson process with intensity λ, and upon entry decide whether to acquire information, for a fixed cost c. Traders who remain uninformed observe the fundamental value with a fixed lag. The fundamental value changes according to a Poisson process with intensity μ, in which case with equal probability can go up or down by k ticks. Each agent can trade at most one unit and have a type $\theta = (\rho, \alpha)$, where ρ is the discount rate and α is a private valuation for the asset. Traders with $\alpha = 0$ are called *speculators*, while those with high α are usually buyers and those with low α are usually sellers. There are cancellation costs: a limit trader can cancel or modify his or her order only at a time that is randomly drawn.

The equilibrium concept used is stationary Markov perfect Bayesian equilibrium and is solved numerically using the Pakes and McGuire (2001) algorithm. Because there are cancellation costs, there are stale limit orders and picking-off risks. Speculators have a high demand for information, but a low desire to trade, so they usually become informed and use limit orders. However, in very volatile times more orders become stale, so in the equilibrium when only speculators are informed, they demand more liquidity via market orders and submit limit orders at more conservative prices. Thus, limit order markets act as a volatility multiplier: a small increase in fundamental volatility can lead to a large increase in price volatility.

Harris (1998) considers the dynamic order submission decisions of some stylized traders: liquidity traders, informed traders, and value traders. Liquidity traders are informed, and their choice of market order versus limit order depends on their deadline. If the deadline by which they must fill their order is distant, liquidity traders use limit orders. Gradually, if their limit orders do not fill, they replace them with more aggressively priced limit orders, and eventually with market orders. Informed traders have transitory private information about the fundamental value, and in general submit market orders to use their "hot information" unless the bid-ask spreads are wide and trading deadlines are distant, in which case they use limit orders to minimize transaction costs. Value-motivated traders have a flow of information and have a cutoff strategy: when they believe the price is far from the fundamental value (and likely to revert quickly), they use market orders. Otherwise, they use limit orders.

Kaniel and Liu (2006) extend the partial equilibrium model of Harris (1998) to a general equilibrium model, similar to Glosten and Milgrom (1985), but with only three trading dates. In their model, informed traders submit limit orders when information is long-lived, to the extent that the limit orders can be even more informative than the market orders.

Roşu (2010) proposes a dynamic model of limit order markets, in which traders can acquire information about a moving fundamental value. As in Roşu (2009), there are no order cancellation costs or monitoring costs, and the same technique is used to construct a stationary Markov perfect equilibrium. The fundamental value v_t moves according to a diffusion process with normal increments. Traders arrive at the market according to a Poisson process with intensity λ, and upon arrival can acquire information: they pay a fixed cost c and observe v_t at the moment of entry. After that, they do not observe v anymore, which means that the precision of their private information decays over time. The resulting equilibrium is pooling: informed traders disguise their information while waiting in the book, and mimic the behavior of the uninformed traders. The informed traders could cancel their limit order at any time and modify it to a market order, but it is shown that they do not have an incentive to do so.

Traders are risk-neutral and have waiting costs proportional to the expected waiting time until execution. The waiting costs of the patient traders are very small, so that the model focuses on a set of states that appears with probability very close to one. In this "average limit order book" one can forget about the shape of the limit order book and focus only on the information content of orders. The model assumes that only patient traders can be informed. If impatient traders can also be informed, some of the quantitative results change, but the qualitative results remain. In equilibrium, impatient traders always submit market orders, while patient traders are either uninformed, in which case they use limit orders, or informed, in which case they submit either a limit order or a market order.

The first set of results concerns the nature of the equilibrium and the strategy of the informed traders. We note that, alongside the fundamental value process, there is also the *efficient price*, which is the expectation of the fundamental value conditional on all public information. In the model, since traders can cancel or revise their orders instantaneously, there are no stale limit orders or picking-off risks. The limit order book always moves up and down along with the efficient price: after each order, all traders modify their limit orders up or down to take into account the update of the efficient price due to the information contained in that order.

The strategy of the informed trader depends on how far the fundamental value, v, is from the efficient price, v^e. The optimal order of the informed trader is: a buy market order (BMO) if v is above v^e plus a cutoff value; a buy limit order (BLO) if v is between v^e and v^e plus the cutoff; a sell limit order (SLO) if v is between v^e minus the cutoff and v^e; and a sell market order (SMO) if v is below v^e minus the cutoff. The cutoff value is proportional to the *efficient volatility*, which is the conditional volatility of the fundamental value given all public information.

Put differently, an informed trader who observes an extreme fundamental value submits a market order, while one who observes a moderate fundamental value submits a limit order. This makes rigorous an intuition present, for example, in Harris (1998), Bloomfield *et al.* (2005), and Hollifield *et al.* (2006). To understand why, we note that in the absence of private information a patient trader would use a limit order in order to take advantage of the bid-ask spread. However, an informed trader who observes, for example, a fundamental value well above the efficient price realizes that the order book will drift upwards due to the action of future informed traders. This reduces the expected profit from a buy limit order, thus making the buy market order more attractive. If the fundamental value is above a cutoff, cashing in on the information advantage with a market order is better than waiting to be compensated for the limit order.

The next set of results regards the price impact of a trade and the efficient price process. Since both limit orders and market orders carry information about the fundamental value, the efficient price adjusts after each type of order. A key result is that all types of orders (BMO, BLO, SLO, SMO) are equally likely on average. First, if market orders were more likely than limit orders, the bid-ask spread would increase as limit orders were consumed by market orders. As the bid-ask spread increased, limit orders would become more likely, to the point where market orders and limit orders are equally likely. Second, if buy orders were more likely than sell orders, price impact would increase on average the efficient price to the point at which buy and sell orders are equally likely. Therefore, all order types are equally likely. This argument also shows that the midpoint between the bid and the ask is very close to the efficient price, so it provides a good empirical proxy for it.

The presence of informed traders ensures that the efficient price approximates the fundamental value. The speed of convergence is increasing in the information ratio: more informed traders make the efficient price converge more quickly to the fundamental value. Moreover, in a stationary equilibrium, the volatility of the efficient price is approximately equal to the fundamental volatility. This result shows that the volatility of the bid-ask spread midpoint is a good proxy for the fundamental volatility.

The average price impact of each type of order has a particularly simple form: Δ for BMO; $u\Delta$ for BLO; $-u\Delta$ for SLO; and $-\Delta$ for SMO, where $u \approx 0.2554$ is a constant and the price impact parameter Δ is proportional to the fundamental volatility and inversely proportional to the square root of total trading activity (the sum of arrival rates of informed and uninformed traders). This implies that the price impact of a limit order is on average about four times smaller than the price impact of a market order and that this ratio ($1/u \approx 3.912$) is independent of all the variables in the model. This result can be tested empirically.

A surprising result is that the price impact parameter Δ is independent of the ratio of the arrival rates of informed and uninformed traders (the *information ratio*). For example, suppose that the information ratio is low and that the market sees a buy market order. A low information ratio means that it is unlikely that the market order comes from an informed trader. This should decrease Δ. At the same time, if the market order does come from an informed trader, this trader knows there is not much competition from other informed traders, so the only reason to submit a market order is if the observed fundamental value v is very far from the efficient price v^e. For this reason Δ should be larger.

The fact that these two effects exactly cancel each other is due to the stationarity of the equilibrium. A stationary equilibrium implies that the volatility between two trades of the fundamental value v and of the efficient price v^e must be equal. However, the volatility of v between two trades only depends on the fundamental volatility and on the average time between two trader arrivals, neither of which depends on the information ratio. On the other hand, since v^e changes between two trades either by $\pm\Delta$ or by $\pm u\Delta$, with equal probability, it follows that the volatility of v^e is proportional to Δ. Therefore the price impact parameter Δ is independent of the information ratio.

The third set of results in Roşu (2010) concerns the shape of the limit order book, as measured by the bid-ask spread or price impact, in relation to trading activity, volatility, and information asymmetry. A surprising result is that the average bid-ask spread is decreasing in the information ratio. In a static model such as that of Glosten (1994), in which the fundamental value is constant, a larger fraction of informed traders increases adverse selection and makes spreads larger. However, with a moving fundamental value, the bid-ask spread has two components: one due to adverse selection costs (proportional to the price impact parameter Δ) and one due to the public uncertainty about the fundamental value (proportional to the efficient volatility σ^e). As explained above, Δ is independent of the information ratio while σ^e is decreasing in the information ratio: more informed traders, smaller public uncertainty.

This suggests another way of estimating the information ratio. The ratio of the intra-day volatility of the spread midpoint to the average bid-ask spread depends only on the information ratio and not on the fundamental volatility or trading activity. This ratio therefore can be used as a measure of the probability of informed trading, in the spirit of Easley *et al.* (2002).

Note that the definition of asymmetric information in Roşu (2010) is different from the typical adverse selection models, such as those of Kyle (1985) or Glosten (1994). Here, informed traders can more accurately be described as "smart" liquidity traders. This feature gives a realistic description of order driven markets in which traders are relatively small and information is decentralized, as opposed to a market dominated by large insiders who know the fundamental value and are present at all times. In fact, as one can see from the results, competition among more "smart" traders leads to *less* adverse selection. Indeed, when the information ratio is higher, efficient prices are usually closer to the fundamental value, and the bid-ask spreads are smaller.

2.4   THE INFORMATION CONTENT OF ORDERS

If informed agents can trade with both limit orders and market orders, both types of orders should have an information content. One way to test that empirically is to look at the price impact after each type of order. Biais *et al.* (1995) find that limit orders do attract future price moves in the same direction, indicating that limit orders contain some information. Kaniel and Liu (2006) study the price informativeness of limit orders and market orders by comparing the conditional probabilities of the bid-ask midpoint moving in the direction of the order right after the order was submitted. With this measure of price informativeness, they find that limit orders are more informative than market orders.

Cao *et al.* (2008) analyze the information content present in limit orders behind the best bid and ask, and find that the order book is indeed moderately informative, in the sense that its contribution to price discovery is about 22 %. The other 78 % comes from the best bid and ask, as well as the last transaction price. Also, imbalances between the bid and ask side in the limit order book are informative, even after controlling for return autocorrelation, inside spread, and trade imbalance. Contrary to the evidence above, Griffiths *et al.* (2000) find that nonmarketable limit orders have a significant price impact in the opposite direction.

Kavajecz and Odders-White (2004) study the connection between technical analysis and liquidity provision. They argue that the limit orders do not reveal just information related to the fundamental value but also discover pockets of depth already in place in the limit order book. Whether these pockets themselves are actually informed is not clear.

Eisler *et al.* (2010) present a VAR framework for the description of the impact of market orders, limit orders, and cancellations. Assuming an additive model of impact, they use an empirical database consisting only of trades and quotes information. They find that the impact of limit orders is similar, but smaller than that of market orders, in agreement with Roşu (2010). Limit order cancellations also impact prices, beyond their effect of attracting limit orders. Latza and Payne (2011) find evidence that both limit orders and market orders have forecasting power for stock returns at very high frequencies. The predictive power of limit order flows is greater and more persistent than that of market order flows. The forecasting power of limit order flows relative to market order flows is larger when both bid-ask spreads and return volatility are high.

Some empirical studies have considered the order submission strategies of various types of institutional or individual traders. Keim and Madhavan (1995) find that indexers and technical traders are more likely to submit market orders, while value traders are more likely to submit limit orders. Ellul *et al.* (2005) provide evidence that orders routed to the automatic execution system of NYSE (as opposed to those routed to the floor auction process) display extreme impatience, yet they appear to be the less information sensitive ones – which indicates that the informed traders need not be impatient in taking advantage of their superior information.

Tóth *et al.* (2011) present an empirical study based on a database where the broker that initiates an order book event can be identified. They find that brokers are very heterogeneous in liquidity provision: some are consistently liquidity providers while others are consistently liquidity takers. The behavior of brokers is strongly conditioned on the actions of other brokers, while they are only weakly influenced by the impact of their own previous orders.

Ranaldo (2004) finds evidence for the waiting costs as the explanation of the choice between limit orders and market orders: limit traders become more aggressive when (1) the own side of the book is thicker; (2) the opposite side of the book is thinner; (3) the bid-ask spread is wider; and (4) the temporary volatility increases. Ranaldo (2004) also finds experimental evidence for Foucault (1999): the bid-ask spread increases in price volatility. Ahn *et al.* (2001) show that market depth (volume of limit order submissions) increases with transitory volatility, and transitory volatility declines after an increase in market depth. If transitory volatility arises from, for example, the ask side, investors submit more limit sell orders than market sell orders. They argue that this is simply evidence for limit order traders who are ready to supply liquidity when this is needed.

Menkhoff *et al.* (2010) identify informed traders by high trading activity and by central trading location. The paper provides evidence from a foreign exchange market that informed traders take advantage of market conditions such as widening spreads or higher volatility, in which case they shift strongly towards limit orders, while uninformed traders respond modestly or not at all. The same is true for changes in market momentum, or changes in depth, but less so for changes in the expected time to execution. Anand *et al.* (2005) identify informed traders by institutional investors, and find that informed traders use market orders at the beginning of the trading day and limit orders later in the day. Furthermore, limit orders submitted by informed traders perform better than limit orders submitted by uninformed (i.e., individual) traders.

Bae *et al.* (2003) find that traders submit more limit orders relative to market orders when the spread is large (also found by Chung *et al.*, 1999), when the order size is large, and when traders expect high transitory price volatility. Goldstein and Kavajecz (2000) find that during circuit breakers and extreme market movements in the NYSE, limit order traders are significantly less willing to supply liquidity and migrate to the floor.

Harris and Hasbrouck (1996) provide evidence from the NYSE SuperDOT limit order book that limit orders perform better than market orders, even after introducing a penalty for unexecuted orders. A similar result is obtained by Wald and Horrigan (2005), who also consider the investor type (information, risk aversion).

Hollifield *et al.* (2004) test empirically whether optimal order submission is monotone in the trader's valuation for the asset. The idea is that, due to the trade-off between price and execution costs, the trader's strategy should depend on the trader's private valuation: if the valuation is above a threshold the trader submits a BMO, if the valuation is not that high the trader submits a BLO, and so on. The paper does not reject the monotonicity restriction for buys and sells considered separately, but it does reject when buys and sells are considered jointly. The expected payoffs from submitting limit orders with low execution probabilities are too low relative to the expected payoffs from submitting limit orders with high execution probabilities. This may be due to not being able to model monitoring costs properly for limit orders with low execution probabilities.

Hollifield *et al.* (2006) use data from the Vancouver exchange to estimate the gains from trade. They find that traders with more extreme private values usually submit orders with low execution risk and low picking-off risk, while traders with moderate private values submit limit orders with higher execution risk and higher picking-off risk.

Lo and Sapp (2005) analyze in an ordered probit model the choice of both price aggressiveness and quantity. They find a trade-off between the two dimensions: more aggressive orders are smaller in size. The competition from increased depth on the same side of the market leads to less aggressive orders in smaller size.

2.5   QUESTIONS FOR FUTURE RESEARCH

As Parlour and Seppi (2008) point out, we know relatively little about limit order markets. In particular, the question about how informed agents choose to trade in such markets is crucial. The extant models are stylized, and it is important to know which findings remain robust to a more realistic specification.

For tractability, most models of limit order markets assume one-unit trading, with risk-neutral traders. If instead risk-neutral agents were allowed to trade more than one unit, they would clear the whole limit order book up to the perceived fundamental value. In fact, under risk-neutrality even a noisy signal would encourage informed traders to use very aggressive order submission strategies. A solution is to allow multi-unit trading, and at the same time to introduce risk aversion in order to make agents trade less. Risk aversion, however, complicates the problem, because one has to explicitly model inventories of risk-averse traders.

Modeling inventories is also related to the possibility of market-makers arising endogenously in limit order markets. In an experimental study, Bloomfield *et al.* (2005) show that informed traders tend to assume both the role of speculators on their private information and of market-makers. Thus, market-making arises endogeneously in markets, and cannot be ignored. However, allowing traders to perform the role of market-makers runs into the difficult problem of modeling inventories.

Understanding the reasons to trade is crucial if we want to understand order choice. Do people trade to hedge nontradeable income or because the investment opportunity sets have shifted? Do they trade because of liquidity shocks? What is the role of delegated asset management? Without an answer to these more general questions, it is difficult to give a definitive answer to the order choice problem.

On the empirical side, endogeneity is a key issue. Several studies, e.g., Ranaldo (2004), find that the bid-ask spread increases in volatility. However, it is not clear which way the causality goes. The theoretical story, e.g., in Foucault (1999), is that volatility determines the bid-ask spread. However, the converse might also hold for mechanical reasons: prices are more volatile when the bid-ask spread is wider.

Another important topic is to find a way to separate waiting costs from information, both theoretically and empirically. Limit orders suffer from both execution costs (waiting costs, monitoring costs) and adverse selection (asymmetric information). Agents can be patient or impatient, and also informed and uninformed. Therefore, being able to identify the different types of costs and the strategies of the various types of traders in limit order markets is a key topic for future research.

REFERENCES

Ahn, H., K. Bae and K. Chan (2001) Limit Orders, Depth and Volatility: Evidence from the Stock Exchange of Hong Kong, *Journal of Finance* **56**, 767–788.

Amihud, Y. and H. Mendelson (1980) Dealership Market: Market-Making with Inventory, *Journal of Financial Economics* **8**, 31–53.

Anand, A., S. Chakravarty and T. Martell (2005) Empirical Evidence on the Evolution of Liquidity: Choice of Market versus Limit Orders by Informed and Uninformed Traders, *Journal of Financial Markets* **8**, 289–309.

Back, K. and S. Baruch (2007) Working Orders in Limit Order Markets and Floor Exchanges, *Journal of Finance* **62**, 1589–1621.

Bae, K., H. Jang and K.S. Park (2003) Traders' Choice between Limit and Market Orders: Evidence from NYSE Stocks, *Journal of Financial Markets* **6**, 517–538.

Biais, B., H. Glosten and C. Spatt (2005) Market Microstructure: A Survey of Microfoundations, Empirical Results, and Policy Implications, *Journal of Financial Markets* **8**, 217–264.

Biais, B., P. Hillion and C. Spatt (1995) An Empirical Analysis of the Limit Order Book and the Order Flow in the Paris Bourse, *Journal of Finance* **50**, 1655–1689.

Biais, B., D. Martimort and J.-C. Rochet (2000) Competing Mechanisms in a Common Value Environment, *Econometrica* **68**, 799–837.

Bloomfield, R., M. O'Hara and G. Saar (2005) The "Make or Take" Decision in an Electronic Market: Evidence on the Evolution of Liquidity, *Journal of Financial Economics* **75**, 165–199.

Bouchaud, J.-P., M. Mezard and M. Potters (2002) Statistical Properties of the Stock Order Books: Empirical Results and Models, *Quantitative Finance* **2**, 251–256.

Cao, C., O. Hansch and X. Wang (2008) The Information Content of an Open Limit-Order Book, *Journal of Futures Markets* **29**, 16–41.

Chakravarty, S. and C. Holden (1995) An Integrated Model of Market and Limit Orders, *Journal of Financial Intermediation* **4**, 213–241.

Chung, K., B. Van Ness and R. Van Ness (1999) Limit Orders and the Bid-Ask Spread, *Journal of Financial Economics* **53**, 255–287.

Cohen, K., S. Maier, R. Schwartz and D. Whitcomb (1981) Transaction Costs, Order Placement Strategy, and Existence of the Bid-Ask Spread, *Journal of Political Economy* **89**, 287–305.

Demsetz, H. (1968) The Cost of Transacting, *Quarterly Journal of Economics* **82**, 33–53.

Easley, D., S. Hvidkjaer and M. O'Hara (2002) Is Information Risk a Determinant of Asset Returns?, *Journal of Finance* **57**, 2185–2221.

Eisler, Z., J.-P. Bouchaud and J. Kockelkoren (2010) The Price Impact of Order Book Events: Market Orders, Limit Orders and Cancellations, Working Paper.

Ellul, A., C. Holden, P. Jain and R. Jennings (2005) Order Dynamics: Recent Evidence from the NYSE, Working Paper.

Foucault, T. (1999) Order Flow Composition and Trading Costs in a Dynamic Limit Order Market, *Journal of Financial Markets* **2**, 99–134.

Foucault, T., O. Kadan and E. Kandel (2005) Limit Order Book as a Market for Liquidity, *Review of Financial Studies* **18**, 1171–1217.

Glosten, L. (1994) Is the Electronic Open Limit Order Book Inevitable?, *Journal of Finance* **49**, 1127–1161.

Glosten, L. and P. Milgrom (1985) Bid, Ask and Transaction Prices in a Specialist Market with Heterogeneously Informed Traders, *Journal of Financial Economics* **14**, 71–100.

Goettler, R., C. Parlour and U. Rajan (2005) Equilibrium in a Dynamic Limit Order Market, *Journal of Finance* **60**, 2149–2192.

Goettler, R., C. Parlour and U. Rajan (2009) Informed Traders and Limit Order Markets, *Journal of Financial Economics* **93**, 67–87.

Goldstein, M. and K. Kavajecz (2000) Trading Strategies during Circuit Breakers and Extreme Market Movements, *Journal of Financial Markets* **7**, 301–333.

Griffiths, M., B. Smith, A. Turnbull and R. White (2000) The Costs and Determinants of Order Aggressiveness, *Journal of Financial Economics* **56**, 65–88.

Handa, P. and R. Schwartz (1996) Limit Order Trading, *Journal of Finance* **51**, 1835–1861.

Handa, P., R. Schwartz and A. Tiwari (2003) Quote Setting and Price Formation in an Order Driven Market, *Journal of Financial Markets* **6**, 461–489.

Harris, L. (1998) Optimal Dynamic Order Submission Strategies in Some Stylized Trading Problems, *Financial Markets, Institutions and Instruments* **7**(2).

Harris, L. and J. Hasbrouck (1996) Market versus Limit Orders: The Superdot Evidence on Order Submission Strategy, *Journal of Financial and Quantitative Analysis* **31**, 213–231.

Hasbrouck, J. and G. Saar (2009) Technology and Liquidity Provision: The Blurring of Traditional Definitions, *Journal of Financial Markets* **12**, 143–172.

Hollifield, B., R. Miller and P. Sandås (2004) Empirical Analysis of Limit Order Markets, *Review of Economic Studies* **71**, 1027–1063.

Hollifield, B., R. Miller, P. Sandås and J. Slive (2006) Estimating the Gains from Trade in Limit-Order Markets, *Journal of Finance* **61**, 2753–2804.

Kaniel, R. and H. Liu (2006) So What Orders Do Informed Traders Use?, *Journal of Business* **79**, 1867–1913.

Kavajecz, K. and E. Odders-White (2004) Technical Analysis and Liquidity Provision, *Review of Financial Studies* **17**, 1043–1071.

Keim, D. and A. Madhavan (1995) Execution Costs and Investment Performance: An Empirical Analysis of Institutional Equity Trades, Working Paper.

Kyle, A.P. (1985) Continuous Auctions and Insider Trading, *Econometrica* **53**(6), 1315–1335.

Large, J. (2009) A Market-Clearing Role for Inefficiency on a Limit Order Book, *Journal of Financial Economics* **91**, 102–117.

Latza, T. and R. Payne (2011) Forecasting Returns and Trading Equities Intra-Day Using Limit Order and Market Order Flows, Working Paper.

Lo, I. and S. Sapp (2005) Price Aggressiveness and Quantity: How Are They Determined in a Limit Order Market?, Working Paper.

Madhavan, A. (2000) Market Microstructure: A Survey, *Journal of Financial Markets* **3**, 205–258.

Menkhoff, L., C. Osler and M. Schmeling (2010) Limit-Order Submission Strategies under Asymmetric Information, *Journal of Banking and Finance* **34**, 2665–2677.

O'Hara, M. (1995) *Market Microstructure Theory*, Blackwell.

Pakes, A. and P. McGuire (2001) Stochastic Algorithms, Symmetric Markov Perfect Equilibrium, and the "Curse" of Dimensionality, *Econometrica* **69**, 1261–1281.

Parlour, C. (1998) Price Dynamics in Limit Order Markets, *Review of Financial Studies* **11**, 789–816.

Parlour, C. and D. Seppi (2008) Limit Order Markets: A Survey, in *Handbook of Financial Intermediation and Banking*, A.V. Thaker and A. Boot (Eds), Elsevier.

Ranaldo, A. (2004) Order Aggressiveness in Limit Order Book Markets, *Journal of Financial Markets* **7**, 53–74.

Rock, K. (1996) The Specialist's Order Book and Price Anomalies, Working Paper.

Roşu, I. (2009) A Dynamic Model of the Limit Order Book, *Review of Financial Studies* **22**, 4601–4641.

Roşu, I. (2010) Liquidity and Information in Order Driven Markets, SSRN eLibrary.

Seppi, D. (1997) Liquidity Provision with Limit Orders and a Strategic Specialist, *Review of Financial Studies* **10**, 103–150.

Tóth, B., Z. Eisler, F. Lillo, J.-P. Bouchaud, J. Kockelkoren and J.D. Farmer (2011) How Does the Market React to Your Order Flow?, Working Paper.

Wald, J. and H. Horrigan (2005) Optimal Limit Order Choice, *Journal of Business* **78**, 597–619.

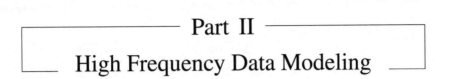

Part II
High Frequency Data Modeling

— 3 —

Some Recent Results on High Frequency Correlation

Nicolas Huth and Frédéric Abergel

3.1 INTRODUCTION

In spite of its significant practical interest, high frequency correlation has not been widely studied in the literature. The main stylized fact known about it is the Epps effect [1979], which states that "correlations among price changes [...] are found to decrease with the length of the interval for which the price changes are measured". Indeed, Figure 3.1 plots the correlation coefficient between the returns of the midquote of BNPP.PA and SOGN.PA, two major French financial stocks, as a function of the sampling period.

The correlation starts from a moderate value, 0.3, for a time scale of a few seconds, and then quickly reaches its asymptotic value, 0.8, after about 15 minutes of trading. Note that the increase in correlation between these two time scales is quite impressive since it is multiplied by more than 2.5. Note, however, that the correlation measured with daily closing prices during the same period is 0.94, still above the seemingly asymptotic value of the previous curve.

In this paper, we consider some empirical issues about high frequency correlation. First, we focus on how to extend the stochastic subordination framework introduced by Clark (1973) to the multivariate case. This allows us to model the random behavior of the covariance matrix of returns and the departure of the multivariate distribution of returns from the Gaussian. Then, we measure high frequency lead/lag relationships with the Hayashi–Yoshida (2005) cross-correlation estimator. Lead/lag

Market Microstructure: Confronting Many Viewpoints. Edited by F. Abergel, J.-P. Bouchaud,
T. Foucault, C.-A. Lehalle and M. Rosenbaum.
© 2012 John Wiley & Sons, Ltd.

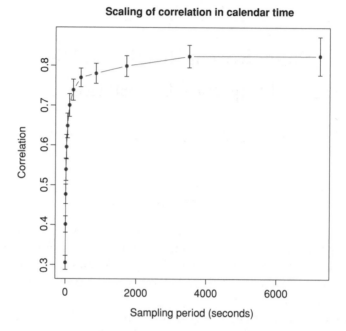

Figure 3.1   Correlation coefficient between the returns of the midquote of BNPP.PA and SOGN.PA as a function of the sampling period.

is of high practical relevance because it can help to build statistical arbitrage strategies through its ability to forecast the short-term evolution of prices. Finally, we compute the intraday profile of correlation, which is also interesting for practitioners such as brokers who split the orders of their clients during the day. The intraday correlation impacts their trading schedule when dealing with a multi-asset portfolio.

The paper is organized as follows. Section 3.2 introduces the dataset. Section 3.3 elaborates on a generalization of event time to the multivariate case. Then, Section 3.4 studies lead/lag relationships at high frequency. Section 3.5 gives some insight into the intraday profile of high frequency correlation. Finally, Section 3.6 concludes and announces further research.

3.2   DATA DESCRIPTION

We have access to the Reuters Tick Capture Engine (RTCE) database, which provides tick-by-tick data on many financial assets (equities, fixed income, forex, futures, commodities, etc.). Four levels of data are available:

- OHLC files: open, high, low, and close prices (on a given trading day);
- trades files: each transaction price and quantity timestamped up to the millisecond;
- quotes files: each quote (best bid and ask) price or quantity modification timestamped up to the millisecond;
- order book files: each limit price or quantity modification timestamped up to the millisecond, up to a given depth, typically ten limits on each side of the order book.

Throughout this study, we will use trades and quotes files. We will sample quotes on a trading time basis so that for each trade we have access to the quotes right before this trade. Trades and quotes data are recorded through different channels, which creates asynchrony between these two information sources. Therefore, a heuristic search algorithm is used to match trades and quotes.

When a trade walks the order book up or down by hitting consecutive limit prices, it is recorded as a sequence of trades with the same timestamp but with prices and quantities corresponding to each limit hit. For instance, assume that the best ask offers 100 shares at price 10 at 200 shares at price 10.01, and that a buy trade arrives for 150 shares. This is recorded as two lines in the trades file with the same timestamp, the first line being 100 shares at 10 and the second line 50 shares at 10.01. As a pre-processing step, we aggregate identical timestamps in the trades files by replacing the price by the volume weighted average price (VWAP) over the whole transaction and the volume by the sum of all quantities consumed. In the previous example, the trade price will thus be $(100 \times 10 + 50 \times 10.01)/(100 + 50) = 10.00333$ and the trade quantity is $100 + 50 = 150$.

The assets we consider are mainly European stocks (except in Section 3.5) and also some major equity index futures. The futures are nearby-maturity futures and are rolled the day before the expiration date. We have data for these assets between 01/03/2010 and 31/05/2010. Except in Section 3.5, we drop the first and last hours of trading because they show a very diferent trading pattern from the rest of the day. By doing so, we limit seasonality effects. The returns we will consider are the returns of the midquote in order to get rid of the bid/ask bounce.

3.3   MULTIVARIATE EVENT TIME

3.3.1   Univariate case

Let us consider an asset whose price fluctuates randomly during the trading hours. Between the $(i-1)$th and the ith trade, the performance of the asset is simply $F_i := P_i/P_{i-1}$. Then, N trades away from the opening price P_0, the total variation is given by the product of these elementary ratios

$$\frac{P_N}{P_0} = \prod_{i=1}^{N} F_i$$

We are then left with the following expression for the relative price increment, i.e., the asset return

$$R_N := \ln\left(\frac{P_N}{P_0}\right) = \sum_{i=1}^{N} \ln(F_i)$$

The asset return is clearly the sum of random variables and we would like to apply a version of the central limit theorem (CLT). The basic CLT is stated for independent and identically distributed random variables, a property that clearly fails to hold if one considers the returns of a financial asset: it has been well documented, and is easily verified experimentally, that absolute values of returns are autocorrelated (Bouchaud *et al.*, 2004). However, the CLT can be extended to the more general case of weakly dependent variables $X_1, \ldots, X_n$ (Whitt, 2002). The main condition for it to hold is the existence of the asymptotic variance

$$\lim_{n\to+\infty} \mathbb{V}\mathrm{ar}\left(\frac{1}{\sqrt{n}}\sum_{i=1}^{n} X_i\right) = \mathbb{V}\mathrm{ar}(X_1) + 2\sum_{k=1}^{+\infty} \mathbb{C}\mathrm{ov}(X_1, X_{1+k})$$

assuming that the X_i's form a weak-sense stationary sequence.

If the sum above is finite, i.e. if the autocorrelation function of $\ln(F_i)$ decays fast enough,[1] then the CLT yields, as $N \to +\infty$,

$$\frac{R_N}{\sqrt{N}} \xrightarrow{d} \mathcal{N}(0, \sigma^2)$$

---

[1] In the case of price returns $\ln(F_i)$, the autocorrelation function decays very fast and can be considered as statistically insignificant after some lag k close to one, even for small time scales (Abergel *et al.*, 2011a). Therefore the above sum is finite in practice.

where $\sigma^2 := \lim_{N \to +\infty} \mathbb{V}\mathrm{ar}\left((1/\sqrt{N}) \sum_{i=1}^{N} \ln(F_i)\right)$ and we have assumed[2] $\mathbb{E}\left(\ln(F_1)\right) = 0$. Hence, there holds, for $N \sim \infty$,

$$R_N \sim \mathcal{N}(0, N\sigma^2)$$

i.e., returns are asymptotically normally distributed with variance proportional to the number of trades when they are sampled in trade time. Recast in the context of stochastic processes, the returns can therefore be viewed as a Brownian motion in a stochastic clock (such processes are called subordinated Brownian motions), the clock being the number of trades.

Note that the same line of reasoning can be used with the traded volume as the stochastic clock. Indeed, the return after a volume V has been traded is

$$R_V = \sum_{i=1}^{N_V} \ln(F_i)$$

$$V = \sum_{i=1}^{N_V} V_i$$

where V_i is the volume traded during transaction i. N_V is the number of transactions needed to reach an aggregated volume V. When scaling with the square root of the traded volume, we get

$$\frac{R_V}{\sqrt{V}} = \sqrt{\frac{N_V}{V}} \frac{\sum_{i=1}^{N_V} \ln(F_i)}{\sqrt{N_V}}$$

$$= \frac{1}{\sqrt{\frac{\sum_{i=1}^{N_V} V_i}{N_V}}} \frac{\sum_{i=1}^{N_V} \ln(F_i)}{\sqrt{N_V}}$$

Since the volume of each transaction is finite, $V \to +\infty$ implies $N_V \to +\infty$. From the law of large numbers, we have $\sum_{i=1}^{N_V} V_i / N_V \to \mathbb{E}(V_1)$ as $N_V \to +\infty$, which is the average volume traded in a single transaction. Thus, applying Slutsky's theorem, we have, when $V \to +\infty$,

$$\frac{R_V}{\sqrt{V}} \xrightarrow{d} \mathcal{N}\left(0, \frac{\sigma^2}{\mathbb{E}(V_1)}\right)$$

---

[2] It is a reasonable assumption since we are dealing with high frequency data.

Now, the number of trades or the traded volume over a time period is obviously random. Therefore, the Δt-return $R_{\Delta t} := \ln(P_{\Delta t}/P_0)$ in calendar time exhibits a random variance $\sigma^2 X_{\Delta t}$, where $X_{\Delta t}$ is either the number of trades or the traded volume occurring during a time period of length Δt. The distribution of calendar time returns $R_{\Delta t}$ can be recovered from subordinated returns $R_{X_{\Delta t}}$ through the application of Bayes' formula[3]

$$P_{R_{\Delta t}}(r) = \int_0^{+\infty} P_{\mathcal{N}(0, x\sigma^2)}(r) P_{X_{\Delta t}}(x) \mathrm{d}x$$

where $P_Z(z)$ is the probability density function of the random variable Z. It is easy to show that the resulting distribution has fatter tails than the Gaussian (Abergel and Huth, in press). As mentioned in the introduction, this mechanism has been extensively studied in the finance literature (Silva, 2005), but only in the univariate framework. We want to generalize it to the multivariate case, which would turn into a stochastic covariance model to take into account the deviation of the empirical multivariate distribution of returns from the multivariate Gaussian.

3.3.2   Multivariate case

We now turn to the more interesting case of $d \in \mathbb{N}^*$ assets. How can we extend the previous framework to take several assets into account? Let us assume that an event time N is defined and that we sample returns $R_N = (R_N^1, \ldots, R_N^d)^T$ according to this time. Using a multivariate CLT, we follow the same line of reasoning as in the previous section and obtain, for $N \sim \infty$,

$$R_N \sim \mathcal{N}(0, N\Sigma)$$

where $\Sigma = \lim_{N \to +\infty} \mathbb{V}\mathrm{ar}\big((1/\sqrt{N}) \sum_{i=1}^N \ln(F_i)\big)$ is now the covariance matrix.

For a given time interval Δt, the respective numbers of trades or traded volumes for each asset $N_{\Delta t}^1, \ldots, N_{\Delta t}^d$ are obviously different, and we need to define a global event time $N_{\Delta t} = f\big(N_{\Delta t}^1, \ldots, N_{\Delta t}^d\big)$. We suggest to use $N_{\Delta t} = \sum_{i=1}^d N_{\Delta t}^i$, which amounts to increment time as soon as a trade occurs on any one of the d assets. This choice seems to us the simplest and most intuitive generalization of the univariate

---

[3] We assume that the distribution of the trading activity $X_{\Delta t}$ (number of trades or traded volume) can be approximated by a continuous distribution.

case, since it amounts to considering a single asset with dimension d: we aggregate the time series of the prices of each asset in chronological order, and then count trades or volumes as in the univariate case.[4]

3.3.3 Empirical results

In this section, we test our theory against high frequency multivariate data. The main statements are:

* Do returns become jointly normal when sampled in trade (respectively volume) time as N (respectively V) grows?
* Is the empirical covariance matrix of returns scaling linearly with N or V?
* What do $P_{N_{\Delta t}}$ and $P_{V_{\Delta t}}$ look like?

We focus on four pairs of assets:

* BNPP.PA/SOGN.PA: BNP Paribas/Société Générale;
* RENA.PA/PEUP.PA: Renault/Peugeot;
* EDF.PA/GSZ.PA: EDF/GDF Suez;
* TOTF.PA/EAD.PA: Total/EADS.

For sampling in trading time, we choose to sample every 2^i trades for $i = 0, 1, \ldots, 12$ ($2^{12} = 4096$). The sampling in calendar and volume time are chosen so that they match the trading time sampling on average. This means that if we sample every N trades, then the corresponding time scale Δt is the average time that it takes to observe N consecutive trades. In the same way, V is the average volume traded after N trades. Since we want to avoid the use of overnight returns[5] and to get approximately the same number of points for each sampling

---

[4] Such a representation makes sense when the orders of magnitude of the liquidity of each of the d assets are similar: consider the extreme case of one heavily traded asset and another one with only one trade per day. In this case, the normality of the couple as $N_{\Delta t}$ increases may fail to appear before an unrealistically large number of trades. A more appropriate clock might thus be to wait until each asset has been updated at least N times, which amounts to choosing $N_{\Delta t} = \min(N_{\Delta t}^1, \ldots, N_{\Delta t}^d)$.

[5] The use of overnight returns would be inappropriate in our framework because there is a significant trading activity during the opening and closing auctions, which would bias the event time clocks. Moreover, we want to focus only on the intraday behavior of returns when there is continuous trading between the starting and ending timestamps of returns.

period, we sample prices with overlap. For instance, assume that we have a series of prices P_1, P_2, P_3, P_4, P_5, and that we sample prices every two trades. Then we get three returns if we sample with overlap, namely $\ln(P_3/P_1)$, $\ln(P_4/P_2)$, $\ln(P_5/P_3)$. On the contrary, if we sample without overlap, we get two returns, $\ln(P_3/P_1)$, $\ln(P_5/P_3)$. The drawback of sampling with overlap is that points cannot be considered independent by construction.

Figure 3.2 displays the QQ-plot of the squared Mahalanobis distance of returns sampled in volume time against chi-square quantiles

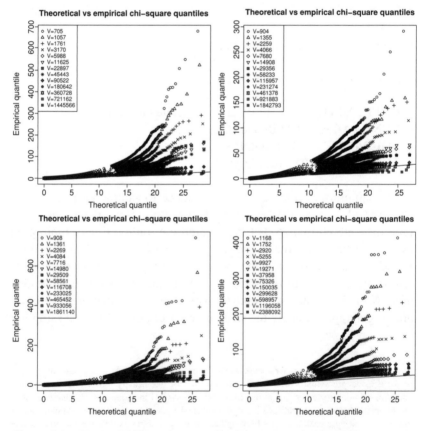

Figure 3.2 QQ-plot of the squared Mahalanobis distance of returns sampled in volume time against chi-square quantiles with two degrees of freedom. The straight line depicts the 45° line. Top left panel: BNPP.PA/SOGN.PA. Top right panel: RENA.PA/PEUP.PA. Bottom left panel: EDF.PA/GSZ.PA. Bottom right panel: TOTF.PA/EAD.PA.

with two degrees of freedom for increasing sampling periods. The Mahalanobis distance of a random vector X is defined as $D^2 = (X - \mu)^T \Sigma^{-1}(X - \mu)$, where μ is its mean and Σ its covariance matrix. Standard computations show that if $X \sim \mathcal{N}_d(\mu, \Sigma)$, then D^2 is distributed according to a chi-square with d degrees of freedom. Thus, for each observed bivariate return $R_{V,i} = (R_{V,i}^1, R_{V,i}^2)^T$, $i = 1, \ldots, n$, we compute its Mahalanobis distance $D_i^2 = (R_{V,i} - \mu)^T \Sigma^{-1}(R_{V,i} - \mu)$, where μ and Σ are respectively the sample average and covariance matrix. We drop duplicates in the vector $(D_1^2, \ldots, D_n^2)$, which creates a new effective sample size n. We then plot the sorted D_i^2 against the chi-square quantiles $F_{\chi^2(2)}^{-1}((i - 0.5)/n)$ for $i = 1, \ldots, n$. Since n is of the order of 10^5 for our sample, we plot a point every 10^3 points and we keep every point in the last 10^3. If the empirical distribution agrees with the theoretical one, then points should lie on the 45° line. We see that the empirical Mahalanobis distances measured in volume time become closer to the chi-square distribution as the sampling period increases. This means that the probability of accepting the hypothesis of bivariate Gaussianity with success becomes larger with the event time scale. Note that for TOTF.PA/EAD.PA, returns sampled with the highest time scale under consideration ($V = 2.38 \times 10^6$) are a bit further from the straight line than other pairs. This might come from the difference of trading activity between these two stocks. The average duration between two trades for TOTF.PA is 3.283 seconds while it is 12.152 seconds for EAD.PA, which is 3.7 times longer. For BNPP.PA/SOGN.PA (respectively RENA.PA/PEUP.PA, EDF.PA/GSZ.PA), this ratio is 1.01 (respectively 1.7, 1.5). Thus the bivariate event time might mostly be affected by TOTF.PA, leaving EAD.PA pretty much unchanged. As we mentioned before, the solution could be either to wait longer (measured in events) or to consider a new event time, such as the time it takes to have both assets updated at least a given number of times.

In comparison with volume time sampling, we plot on Figure 3.3 the same QQ-plot as on Figure 3.2, along with trading and calendar time sampling. We only show for visual clarity the results for the pair BNPP.PA/SOGN.PA and for four selected sampling periods. The findings are similar on the other pairs tested. From this figure it is clear that returns sampled in volume or trading time are closer to a bivariate Gaussian than calendar time returns, especially as the sampling period increases. Gaussianity seems even more plausible for volume time returns than for trading time returns.

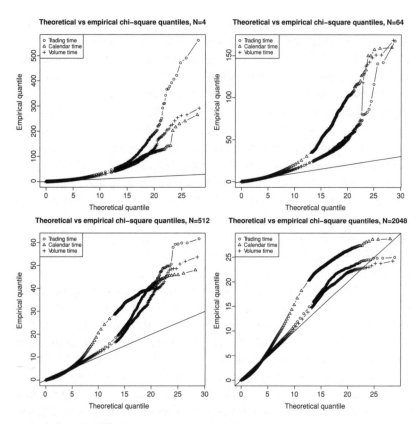

Figure 3.3 QQ-plot of the squared Mahalanobis distance of returns sampled in trading, volume, and calendar time against chi-square quantiles with two degrees of freedom for BNPP.PA/SOGN.PA. Top left panel: $N = 4$. Top right panel: $N = 64$. Bottom left panel: $N = 512$. Bottom right panel: $N = 2048$.

We now consider the scaling of the covariance matrix of returns in event time. Figure 3.4 (respectively 3.5) plots the realized variance (respectively covariance) of returns sampled in trading and volume time as a function of the sampling period, along with a linear fit. Clearly, the linearity of the covariance matrix as a function of either the volume or trading time is in agreement with the data. However, for very large sampling periods, the linearity tends to break down, but this might come from the shortage of data.

Figure 3.6 presents the survival function[6] of the aggregated volume $V_{\Delta t}$ on a semi-log scale for four sampling periods Δt. We consider

---

[6] The survival function of a random variable X is defined as $S(x) = \mathbb{P}(X > x)$.

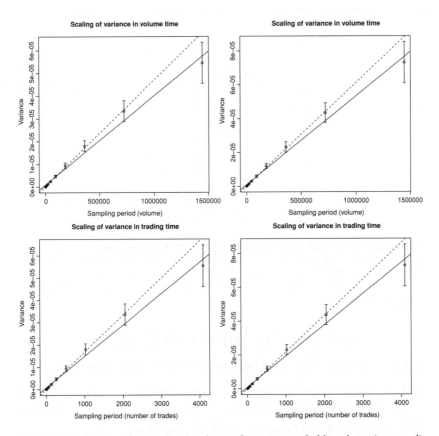

Figure 3.4 Scaling of the realized variance of returns sampled in volume (top panel) and trading (bottom panel) time as a function of the sampling period. The solid (respectively dotted) line shows the best linear fit with ordinary least squares on all points (respectively on all points except the last one). Left panel: BNPP.PA. Right panel: SOGN.PA.

four potential theoretical distributions as a comparison with the empirical one: Poisson, gamma, inverse-gamma and log-normal. We fit the parameters in order to match the first two moments of the empirical distribution. The empirical distribution lies somewhere in between the gamma distribution (exponential tail) and the inverse-gamma or log-normal distribution (heavy tails). Such a distribution for the subordinator respectively results in either a hyperbolic (exponential tails) or power-law (in the tails) distribution for price returns, which is in agreement with the deviation of the empirical distribution from the Gaussian.

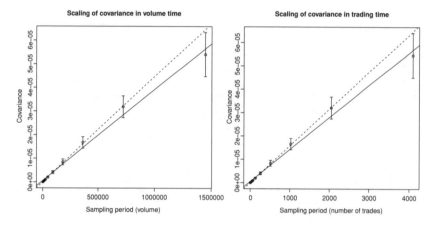

Figure 3.5 Scaling of the realized covariance of returns sampled in volume and trading time as a function of the sampling period for BNPP.PA/SOGN.PA. The solid (respectively dotted) line shows the best linear fit with ordinary least squares on all points (respectively on all points except the last one). Left panel: volume time. Right panel: trading time.

3.4 HIGH FREQUENCY LEAD/LAG

3.4.1 The Hayashi–Yoshida cross-correlation function

In Hayashi and Yoshida (2005), the authors introduce a new[7] estimator of the linear correlation coefficient between two asynchronous diffusive processes. Given two Itô processes X, Y such that

$$dX_t = \mu_t^X dt + \sigma_t^X dW_t^X$$
$$dY_t = \mu_t^Y dt + \sigma_t^Y dW_t^Y$$
$$d\langle W^X, W^Y \rangle_t = \rho_t dt$$

and observation times $0 = t_0 < t_1 < \cdots < t_{n-1} < t_n = T$ for X and $0 = s_0 < s_1 < \cdots < s_{m-1} < s_m = T$ for Y, which must be independent from X and Y, they show that the following quantity

$$\sum_{i,j} r_i^X r_j^Y \mathbb{1}_{\{O_{ij} \neq \emptyset\}}$$
$$O_{ij} =]t_{i-1}, t_i] \cap]s_{j-1}, s_j]$$
$$r_i^X = X_{t_i} - X_{t_{i-1}}$$
$$r_j^Y = Y_{s_j} - Y_{s_{j-1}}$$

---

[7] In fact, a very similar estimator was already designed by De Jong and Nijman (1997).

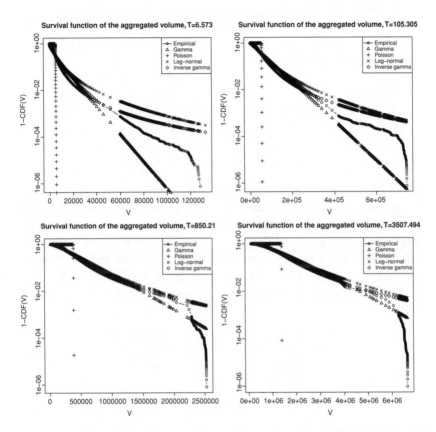

Figure 3.6 Distribution of the aggregated volume $V_{\Delta t}$ for BNPP.PA/SOGN.PA and four sampling periods Δt. Top left panel: $\Delta t = 6.573$ seconds. Top right panel: $\Delta t = 105.305$ seconds. Bottom left panel: $\Delta t = 850.21$ seconds. Bottom right panel: $\Delta t = 3507.494$ seconds.

is an unbiased and consistent estimator of $\int_0^T \sigma_t^X \sigma_t^Y \rho_t dt$ as the largest mesh size goes to zero, as opposed to the standard previous-tick covariance estimator (Griffin and Oomen, 2011; Zhang, 2011). In practice, it sums every product of increments as soon as they share any overlap of time. In the case of constant volatilities and correlation, it provides a consistent estimator for the correlation

$$\hat{\rho} = \frac{\sum_{i,j} r_i^X r_j^Y \mathbb{1}_{\{O_{ij} \neq \emptyset\}}}{\sqrt{\sum_i \left(r_i^X\right)^2 \sum_j (r_j^Y)^2}}$$

Recently, in Hoffman *et al.* (2010), the authors generalize this estimator to the whole cross-correlation function. They use a lagged version of the original estimator

$$\hat{\rho}(\ell) = \frac{\sum_{i,j} r_i^X r_j^Y \mathbb{1}_{\left\{ O_{ij}^\ell \neq \emptyset \right\}}}{\sqrt{\sum_i \left(r_i^X \right)^2 \sum_j \left(r_j^Y \right)^2}}$$

$$O_{ij}^\ell =]t_{i-1}, t_i] \cap]s_{j-1} - \ell, s_j - \ell]$$

It can be computed by shifting all the timestamps of Y and then using the Hayashi–Yoshida estimator. They define the lead/lag time as the lag that maximizes $|\hat{\rho}(\ell)|$. In the following we will not estimate the lead/lag time but rather decide if one asset leads the other by measuring the asymmetry of the cross-correlation function between the positive and negative lags. More precisely, we state that X leads Y if X forecasts Y more accurately than Y does for X. Formally speaking, X is leading Y if

$$\frac{\left\| r_t^Y - \text{Proj}\left(r_t^Y | \vec{r}_{t-}^X \right) \right\|}{\left\| r^Y \right\|} < \frac{\left\| r_t^X - \text{Proj}\left(r_t^X | \vec{r}_{t-}^Y \right) \right\|}{\left\| r^X \right\|}$$

$$\Longleftrightarrow \frac{\left\| \varepsilon^{YX} \right\|}{\left\| r^Y \right\|} < \frac{\left\| \varepsilon^{XY} \right\|}{\left\| r^X \right\|}$$

where $\text{Proj}(r_t^Y | \vec{r}_{t-}^X)$ denotes the projection of r_t^Y on the space spanned by $\vec{r}_{t-}^X := \left\{ r_s^X, s < t \right\}$. We will only consider the ordinary least squares setting, i.e. $\text{Proj}(r_t^Y | \vec{r}_{t-}^X) = \mu + \int_{]0,\bar{\ell}]} \beta_s r_{t-s}^X ds$ and $\|X\|^2 = \mathbb{V}\text{ar}(X)$. In practice, we compute the cross-correlation function on a discrete grid of lags so that $\int_{]0,\bar{\ell}]} \beta_s r_{t-s}^X ds = \sum_{i=1}^{p} \beta_i r_{t-\ell_i}^X$. It is easy to show (see Appendix A) that

$$\frac{\left\| \varepsilon^{YX} \right\|^2}{\left\| r^Y \right\|^2} = 1 - (C^{YX})^T (C^{XX} C^{YY})^{-1} C^{YX}$$

$$C^{YX} = (\mathbb{C}\text{ov}(Y_t, X_{t-\ell_1}), \ldots, \mathbb{C}\text{ov}(Y_t, X_{t-\ell_p}))^T$$

$$C^{YY} = \mathbb{V}\text{ar}(Y_t)$$

$$C^{XX} = (\mathbb{C}\text{ov}(X_{t-\ell_i}, X_{t-\ell_j}), i, j = 1, \ldots, p)$$

$(C^{YX})^T (C^{XX} C^{YY})^{-1} C^{YX}$ measures the correlation between Y and X. Indeed, X is a good predictor of Y if both are highly correlated. If we assume, furthermore, that the predictors X are uncorrelated, we can show that

$$\frac{\left\| \varepsilon^{YX} \right\|}{\left\| r^Y \right\|} < \frac{\left\| \varepsilon^{XY} \right\|}{\left\| r^X \right\|}$$

$$\Longleftrightarrow \sum_{i=1}^{p} \rho^2(\ell_i) > \sum_{i=1}^{p} \rho^2(-\ell_i)$$

$$\Longleftrightarrow \text{LLR} := \frac{\sum_{i=1}^{p} \rho^2(\ell_i)}{\sum_{i=1}^{p} \rho^2(-\ell_i)} > 1$$

The asymmetry of the cross-correlation function, as defined by the LLR (standing for the lead/lag ratio) measures lead/lag relationships. Our indicator tells us which asset is leading the other for a given pair, but we might also wish to consider the strength and the characteristic time of this lead/lag relationship. Therefore, the maximum level of the cross-correlation function and the lag at which it occurs must also be taken into account.

In the following empirical study, we measure the cross-correlation function between variations of midquotes of two assets; i.e. X and Y are midquotes. The observation times will be tick times. Tick time is defined as the clock that increments each time there is a nonzero variation of the midquote between two trades (not necessarily consecutive). It does not take into account the nil variations of the midquote, contrary to trading time.

3.4.2 Empirical results

Figure 3.7 shows the tick time Hayashi–Yoshida cross-correlation functions computed on four pairs of assets:

- FCE/FSMI: future/future;
- FCE/TOTF.PA: future/stock;
- RENA.PA/PEUP.PA: stock/stock;
- FSMI/NESN.VX: future/stock.

We choose the following grid of lags (in seconds):

$$0, 0.01, 0.02, \ldots, 0.1, 0.2, \ldots, 1, 2, \ldots, 10, 15, 20,$$
$$30, \ldots, 120, 180, 240, 300$$

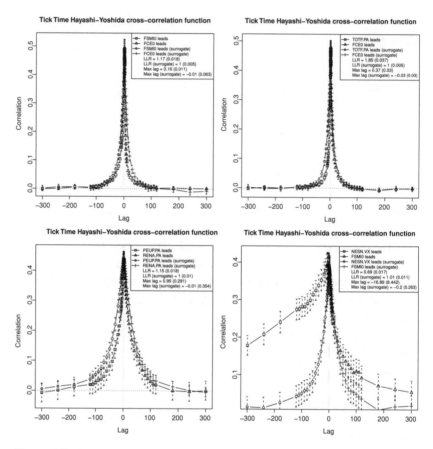

Figure 3.7 Tick time Hayashi–Yoshida cross-correlation function. Top left panel: FCE/FSMI. Top right panel: FCE/TOTF.PA. Bottom left panel: RENA.PA/PEUP.PA. Bottom right panel: FSMI/NESN.VX.

We consider that there is no correlation after five minutes of trading on these assets, which seems to be empirically justified on Figure 3.7, except for the FSMI/NESN.VX case. Figure 3.8 is similar to Figure 3.7, but zooms on lags smaller than 10 seconds. In order to assess the robustness of our empirical results against the null hypothesis of no genuine lead/lag relationship but only artificial lead/lag, we build a surrogate dataset. For two assets and for a given trading day, we generate two synchronously correlated Brownian motions with the same correlation as the two assets $\rho = \hat{\rho}_{HY}(0)$ on $[0, T]$, T being the duration of a trading day, with a mesh of 0.01 second. Then we sample these

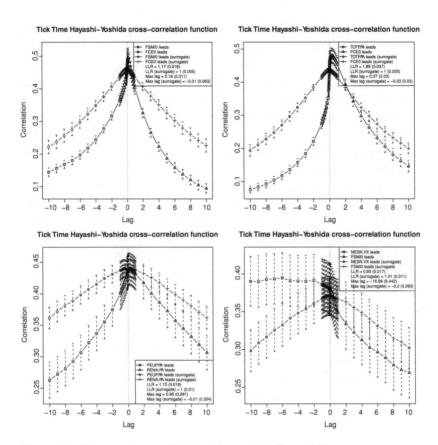

Figure 3.8   Zoom on lags smaller than 10 seconds in Figure 3.7.

Brownian motions along the true timestamps of the two assets, so that the surrogate data have the same timestamp structure as the original data. The error bars indicate the 95 % confidence interval for the average correlation over all trading days.[8]

For the FCE/FSMI pair (future versus future), the cross-correlation vanishes very quickly and there is less than 5 % of correlation at 30 seconds. We observe that there is more weight on the side where FCE leads with an LLR of 1.17 and a maximum correlation at 0.16 seconds. The pair FCE/TOTF.PA involves a future on an index with a stock being

---

[8] Assuming our dataset is made of D uncorrelated trading days, the confidence interval for the average correlation $\bar{\rho}_D = (1/D)\sum_{d=1}^{D} \rho_d$ is $[\bar{\rho}_D \pm 1.96\sigma_D/\sqrt{D}]$, where $\sigma_D^2 = \frac{1}{D}\sum_{d=1}^{D} \rho_d^2 - \bar{\rho}_D^2$. By doing so, we neglect the variance of the correlation estimator inside a day.

part of this index. Not surprisingly, the future leads by 0.37 seconds. This pair shows the biggest amount of lead/lag as measured by the LLR (1.85). The RENA.PA/PEUP.PA case compares two stocks in the French automobile industry. The cross-correlation is the most symmetric of the four shown with an LLR of 1.15. Finally, the FSMI/NESN.VX pair is interesting because the stock leads the future on the index where it belongs. Indeed, this result might be explained by the fact that NESN.VX is the largest market capitalization in the SMI, about 25 %. The asymmetry is quite strong (LLR = 0.69) and the maximum lag is 16.89 seconds, which is very large, but there is a significant amount of noise on this average lag. We also see that there still seems to be correlation after five minutes. The difference between the maximum correlation and the correlation at lag zero is 4.5 % for FCE/FSMI, 4.7 % for FCE/TOTF.PA, 1.4 % for RENA.PA/PEUP.PA, and 2.4 % for FSMI/NESN.VX, which confirms that the lead/lag is less pronounced for RENA.PA/PEUP.PA. The LLR for surrogate data is equal to one and the maximum lag is very close to zero for the four pairs of assets.[9] This strong contrast between real and surrogate data suggests that there are genuine lead/lag relationships between these assets that are not solely due to the difference in the levels of trading activity.

A more detailed study of lead/lag relationships, and especially their link with liquidity, will be available in Abergel and Huth (forthcoming 2012b).

3.5   INTRADAY SEASONALITY OF CORRELATION

Trading activity on financial markets is well known to display intraday seasonality (Abergel et al., 2011a; Admati and Pfleiderer, 1988; Andersen and Bollerslev, 1997; Chan et al., 1995). Seasonality appears on many quantities of interest, such as volatility, transaction volume, bid/ask spread, market and limit orders arrivals, etc. For instance, the intraday pattern of the traded volume on European equity stocks obeys an asymmetric U-shape: big volumes at the opening of the market, then it decreases until lunch time where it reaches the minimum, after 13:30[10] it starts to rise again, peaks at 14:30 (announcement of macroeconomic figures), it changes regime at 15:30 (NYSE and NASDAQ

---

[9] In fact, it can be assumed to be zero with a confidence level of 95%.

[10] In the following, we will always use Central European Time.

openings), peaks at 16:00 (other macroeconomic figures), and finally
rallies to reach its highest level at the close of the market. Therefore,
the intraday seasonality seems to be highly connected with both the human activity and the arrival of significant information. We believe that
huge volumes at the opening are due to the discovery of both corporate
news and figures (earnings, dividends, etc.) before the market opens, the
information coming from other international market performances and
the adjustment of positions taken the day before, while the peak at the
close is made by large investors such as derivatives traders and portfolio
managers who benchmark on closing prices.

In order to compute the intraday profile of correlation, or any other
quantity of interest, we cut trading days into 5 minute bins spanning the
whole day from the open to the close of the market. For instance, on the
CAC40 universe, the market opens at 9:00 and closes at 17:30, which
leads to $8.5 \times 12 = 102$ bins. On each day, we compute statistics on
each time slice and then we average over days for each slice. We end
up with an average statistics for each 5 minute bin. More precisely, for
a given bin $b = 1, \ldots, B$, the resulting statistics is

$$S(b) = \frac{1}{n_{\text{days}}} \sum_{d=1}^{n_{\text{days}}} S_d(b)$$

where $S_d(b)$ is the statistics computed on day d and bin b. In order to
compare the results from one universe to the other, we normalize the
intraday profile by the average value of the profile

$$\tilde{S}(b) = \frac{S(b)}{\frac{1}{B} \sum_{b=1}^{B} S(b)}$$

Since we have data for many stocks, we display cross-sectional results; i.e., we compute a statistics independently on each asset (or pair
of assets if we are interested in bivariate statistics) and we typically plot
the probability distribution of this statistics over the universe.

We focus our study on four universes of stocks:

- the 40 assets composing the French index CAC40 on 01/03/2010
  (CAC universe);
- the 30 most liquid[11] assets from the English index Footsie100 on
  01/03/2010 (FTSE universe);

---

[11] We use here the average daily number of trades as a rough criterion of liquidity.

- the 30 assets comprising the US index DJIA on 01/03/2010, plus major financial and IT stocks, 40 US stocks altogether (NY universe);
- the 30 assets composing the Asian index TopixCore30 on 01/03/2010 (TOPIX universe).

We use the Hayashi–Yoshida (2005) estimator for covariance and the standard realized volatility estimator (Barndorff-Nielsen and Shephard, 2002). We consider midquotes sampled in trading time, i.e. X_{t_i} (resp. Y_{s_j}) is the midquote of asset X (resp. Y) just before the trade that occurred at time t_i (resp. s_j) on X (resp. Y).

3.5.1   Empirical results

Figure 3.9 plots the intraday profile of correlation for the four universes and Figure 3.10 zooms on cross-sectional medians of profiles normalized by their average.[12] The CAC and FTSE correlation profiles are very similar and show an upward trend. The correlation is substantially weak at the open and steadily increases until 14:00; then there is a sudden strong upward jump at 14:30 when most of the US macroeconomic figures are announced.[13] At 15:30 (NYSE and NASDAQ markets open), we observe another sharp jump in correlation, followed by another jump at 16:00 when other macroeconomic figures are known by market participants. After 16:00, correlation tends to decrease to roughly 60 % (respectively 70 %) of its daily average at the close for the CAC (respectively FTSE) universe. Another remarkable pattern in this profile is that there is always a downard trend starting 15 or 20 minutes before abrupt jumps.

Regarding the NY universe, the correlation is also very low at the open and increases up to 16:00, where the aforementioned jump related to US figures occurs. We do not observe a significant impact when European stock markets close (17:30), in contrast to the noteworthy impact of US

---

[12] The whisker plots we present display a box ranging from the first to the third quartile with the median in between and whiskers extending to the most extreme point that is no more than 1.5 times the interquartile range from the box. These are the default settings in the boxplot function of R.

[13] The figures released at 14:30 are the Consumer Price Index, the Durable Goods Report, the Employee Cost Index, the Existing Home Sales, the Factory Orders Report, the Gross Domestic Product, the Housing Starts, the Jobless Claims Report, the Personal Income and Outlays, the Producer Price Index, the Productivity Report, the Retail Sales Report, and the Trade Balance Report. Those released at 16:00 are the Consumer Confidence Index, the Non-Manufacturing Report, the Purchasing Managers Index, and the Wholesale Trade Report. All of these figures are released on a monthly basis, except the GDP, which is announced quarterly.

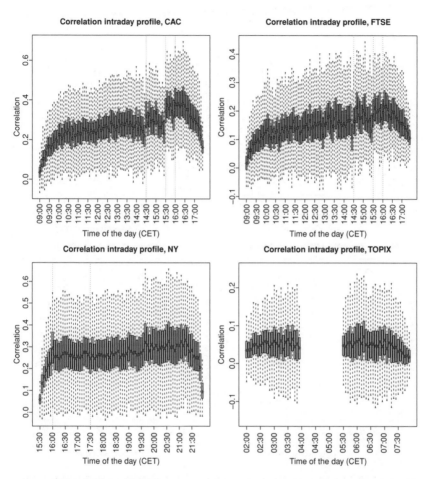

Figure 3.9   Intraday profile of correlation (cross-sectional distribution). Top left panel: CAC universe. Top right panel: FTSE universe. Bottom left panel: NY universe. Bottom right panel: TOPIX universe.

markets opening on Europe. The upward trend continues until 21:15, after which the correlation drops to reach 40 % of its average daily level. Most of this massive decrease in correlation is realized during the last 10 minutes of the trading session.

The intraday profile for the TOPIX universe is cut into two pieces because of the trading halt on the Tokyo Stock Exchange between 03:00 and 04:30. Both trading sessions tend to be similar to the patterns already observed on other universes: a global upward trend with a drop at the

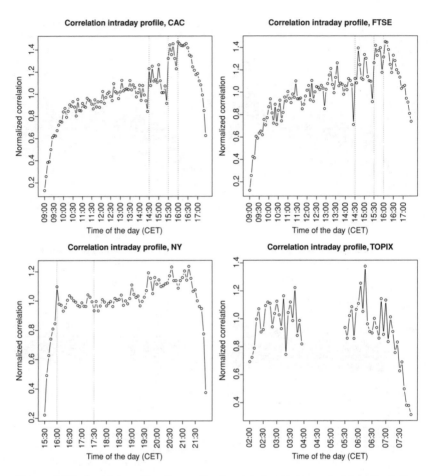

Figure 3.10 Intraday profile of normalized correlation (cross-sectional median). Top left panel: CAC universe. Top right panel: FTSE universe. Bottom left panel: NY universe. Bottom right panel: TOPIX universe.

close. Note that the gap between the correlation at the first close and at the second open is quite small, roughly 10 % of the average daily level.

Finally, we remark that the TOPIX cross-sectional distribution of correlation is the tightest and smallest, with an average correlation of about 5 % and many negatively correlated stocks, while the three other universes exhibit about 25 % of the average correlation, with not very much negative correlation.

The modeling of this intraday correlation pattern with nonstationary Hawkes processes will be studied in Abergel and Huth (forthcoming 2012a).

3.6 CONCLUSION

This paper provides some recent empirical results on high frequency correlation. We introduce a generalization of the univariate event time to take into account several assets. The resulting model for the distribution of returns fits the data quite well. We observe significant lead/lag relationships at high frequency, especially in the future/stock case. Finally, we study the intraday pattern of correlation and find a seemingly universal pattern, where correlation starts from small values and increases throughout the day, but substantially drops one hour before the closing of the market.

Regarding further research, lead/lag relationships will be investigated in more detail in Abergel and Huth (forthcoming 2012b), and we also plan to use the branching structure of Hawkes processes (Ogata *et al.*, 2002) to estimate the distribution of the lead/lag time. A forthcoming paper by Abergel and Huth (2012a) will be devoted to the calibration of the intraday correlation pattern with nonstationary Hawkes processes using the EM algorithm introduced in Lewis and Mohler (2011).

ACKNOWLEDGMENT

The authors would like to thank the members of the Natixis statistical arbitrage R&D team for fruitful discussions.

REFERENCES

Abergel, F. and N. Huth (forthcoming 2012a) High Frequency Correlation Intraday Profile. Empirical Facts.

Abergel, F. and N. Huth (forthcoming 2012b) High Frequency Lead/Lag Relationships. Empirical Facts.

Abergel, F. and N. Huth (in press). The Times Change: Multivariate Subordination. Empirical Facts, to appear in *Quantitative Finance*.

Abergel, F., A. Chakraborti, I. Muni Toke and M. Patriarca (2011a) Econophysics Review: 1. Empirical Facts, *Quantitative Finance* **11**(7), 991–1012.

Abergel, F., A. Chakraborti, I. Muni Toke and M. Patriarca (2011b) Econophysics Review: 2. Agent-Based Models, *Quantitative Finance* **11**(7), 1013–1041.

Admati, A. and P. Pfleiderer (1988) A Theory of Intraday Patterns: Volume and Price Variability, *Review of Financial Studies* **1**(1), 3–40.

Andersen, T. and T. Bollerslev (1997) Intraday Periodicity and Volatility Persistence in Financial Markets, *Journal of Empirical Finance* **4**, 115–158

Barndorff-Nielsen, O. and N. Shephard (2002) Econometric Analysis of Realized Volatility and Its Use in Estimating Stochastic Volatility Models, *Journal of the Royal Statistical Society, Series B (Statistical Methodology)* **64**(2), 253–280.

Bouchaud, J.-P., Y. Gefen, M. Potters and M. Wyart (2004) Fluctuations and Response in Financial Markets: The Subtle Nature of "Random" Price Changes, *Quantitative Finance* **4**(2), 176–190.

Chan, K., Y.P. Chung and H. Johnson (1995) The Intraday Behavior of Bid-Ask Spreads for NYSE Stocks and CBOE Options, *Journal of Financial and Quantitative Analysis* **30**(3), 329–346.

Clark, P.K. (1973) A Subordinated Stochastic Process Model with Finite Variance for Speculative Prices, *Econometrica* **41**, 135–155.

De Jong, F. and T. Nijman (1997) High Frequency Analysis of Lead–Lag Relationships between Financial Markets, *Journal of Empirical Finance* **4**(2–3), 259–277.

Epps, T.W. (1979) Comovements in Stock Prices in the Very Short-Run, *Journal of the American Statistical Association* **74**, 291–298.

Griffin, J.E. and R.C.A. Oomen (2011) Covariance Measurement in the Presence of Non-Synchronous Trading and Market Microstructure Noise, *Journal of Econometrics* **160**(1), 58–68.

Hayashi, T. and N. Yoshida (2005) On Covariance Estimation of Non-Synchronously Observed Diffusion Processes, *Bernoulli* **11**(2), 359–379.

Hoffmann, M., M. Rosenbaum and N. Yoshida (2010) Estimation of the Lead–Lag Parameter From Nonsynchronous Data, to Appear in *Bernoulli*.

Lewis, E. and G. Mohler (2011) A Nonparametric EM algorithm for Multiscale Hawkes Processes, Working Paper.

Ogata, Y., D. Vere-Jones and J. Zhuang (2002) Stochastic Declustering of Space–Time Earthquake Occurrences, *Journal of the American Statistical Association* **97**, 369–380.

Silva, A.C. (2005) Applications of Physics to Finance and Economics: Returns, Trading Activity and Income. PhD Thesis.

Whitt, W. (2002) Stochastic-Process Limits, *Springer*.

Zhang, L. (2011) Estimating Covariation: Epps Effect, Microstructure Noise, *Journal of Econometrics* **160**(1), 33–47.

— 4 —

Statistical Inference for Volatility and Related Limit Theorems

Nakahiro Yoshida

4.1 INTRODUCTION

This chapter provides a brief overview of some recent developments in statistical inference for stochastic processes from probabilistic and statistical aspects. We will discuss mainly three topics, that is, quasi likelihood analysis for semimartingales, nonsynchronous covariance estimation, and asymptotic expansion that can apply to finance.

In Sections 4.2 and 4.3, we will discuss *quasi likelihood analysis* (QLA) for semimartingales. In this article, the QLA means an asymptotic theory that provides asymptotic distribution of the quasi maximum likelihood and quasi Bayesian estimators (polynomial type), large deviation estimates for the quasi likelihood random field, and tail probability estimates for these estimators with their convergence of moments as a result. One cannot avoid such kinds of tail probability estimates when developing the very basic fields in standard theoretical statistics.

Section 4.4 is devoted to the problem of nonsynchronous covariance estimation. Statistical inference for stochastic processes under an irregular sampling scheme requires new developments in limit theorems. Among various irregularities, the nonsynchronicity gives challenging problems. Ad hoc interpolation causes bias in covariance estimation. The problem is how to construct a suitable estimator and to prove probabilistic performance of the estimator. Nonsynchronicity is not standard in stochastic analysis in which time related to measurability is rigid. However, the model is defined in terms of the stochastic analysis and we need it to address limit theorems under the nonsynchronicity. What is most important in the nonsynchronous estimation is that this concept

Market Microstructure: Confronting Many Viewpoints. Edited by F. Abergel, J.-P. Bouchaud, T. Foucault, C.-A. Lehalle and M. Rosenbaum.
© 2012 John Wiley & Sons, Ltd.

has brought relativization of time. The concept of lead-lag can be treated thanks to the relativization.

In Section 4.5, we will briefly mention Project YUIMA II in order to develop an R-package YUIMA for statistical inference and simulation for stochastic differential equations.

An asymptotic expansion scheme gives a numerical method in option pricing. In Section 4.6, we will discuss this scheme. There are three approaches: martingale expansion (global approach), mixing expansion (local approach), and small σ expansion (perturbation method). The third method has already been applied to option pricing and implemented by the YUIMA package. Recently an essential progress was made for martingale expansion. The estimator of the volatility parameter has an asymptotically mixed normal distribution, in general. In order to go into a further approximation, we need a method that gives asymptotic expansion in the mixed normal limit. A new device is necessary since classical methods of asymptotic expansion cannot apply in this situation.

4.2 QLA FOR AN ERGODIC DIFFUSION PROCESS

Consider a d-dimensional stationary diffusion process satisfying the stochastic differential equation

$$dX_t = a(X_t, \theta_2)dt + b(X_t, \theta_1)dw_t, \qquad X_0 = x_0$$

Here w_t is an r-dimensional standard Wiener process independent of the initial value x_0, and θ_1 and θ_2 are unknown parameters with $\theta_i \in \Theta_i \subset \mathbb{R}^{m_i}$. The distribution of x_0 possibly depends on the parameters. The true value of the unknown parameter will be denoted by $\theta^* = (\theta_1^*, \theta_2^*)$.

We assume the following condition.

[D1] (i) The mappings $a : \mathbb{R}^d \times \Theta_2 \to \mathbb{R}^d$ and $b : \mathbb{R}^d \times \Theta_1 \to \mathbb{R}^d$ have continuous derivatives satisfying

$$\sup_{\theta_2 \in \Theta_2} |\partial_{\theta_2}^i a(x, \theta_2)| \leq C(1 + |x|)^C \qquad (0 \leq i \leq 4)$$

and

$$\sup_{\theta_1 \in \Theta_1} |\partial_x^j \partial_{\theta_1}^i b(x, \theta_1)| \leq C(1 + |x|)^C \quad (0 \leq i \leq 4; 0 \leq j \leq 2)$$

for some constant C.

(ii) The $d \times d$ matrix $B(x, \theta_1) = b^{\otimes 2}(x, \theta_1)$ is elliptic uniformly in (x, θ_1).

(iii) For some constant C,

$$\sup_{\theta_2 \in \Theta_2} |a(x_1, \theta_2) - a(x_2, \theta_2)| + \sup_{\theta_1 \in \Theta_1} |b(x_1, \theta_1) - b(x_2, \theta_1)|$$

$$\leq C|x_1 - x_2| \quad (x_1, x_2 \in \mathbb{R}^d).$$

(iv) $X_0 \in \bigcap_{p>0} L^p(P_{\theta^*})$.

In this section, we assume a mixing property for X.

[D2]   There exists a positive constant a such that

$$\alpha_X(h) \leq a^{-1}e^{-ah} \quad (h > 0),$$

where

$$\alpha_X(h) = \sup_{t \in \mathbb{R}_+} \sup_{\substack{A \in \sigma[X_r : r \leq t], \\ B \in \sigma[X_r : r \geq t+h]}} |P_{\theta^*}[A \cap B] - P_{\theta^*}[A]P_{\theta^*}[B]|$$

In order to estimate the unknown parameters with the discrete-time observations $\mathbf{x}_n = (X_{t_i})_{i=0}^n$, where $t_i = ih$ with $h = h_n$ depending on $n \in \mathbb{N}$, we consider a quasi-likelihood function

$$p_n(\mathbf{x}_n, \theta) = \prod_{i=1}^n \frac{1}{(2\pi h)^{d/2}|B(X_{t_{i-1}}, \theta_1)|^{1/2}}$$

$$\times \exp\left(-\frac{1}{2h} B(X_{t_{i-1}}, \theta_1)^{-1}[(\Delta_i X - ha(X_{t_{i-1}}, \theta_2))^{\otimes 2}]\right)$$

with $\Delta_i X = X_{t_i} - X_{t_{i-1}}$.

For the sampling scheme, we will assume that $h \to 0$, $nh \to \infty$, and $nh^2 \to 0$ as $n \to \infty$. Moreover, we assume that for some positive constant ϵ_0, $nh \geq n^{\epsilon_0}$ for large n.

The quasi log likelihood random field is defined by

$$\mathbb{H}_n(\theta_1, \theta_2) = \log\left\{(2\pi h)^{nd/2} p_n(\mathbf{x}_n, \theta)\right\} \tag{4.1}$$

The scaling limit of $\log p_n(\mathbf{x}_n, \theta)/p_n(\mathbf{x}_n, \theta^*) = \mathbb{H}_n(\theta_1, \theta_2) - \mathbb{H}_n(\theta_1^*, \theta_2^*)$ gives

$$\mathbb{Y}_1(\theta_1; \theta^*) = -\frac{1}{2}\int_{\mathbb{R}^d}\left\{\text{Tr}(B(x, \theta_1)^{-1}B(x, \theta_1^*) - I_d)\right.$$

$$\left. + \log\frac{|B(x, \theta_1)|}{|B(x, \theta_1^*)|}\right\}\nu(dx)$$

where ν is a unique invariant probability measure of X. The integrand on the right-hand side of the above equation is non-negative. An identifiability condition in the present situation is as follows:

[D3]   There exists a positive constant $\chi(\theta^*)$ such that $\mathbb{Y}_1(\theta_1; \theta^*) \leq -\chi(\theta^*)|\theta_1 - \theta_1^*|^2$ for all $\theta_1 \in \Theta_1$ and $\theta_2 \in \Theta_2$.

Without this condition, we cannot expect the existence of a $\sqrt{n}$-consistent estimator of θ_1. A sufficient condition for [D3] is that the parametric model can be extended continuously to a compact set including Θ_1 and $\mathbb{Y}_1 \neq 0$ for $\theta_1 \neq \theta_1^*$.

The Ibragimov–Has'minskii–Kutoyants (Ibragimov and Has'minskii, 1972, 1973, 1981; Kutoyants (1984, 1994, 1998, 2004) program suggests that any asymptotic behavior of a QLA estimator is deduced from that of the statistical random field $p_n(\mathbf{x}_n, \theta)$. Guided by this philosophy, we associate with $\mathbb{H}_n(\theta_1, \theta_2)$ the statistical random field

$$\mathbb{Z}_n^1(u_1; \theta_1^*, \theta_2) = \exp\left\{ \mathbb{H}_n(\theta_1^* + n^{-1/2}u_1, \theta_2) - \mathbb{H}_n(\theta_1^*, \theta_2) \right\}$$

for $u_1 \in \mathbb{U}_n^1(\theta_1^*) = \{u_1 \in \mathbb{R}^{m_1}; \theta_1^* + n^{-1/2}u_1 \in \Theta_1\}$. Let $V_n^1(r, \theta_1^*) = \{u_1 \in \mathbb{U}_n^1(\theta_1^*); r \leq |u_1|\}$. Then the polynomial type large deviation (PLD) inequality (Yoshida, 2005) gives

$$P_{\theta^*}\left[\sup_{(u_1, \theta_2) \in V_n^1(r, \theta_1^*) \times \Theta_2} \mathbb{Z}_n^1(u_1; \theta_1^*, \theta_2) \geq e^{-r} \right] \leq \frac{C_L}{r^L} \quad (r > 0, \ n \in \mathbb{N})$$

(4.2)

for $L > 0$, where C_L is a constant depending on L.

Let us assume that $p_n(\mathbf{x}_n, \theta)$ can extend continuously to the boundary of $\Theta_1 \times \Theta_2$. A typical estimator of the QLA is the quasi maximum likelihood estimator (QMLE) $\hat{\theta}_n = (\hat{\theta}_{1,n}, \hat{\theta}_{2,n})$ that maximizes $p_n(\mathbf{x}_n, \theta)$ in $\theta = (\theta_1, \theta_2) \in \Theta = \Theta_1 \times \Theta_2$. Then as a consequence of (4.2), we obtain polynomial type large deviation estimates for the tail probability of $\sqrt{n}(\hat{\theta}_{1,n} - \theta_1^*)$. Indeed, if $|\sqrt{n}(\hat{\theta}_{1,n} - \theta_1^*)| \geq r$, then

$$\sup_{(u_1, \theta_2) \in V_n^1(r, \theta_1^*) \times \Theta_2} \mathbb{Z}_n^1(u_1; \theta_1^*, \theta_2) \geq 1$$

and this event admits (4.2). In particular, this ensures the boundedness of the moments

$$\sup_{n \in \mathbb{N}} P_{\theta^*}\left[|\sqrt{n}(\hat{\theta}_{1,n} - \theta_1^*)|^p \right] < \infty$$

for $p > 0$. It should be noted that $\hat{\theta}_{1,n}$ is *any* sequence of QMLEs.

Next, set

$$\mathbb{Z}_n^2(u_2; \hat{\theta}_{1,n}, \theta_2^*) = \exp\left(\mathbb{H}_n(\hat{\theta}_{1,n}, \theta_2^* + (nh)^{-1/2}u_2) - \mathbb{H}_n(\hat{\theta}_{1,n}, \theta_2^*)\right)$$

The scaling limit of $\log p_n(\mathbf{x}_n, \theta^1)/p_n(\mathbf{x}_n, \theta^*) = \mathbb{H}_n(\theta_1^*, \theta_2) - \mathbb{H}_n(\theta_1^*, \theta_2^*)$ yields

$$\mathbb{Y}_2(\theta_2; \theta^*) = -\frac{1}{2} \int_{\mathbb{R}^d} B(x, \theta_1^*)^{-1}[(a(x, \theta_2) - a(x, \theta_2^*))^{\otimes 2}] \, v(dx).$$

(4.3)

The identifiability of θ_2 is as follows.

[D4]   There exists a positive constant $\chi'(\theta^*)$ such that $\mathbb{Y}_2(\theta_2; \theta^*) \leq -\chi'(\theta^*)|\theta_2 - \theta_2^*|^2$ for all $\theta_2 \in \Theta_2$.

To deduce the properties of $\hat{\theta}_{2,n}$, we consider the statistical random field

$$\mathbb{Z}_n^2(u_2; \hat{\theta}_{1,n}, \theta_2^*) = \exp\left(\mathbb{H}_n(\hat{\theta}_{1,n}, \theta_2^* + (nh)^{-1/2}u_2) - \mathbb{H}_n(\hat{\theta}_{1,n}, \theta_2^*)\right)$$

for $u_2 \in \mathbb{U}_n^2(\theta_2^*) = \{u_2 \in \mathbb{R}^{m_2}; \theta_2^* + (nh)^{-1/2}u_2 \in \Theta_2\}$. The scaling is now $\sqrt{nh}$. Let $V_n^2(r, \theta_2^*) = \{u_2 \in \mathbb{U}_n^2(\theta_2^*); r \leq |u_2|\}$. Applying the PLD of Yoshida (2005) again, but this time for the statistical random fields $\mathbb{Z}_n^2(u_2; \hat{\theta}_{1,n}, \theta_2^*)$, we obtain the PLD inequality

$$P_{\theta^*}\left[\sup_{u_2 \in V_n^2(r, \theta_2^*)} \mathbb{Z}_n^2(u_2; \hat{\theta}_{1,n}, \theta_2^*) \geq e^{-r}\right] \leq \frac{C_L}{r^L} \qquad (r > 0, \ n \in \mathbb{N}).$$

(4.4)

In quite the same way as for θ_1, Inequality (4.4) entails polynomial type large deviation estimates for the tail probability of $\hat{\theta}_{2,n}$, which corresponds to one of the maximizers of $\mathbb{Z}_n^2(\cdot; \hat{\theta}_{1,n}, \theta_2^*)$ and equivalently the boundedness of the moments of the estimator:

$$\sup_{n \in \mathbb{N}} P_{\theta^*}\left[|\sqrt{nh}(\hat{\theta}_{2,n} - \theta_2^*)|^p\right] < \infty$$

for $p > 0$.

Define random fields $\mathbb{Z}_n(u_1, u_2; \theta^*)$ on $\mathbb{U}_n^1(\theta_1^*) \times \mathbb{U}_n^2(\theta_2^*)$ by

$$\mathbb{Z}_n(u_1, u_2; \theta^*) = \exp\left\{\mathbb{H}_n(\theta_1^\dagger, \theta_2^\dagger) - \mathbb{H}_n(\theta_1^*, \theta_2^*)\right\},$$

where $\theta_1^\dagger = \theta_1^* + n^{-1/2}u_1$, $u_1 \in \mathbb{U}_n^1(\theta_1^*)$ and $\theta_2^\dagger = \theta_2^* + (nh)^{-1/2}u_2$, $u_2 \in \mathbb{U}_n^2(\theta_1^*)$. By the PLD inequalities, it is possible to extend $\mathbb{Z}_n(., .; \theta^*)$

to a random field on $\mathbb{R}^{m_1} \times \mathbb{R}^{m_2}$ by a discounting factor and the extended random field becomes a random variable taking values in $\hat{C}(\mathbb{R}^{m_1+m_2})$, the set of continuous functions that tends to 0 as $|(u_1, u_2)| \to \infty$. $\hat{C}(\mathbb{R}^{m_1+m_2})$ is a separable Banach space with uniform norm.

Set

$$\Gamma_1(\theta^*)\left[u_1^{\otimes 2}\right] = \frac{1}{2} \int \left\{ \partial_{\theta_1}^2 B^{-1}(x, \theta_1)\left[u_1^{\otimes 2}, B(x, \theta_1^*)\right] \right.$$
$$+ \left. \partial_{\theta_1}^2 \log \frac{|B(x, \theta_1)|}{|B(x, \theta_1^*)|}\left[u_1^{\otimes 2}\right]\right\}\bigg|_{\theta_1 = \theta_1^*} \nu(\mathrm{d}x)$$
$$= \frac{1}{2} \int \mathrm{tr}\left\{ B^{-1}(\partial_{\theta_1} B) B^{-1}(\partial_{\theta_1} B)(x, \theta_1^*)\left[u_1^{\otimes 2}\right] \right\} \nu(\mathrm{d}x)$$

for $u_1 \in \mathbb{R}^{m_1}$, and

$$\Gamma_2(\theta^*)\left[u_2^{\otimes 2}\right] = \int_{\mathbb{R}^d} B(x, \theta_1^*)^{-1}\left[\partial_{\theta_2} a(x, \theta_2^*)[u_2], \partial_{\theta_2} a(x, \theta_2^*)[u_2]\right] \nu(\mathrm{d}x)$$

for $u_1 \in \mathbb{R}^{m_2}$.

Prepare random vectors $\Delta_i \sim N_{m_i}(0, \Gamma_i(\theta^*))$ $(i = 1, 2)$ such that Δ_1 and Δ_2 are independent. Define $\mathbb{Z}(u_1, u_2; \theta^*)$ by

$$\mathbb{Z}(u_1, u_2; \theta^*) = \exp\left\{ \Delta_1[u_1] + \Delta_2[u_2] \right.$$
$$- \left. \frac{1}{2}\left(\Gamma_1(\theta^*)\left[u_1^{\otimes 2}\right] + \Gamma_2(\theta^*)\left[u_2^{\otimes 2}\right]\right)\right\}$$

We denote by C_R the space of continuous functions on $\{(u_1, u_2); |(u_1, u_2)| \leq R\}$ and equip the uniform topology. It is easy to prove the weak convergence

$$\mathbb{Z}_n(\cdot, \cdot; \theta^*) \to^d \mathbb{Z}(\cdot, \cdot; \theta^*) \tag{4.5}$$

in C_R as $n \to \infty$ for each $R > 0$. In fact, the finite-dimensional convergence follows from a central limit theorem and tightness is easy to see on C_R.[1] Therefore, the PLD inequalities imply that the convergence (4.5) also takes place in $\hat{C}(\mathbb{R}^{m_1+m_2})$. The convergence of $(\hat{\theta}_{1,n}, \hat{\theta}_{2,n})$ follows from this convergence by the continuous mapping theorem. Since we already have the L^p-boundedness of the QMLE, we obtain the following theorem.

---

[1] The pointwise convergence $\mathbb{Z}_n(u_1, u_2; \theta^*) \to^d \mathbb{Z}(u_1, u_2; \theta^*)$ in particular means that $\mathbb{Z}_n(\cdot, \cdot; \theta^*)$ is locally asymptotically normal (LAN) at θ^* if we abuse this terminology for the quasi likelihood.

Theorem 1 *For any sequence of the maximum likelihood type estimators for* $\theta = (\theta_1, \theta_2)$,

$$\left(\sqrt{n}(\hat{\theta}_1 - \theta_1^*), \sqrt{nh}(\hat{\theta}_2 - \theta_2^*)\right) \to^d (\zeta_1, \zeta_2)$$

$$\sim N_{m_1+m_2}(0, \operatorname{diag}[\Gamma_1(\theta^*)^{-1}, \Gamma_2(\theta^*)^{-1}])$$

as $n \to \infty$. *Moreover,*

$$E_{\theta^*}[f(\sqrt{n}(\hat{\theta}_1 - \theta_1^*), \sqrt{nh}(\hat{\theta}_2 - \theta_2^*))] \to \mathbb{E}[f(\zeta_1, \zeta_2)]$$

as $n \to \infty$ *for all continuous functions* f *of at most polynomial growth.*

Prakasa Rao (1983, 1988) presented asymptotic results for an ergodic diffusion process under a sampling scheme. The joint weak convergence was presented in Yoshida (1992c) for a sampled diffusion process. Kessler (1997) applied a local Gaussian approximation with higher order correction terms to relax the rate of convergence of h to zero. Theorem 1 is from Yoshida (2005, 2006). Uchida (2010a) and Yoshida and Uchida (2010) proved convergence of moments of the adaptive quasi maximum likelihood estimators at a general sampling rate as well as the limit distribution. The tail probability estimate of polynomial type is inevitable for rigorously developing very basic asymptotic statistical theory, for example, prediction, model selection, asymptotic expansion, and higher-order decision theory among many fields involving such estimates. Uchida (2010b) proposed a contrast-based information criterion and proved its validity through technical arguments with the Malliavin calculus and the PLD. The PLD was applied in Masuda (2010) to drift estimation of a discretely observed Ornstein–Uhlenbeck process driven by a possibly heavy-tailed symmetric Lévy process with positive activity index.

The Ibragimov–Has'minskii–Kutoyants program applies to Bayesian type estimators for the diffusion process by the PLD. The adaptive Bayesian type estimator (ABE) is defined as follows. Here we only consider the quadratic loss function to make Bayesian estimators, for simplicity. Define a Bayesian type estimator $\tilde{\theta}_{1,n}$ by

$$\tilde{\theta}_{1,n} = \left\{ \int_{\Theta_1} \exp\left(\mathbb{H}_n(\theta_1, \theta_2^*)\right) \pi_1(\theta_1) \, d\theta_1 \right\}^{-1}$$

$$\times \int_{\Theta_1} \theta_1 \exp\left(\mathbb{H}_n(\theta_1, \theta_2^{\star})\right) \pi_1(\theta_1) \, d\theta_1$$

where θ_2^* is a known dummy value of θ_2, and $\pi_1(\theta_1) \, d\theta_1$ is a prior distribution of θ_1, bounded from below. Given the estimator $\tilde{\theta}_{1,n}$ for θ_1, we define a Bayesian type estimator $\tilde{\theta}_{2,n}$ by

$$\tilde{\theta}_{2,n} = \left\{ \int_{\Theta_2} \exp\left(\mathbb{H}_n(\tilde{\theta}_{1,n}, \theta_2)\right) \pi_2(\theta_2) \, d\theta_2 \right\}^{-1}$$
$$\times \int_{\Theta_2} \theta_2 \exp\left(\mathbb{H}_n(\tilde{\theta}_{1,n}, \theta_2)\right) \pi_2(\theta_2) \, d\theta_2$$

where $\pi_2(\theta_2) \, d\theta_2$ is a prior distribution of θ_2, bounded from below. It is possible to replace $\tilde{\theta}_{1,n}$ by another suitable estimator of θ_1, in general, for our purpose. A simultaneous Bayesian type estimator can be defined. However, the ABE has a computational advantage because the dimension of integration is lower. It is crucial in practical applications.

By definition, we have

$$\sqrt{n}(\tilde{\theta}_{1,n} - \theta_1^*) = \left\{ \int_{\mathbb{U}_n^1(\theta_1^*)} \mathbb{Z}_n^1(u_1; \theta_1^*, \theta_2^{\star}) \pi_1(\theta_1^* + n^{-1/2}u_1) \, d\theta_1 \right\}^{-1}$$
$$\times \int_{\mathbb{U}_n^1(\theta_1^*)} u_1 \, \mathbb{Z}_n^1(u_1; \theta_1^*, \theta_2^{\star}) \pi_1\left(\theta_1^* + n^{-1/2}u_1\right) \, d\theta_1$$

and a similar representation of $\sqrt{nh}(\tilde{\theta}_{2,n} - \theta_2^*)$. Since each Bayesian estimator consists of integrals of a random field and its asymptotic properties are available, we can investigate the asymptotic behavior of the Bayesian estimators.

Theorem 2 *For the ABE $(\tilde{\theta}_{1,n}, \tilde{\theta}_{2,n})$ for $\theta = (\theta_1, \theta_2)$, it holds that*

$$(\sqrt{n}(\tilde{\theta}_{1,n} - \theta_1^*), \sqrt{nh}(\tilde{\theta}_{2,n} - \theta_2^*)) \to^d (\zeta_1, \zeta_2)$$
$$\sim N_{m_1+m_2}(0, \text{diag}\,[\Gamma_1(\theta^*)^{-1}, \Gamma_2(\theta^*)^{-1}])$$

as $n \to \infty$. Moreover,

$$E_{\theta^*}[f(\sqrt{n}(\tilde{\theta}_1 - \theta_1^*), \sqrt{nh}(\tilde{\theta}_2 - \theta_2^*))] \to \mathbb{E}[f(\zeta_1, \zeta_2)]$$

as $n \to \infty$ for all continuous functions f of at most polynomial growth.

The adaptive Bayesian type estimator was defined in Yoshida (2005) and applied to the diffusion process. A simultaneous Bayesian type estimator was also treated. Ogihara and Yoshida (2011) proposed the QLA for the jump diffusion processes and proved limit theorems and convergence of moments for the ABE as well as the QMLE. The estimator that is characterized as a root of a random estimating equation, as it is often called a "Z-estimator", is within our scope. Obviously, finding a root is reduced to a minimum/maximum optimization problem.

4.3   QLA FOR VOLATILITY IN THE FINITE TIME-HORIZON

Consider an m-dimensional Itô process satisfying the stochastic differential equation

$$dY_t = b_t dt + \sigma(X_t, \theta) dw_t, \quad t \in [0, T] \tag{4.6}$$

where w is an r-dimensional standard Wiener process on some stochastic basis $(\Omega, \mathcal{F}, (\mathcal{F}_t)_{t \in [0,T]}, P)$ and b and X are progressively measurable processes with values in $\mathbb{R}^m$ and $\mathbb{R}^d$, respectively. The process σ is an $\mathbb{R}^m \otimes \mathbb{R}^r$-valued function defined on $\mathbb{R}^d \times \Theta$, Θ being a bounded domain in $\mathbb{R}^p$. For example, when $b_t = b(Y_t, t)$ and $X_t = (Y_t, t)$, Y is a time-inhomogeneous diffusion process.

The unknown parameter θ will be estimated based on the data $\mathbf{Z}_n = (X_{t_k}, Y_{t_k})_{0 \le k \le n}$ with $t_k = kh$ for $h = h_n = T/n$. The process b is unobservable, completely unknown to the observer. Here T is fixed and consistent estimation of the drift term is impossible unless the diffusion is degenerate. This is a semiparametric estimation problem.

Asymptotic theory of estimation of the volatility parameter with high frequency data observed on a fixed interval has been developed. Dohnal (1987) showed the local asymptotic mixed normality (LAMN) property for the likelihood. Genon-Catalot and Jacod (1993, 1994) proposed contrast functions for diffusion processes, proving the asymptotic mixed normality of the minimum contrast estimator.

We will see the asymptotic mixed normality and convergence of moments of both the maximum likelihood type estimator and the Bayesian type estimator for a quasi-likelihood function. The Ibragimov–Has'minskii–Kutoyants scheme is applied. A key point is to obtain the polynomial type large deviation inequality for the statistical random field.

The quasi log likelihood function is given by

$$\mathbb{H}_n(\theta) = -\frac{nm}{2} \log(2\pi h) - \frac{1}{2} \sum_{k=1}^{n} \left\{ \log \det S(X_{t_{k-1}}, \theta) \right.$$

$$\left. + h^{-1} S^{-1}(X_{t_{k-1}}, \theta)[(\Delta_k Y)^{\otimes 2}] \right\}$$

where $S = \sigma^{\otimes 2}$, the nondegeneracy of which will be assumed. The unknown drift process b is not used.

The quasi maximum likelihood estimator $\hat{\theta}_n$ is defined as

$$\mathbb{H}_n(\hat{\theta}_n) = \sup_{\theta \in \Theta} \mathbb{H}_n(\theta) \qquad (4.7)$$

The quasi Bayesian estimator (QBE) $\tilde{\theta}_n$ for the prior density $\pi : \Theta \to \mathbb{R}_+$ is defined by

$$\tilde{\theta}_n = \left(\int_\Theta \exp(\mathbb{H}_n(\theta))\pi(\theta)\mathrm{d}\theta \right)^{-1} \int_\Theta \theta \exp(\mathbb{H}_n(\theta))\pi(\theta)\mathrm{d}\theta \qquad (4.8)$$

We assume that π is continuous and $0 < \inf_{\theta \in \Theta} \pi(\theta) \leq \sup_{\theta \in \Theta} \pi(\theta) < \infty$. The true value of θ is denoted by θ^*.

Let $\mathbb{U}_n = \{u \in \mathbb{R}^p; \ \theta^* + n^{-1/2}u \in \Theta\}$. Define the random field $\mathbb{Z}_n(u)$ $(u \in \mathbb{U}_n)$ by

$$\mathbb{Z}_n(u) = \exp\left\{ \mathbb{H}_n\left(\theta^* + \frac{1}{\sqrt{n}}u \right) - \mathbb{H}_n(\theta^*) \right\}$$

Let

$$\mathbb{Z}(u) = \exp\left(\Gamma(\theta^*)^{1/2}\zeta[u] - \frac{1}{2}\Gamma(\theta^*)[u, u] \right)$$

where $\Gamma(\theta^*) = (\Gamma^{ij}(\theta^*))_{i,j=1,\ldots,p}$ with

$$\Gamma^{ij}(\theta^*) = \frac{1}{2T} \int_0^T \mathrm{tr}\left((\partial_{\theta_i}S)S^{-1}(\partial_{\theta_j}S)S^{-1}(X_t, \theta^*) \right) \mathrm{d}t$$

and ζ is a p-dimensional standard normal random variable independent of $\Gamma(\theta^*)$.

We need standard regularity conditions to derive asymptotic properties of the estimators though we do not write them here. See Uchida and Yoshida (2011) for details. That said, we should recall a problem of identifiability. A key index that evaluates the separation of statistical models is

$$\chi_0 = \inf_{\theta \neq \theta^*} \frac{-\mathbb{Y}(\theta)}{|\theta - \theta^*|^2}$$

where

$$\mathbb{Y}(\theta) = -\frac{1}{2T} \int_0^T \left\{ \log\left(\frac{\det S(X_t, \theta)}{\det S(X_t, \theta^*)} \right) + \mathrm{tr}\left(S^{-1}(X_t, \theta)S(X_t, \theta^*) - I_d \right) \right\}\mathrm{d}t$$

Naturally, the field $\mathbb{Y}(\theta)$ came from $\mathbb{H}_n(\theta) - \mathbb{H}_n(\theta^*)$. Differently from the ergodic case, $\mathbb{Y}(\theta)$ is *random* since it involves X_t. A quantitative estimate of χ_0 is necessary to construct a QLA that can catch more information about the estimators than just limit theorems. We set the following condition.[2]

[H2] For every $L > 0$, there exists $c_L > 0$ such that

$$P\left[\chi_0 \leq r^{-1}\right] \leq \frac{c_L}{r^L}$$

for all $r > 0$.

Condition [H2] enables the PLD to be obtained for $\mathbb{Z}_n(u)$:

$$P\left[\sup_{u \in \mathbb{R}^p : |u| \geq r} \mathbb{Z}_n(u) \geq e^{-r}\right] \leq \frac{C_L}{r^L} \qquad (r > 0) \qquad (4.9)$$

and the convergence

$$\mathbb{Z}_n \to^{d_s} \mathbb{Z} \qquad \text{in } \hat{C}(\mathbb{R}^p)$$

as $n \to \infty$ for the extended $\mathbb{Z}_n$, where d_s means stable convergence (with respect to the original universe). Let ζ denote a p-dimensional standard normal vector, on an extension of the original probability space, independent of $\Gamma(\theta^*)$.

In this way, we have for the QMLE

Theorem 3   (a) $\sqrt{n}(\hat{\theta}_n - \theta^*) \to^{d_s} \Gamma(\theta^*)^{-1/2}\zeta$ *as* $n \to \infty$.
(b) *For all continuous functions f of at most polynomial growth,*

$$E\left[f(\sqrt{n}(\hat{\theta}_n - \theta^*))\right] \to \mathbb{E}\left[f(\Gamma(\theta^*)^{-1/2}\zeta)\right]$$

as $n \to \infty$.

For the QBE, by setting $\tilde{u}_n = \sqrt{n}(\tilde{\theta}_n - \theta^*)$,

$$\tilde{u}_n = \left(\int_{\mathbb{U}_n} \mathbb{Z}_n(u)\pi(\theta^* + (1/\sqrt{n})u)du\right)^{-1} \int_{\mathbb{U}_n} u\,\mathbb{Z}_n(u)$$
$$\times \pi(\theta^* + (1/\sqrt{n})u)du \qquad (4.10)$$

---

[2] We keep the same name for this condition as Uchida and Yoshida (2009, 2011).

Let

$$\tilde{u} = \left(\int_{\mathbb{R}^p} \mathbb{Z}(u)du \right)^{-1} \int_{\mathbb{R}^p} u\,\mathbb{Z}(u)du \quad \left(= \Gamma(\theta^*)^{-1/2}\zeta \right) \quad (4.11)$$

Theorem 4   (a) $\sqrt{n}(\tilde{\theta}_n - \theta^*) \to^{d_s} \Gamma(\theta^*)^{-1/2}\zeta$ *as $n \to \infty$.*
(b) *For all continuous functions f of at most polynomial growth,*

$$E\left[f(\sqrt{n}(\tilde{\theta}_n - \theta^*)) \right] \to \mathbb{E}\left[f(\Gamma(\theta^*)^{-1/2}\zeta) \right]$$

as $n \to \infty$.

Condition [H2] implies the PLD inequality (4.9). The limit theorem with a mixed Gaussian limit and the tightness argument imply $\mathbb{Z}_n \to^{d_s} \mathbb{Z}$ in $C(\{|u| \le R\})$ for every $R > 0$. The PLD plus $\mathbb{Z}_n \to^{d_s} \mathbb{Z}$ implies the QLA in the above theorems. Hence, the problem is how to verify [H2]. A sufficient condition for [H2] is that

$$\underset{\substack{\omega \in \Omega \\ \theta \in \Theta \setminus \{\theta_*\} \\ t \in [0,T]}}{\text{ess. inf}} \left\{ \log \left(\frac{\det S(X_t, \theta)}{\det S(X_t, \theta^*)} \right) \right.$$

$$\left. + \text{tr}\left(S^{-1}(X_t, \theta)S(X_t, \theta^*) - I_d \right) \right\} / |\theta - \theta^*|^2 > 0$$

However, it is too naïve as it breaks, for example, in a simple model

$$dX_t = \left(1 + X_t^2 \right)^{\theta} dw_t, \qquad X_0 = 0$$

This statistical model is completely degenerate at $t = 0$. The state of separation between models strongly depends on randomness remaining in the limit. The existence of a local section of a certain tensor bundle validates [H2], even in such a nondegenerate case (Uchida and Yoshida, 2009, 2011).

For a concluding comment, there are still important questions related to QLA: jump diffusions in finite-time horizon, irregular sampling, nonsynchronous sampling, and inference under microstructure noise.

4.4   NONSYNCHRONOUS COVARIANCE ESTIMATION

4.4.1   Consistent estimator

Let $(X_t, Y_t)_{t \in \mathbb{R}_+}$ be a two-dimensional Itô process defined on a stochastic basis $\mathcal{B} = (\Omega, \mathcal{F}, \mathbf{F}, P)$ with $\mathbf{F} = (\mathcal{F}_t)_{t \in \mathbb{R}_+}$. A semiparametric problem is to estimate the (possibly random) "parameter" $\theta = [X, Y]_T$. If the

two sequences of data are synchronously observed, the sum of products
of increments of X and Y up to T

$$\mathrm{RCOV}_T = \sum_i \Delta_i X \Delta_i Y$$

is a natural estimator of θ because it converges in probability to θ if
the maximum lag of the time points tends to 0 in probability, as is well
known. Indeed, we can regard RCOV_T as a definition of $[X, Y]_T$.

If the sampling times of X and Y are different, the estimation problem
becomes nontrivial. In the nonsynchronous sampling scheme, we con-
sider families $\Pi_1 = \{I^i, i = 1, \ldots, N_1\}$ and $\Pi_2 = \{J^j, j = 1, \ldots, N_2\}$
of partitions of the interval $[0, T]$ corresponding to the observing times
of X and Y, respectively.[3] The increments are given by $\Delta_i X = \int_{I^i} dX_t$
and $\Delta_j Y = \int_{J^j} dY_t$.

If one wants to apply the "realized volatility" estimator to the nonsynchronous data, an interpolation such as previous-tick interpolation
and linear interpolation will be necessary. However, it is known that
such a naïve synchronization causes estimation bias. Nonsynchronicity
causes the "Epps effect".

For estimation of θ, Hayashi and Yoshida (2005) proposed

$$\hat{\theta} = \sum_i \sum_j \Delta_i X \Delta_j Y \, 1_{\{I^i \cap J^j \neq \emptyset\}}$$

This estimator has some advantages. No interpolation is used so it does
not depend on any tuning parameter such as the grid size. It is a finite
sum and no cut-off number is involved. The summation is essentially
one-dimensional. It attains asymptotically minimum variance.

Theoretical statistics requires some basic asymptotic properties: consistency of the estimator, asymptotic distribution of the error, efficiency
and optimality, and precise approximation to the error distribution. The
estimator $\hat{\theta}$ is consistent: $\hat{\theta} \to^P \theta$ whenever $\max_{i,j}\{|I^i|, |J^j|\} \to^P 0$
(Hayashi and Yoshida, 2005; Hayashi and Kusuoka, 2008).

4.4.2 Functional limit theorem

We will discuss a limit theorem of the nonsynchronous covariance estimator. Suppose that (X, Y) satisfies the stochastic differential equations

$$\begin{cases} dX = a_t^X dt + b_t^X dB_t^X, & X_0 = x_0 \\ dY = a_t^Y dt + b_t^Y dB_t^Y, & Y_0 = y_0 \end{cases}$$

---

[3] It does not matter up to the first order asymptotic results whether the observations at T are
available or not.

on the stochastic basis $\mathcal{B}$. Here $B^X = (B_t^X)_{t \in \mathbb{R}_+}$ and $B^Y = (B_t^Y)_{t \in \mathbb{R}_+}$ are standard Wiener processes with correlation $d\langle B^X, B^Y \rangle = \rho_t dt$, and a^X, a^Y, b^X, b^Y, and ρ are progressively measurable processes such that $\int_0^T (|a_t^X| + |a_t^Y| + |b_t^X|^2 + |b_t^Y|^2) dt < \infty$ a.s. for every $T > 0$.

Let $(S^i)_{i \in \mathbb{Z}_+}$ and $(T^j)_{j \in \mathbb{Z}_+}$ denote sampling times of X and Y, respectively. They are sequences of stopping times that are increasing a.s., $S^i \uparrow \infty$ and $T^j \uparrow \infty$ and $S^0 = 0$, $T^0 = 0$. We assume that the observation times depend on $n \in \mathbb{N}$, e.g., $S^i = S^i(n)$. We define a functional version of the *nonsynchronous covariance process* by

$$C_t^n = \sum_{i,j \in \mathbb{N}: S_i \leq t, \, T_j \leq t} (X_{S_i} - X_{S_{i-1}})(Y_{T_j} - Y_{T_{j-1}}) 1_{\{(S_{i-1}, S_i] \cap (T_{j-1}, T_j] \neq \emptyset\}}$$

Write $I(t) = I \cap [0, t)$ for an interval $I \subset \mathbb{R}_+$. The length of I is denoted by $|I|$. Let $I^i = [S^{i-1}, S^i)$ and $J^j = [T^{j-1}, T^j)$. We associate the sampling scheme $\{(S^i), (T^j)\}$ with the following nondecreasing functions:

$$H_n^1(t) = \sum_i |I^i(t)|^2, \qquad \qquad H_n^2(t) = \sum_j |J^j(t)|^2$$

$$H_n^{1 \cap 2}(t) = \sum_{i,j} |(I^i \cap J^j)(t)|^2, \qquad H_n^{1*2}(t) = \sum_{i,j} |I^i(t)||J^j(t)|K_t^{ij}$$

Assume that there exist positive numbers $b_n \to 0$ and random functions h^k such that for every $t \in \mathbb{R}_+$, $b_n^{-1} H_n^k(t) \xrightarrow{p} H^k(t)$ as $n \to \infty$ for $H^k = \int_0^t h_s^k ds$, $k = 1, 2, 1 \cap 2, 1*2$. Introducing a *strong predictability* of sampling times, Hayashi and Yoshida proved stable convergence of the nonsynchronous covariation process C^n:

$$b_n^{-1/2}(C^n - [X, Y]) \to^{d_s} \int_0^{\cdot} \gamma_s d\tilde{w}_s \qquad \text{in } \mathbb{D}(\mathbb{R}_+) \qquad (4.12)$$

as $n \to \infty$, where $\tilde{w}$ is a Wiener process independent of $\mathcal{F}$ and the process γ is given by

$$\gamma_s = \sqrt{(b_s^X b_s^Y)^2 h_s^{1*2} + (b_s^X b_s^Y \rho_s)^2 (h_s^1 + h_s^2 - h_s^{1 \cap 2})} \qquad (4.13)$$

See Hayashi and Yoshida (2008a, 2008b, 2011) for details.

Example 1 (Poisson sampling)   The partitions Π_i are given by independent Poisson random measures on $[0, T]$ with intensities np_i, $i = 1, 2$. Suppose that $\Pi = (\Pi_1, \Pi_2)$ is independent of (X, Y). If the functions σ_1, σ_2, and ρ are continuous, then the sequence $\sqrt{n}(\hat{\theta}_n - \theta)$

converges in distribution to a centered Gaussian random variable with variance

$$c = \left(\frac{2}{p_1} + \frac{2}{p_2} \right) \int_0^T \sigma_{1,t}^2 \sigma_{2,t}^2 \left(1 + \rho_t^2 \right) dt - \frac{2}{p_1 + p_2} \int_0^T (\sigma_{1,t} \sigma_{2,t} \rho_t)^2 dt$$

For nonsynchronous covariance estimation, Malliavin and Mancino (2002) proposed a Fourier transform based estimator. Hoshikawa *et al.* (2008) compared the performance of various nonsynchronous covariance estimators. Mykland (2010) considered the HY-estimator from the aspect of Gaussian analysis. Bergomi (2010) pointed out the HY-estimator appears in the context of option pricing.

For nonsynchronicity with microstructure noise, Ubukata and Oya (2008) discussed detection of microstructure noise and estimation of the autocovariance. Robert and Rosenbaum (2010a, 2010b) gave a new insight into the nonsynchronous covariance estimator under microstructure noise, introducing the notion of the uncertainty zone. Recently, Bibinger (2011a, 2011b) proposed a rate-optimal estimator of a new version of the nonsynchronous covariance estimator to overcome the microstructure noise. There are many studies on variance estimation in the presence of microstructure noise. Among which are Zhou (1996), Bandi and Russell (2005), Bandi *et al.* (2008), Zhang *et al.* (2005), and Hansen and Lunde (2006).

As for the power and bipower variations, Barndorff-Nielsen and Shephard (2004) discussed robustness of the estimator. Barndorff-Nielsen *et al.* (2006) proved central limit theorems for power and bipower variations. Podolskij and Vetter (2009) provided a central limit theorem for the modulated bipower variation that has rate $n^{1/4}$. Hayashi *et al.* (2008) proved asymptotic mixed normality for a general irregular sampling scheme.

It is possible to derive asymptotic expansion of the HY-estimator in the case without feedback to the diffusion coefficient, where the first order limit is central (Dalayan and Yoshida, 2011).

4.4.3   Application of YUIMA

In the R-package YUIMA (see Section 4.5), all simulation schemes, subsampling, and inference are designed to work on both regular or irregular sampling times. For an example, we apply YUIMA package to nonsynchronous covariance estimation. High frequency data consisting of nonsynchronously observed stock prices of four companies ("ba", "ge", "gm", "cc") were input and combined to make the YUIMA object "all.yuima". We applied function "cce" to output covariance estimates for all pairs of companies, and obtained the table below.

```
> load(file="ba.data")
> load(file="ge.data")
> load(file="gm.data")
> load(file="cc.data")
> all.yuima<-cbind.yuima(ba.data,ge.data,gm.data,cc.data)
> cce(all.yuima)
```

	ba	ge	gm	cc
ba	9.138171e-04	7.284301e-05	1.139381e-04	1.220833e-04
ge	7.284301e-05	8.312598e-04	5.703226e-05	8.153857e-05
gm	1.139381e-04	5.703226e-05	3.617391e-04	5.319538e-05
cc	1.220833e-04	8.153857e-05	5.319538e-05	3.014167e-04

4.4.4   Lead–lag estimation

What is most important in the nonsynchronous estimation is that this concept has brought relativization of time. If the observed multidimensional data had time lags between elements, the standard estimation methods for synchronously observed semimartingales would lose validity. Indeed, such a phenomenon is observed in high-frequency financial data. The lag estimation will be the first question in this situation.

Let $X = (X_t)_{t\in\mathbb{R}_+}$ and $Y = (Y_t)_{t\in[-\theta^*,\infty)}$ be Itô processes for a suitable filtration, and assume that $Y = (Y_t)_{t\in\mathbb{R}_+}$ is given by $Y_t = Y_{t-\theta^*}$. Estimation of θ^* deserves investigation because it gives information of the leader/follower relation between two companies that is, when $\theta^* > 0$; X is regarded as the leader and Y as the follower.

Suppose that X and Y are possibly nonsynchronously, randomly observed on the time interval $[0, T]$ and write I and J for subintervals corresponding to two consecutive data of X and Y, respectively. Denote by J_θ the interval $(\min J + \theta, \max J + \theta]$. Hoffmann et al. (2010) proposed the lead–lag estimator

$$\hat{\theta} = \text{argmax} \, |U(\theta)|$$

where

$$U(\theta) = \sum_{I,J:\bar{I} \leq T} X(I)Y(J)1_{\{I \cap J_{-\theta} \neq \emptyset\}}$$

We introduce parameter $n \in \mathbb{N}$ for asymptotic analysis. In typical examples, the intensities of the observation times on $[0, T]$ are proportional to n. Write $\hat{\theta}_n$ for $\hat{\theta}$. The intervals I and J form triangular arrays of sequences of subintervals depending on n. We can prove the consistency of $\hat{\theta}_n$ with the rate of convergence.

Theorem 5 *Under certain regularity conditions,*

$$\bar{r}_n^{-1}(\hat{\theta}_n - \theta^*) \to^P 0, \qquad n \to \infty$$

on the event $\{[X, \overset{\circ}{Y}]_T \neq 0\}$ *for a sequence of positive constants* $\bar{r}_n$ *tending to 0 as* $n \to \infty$ *such that* $r_n/\bar{r}_n \to^P 0$ *as* $n \to \infty$. *Here* r_n *is the maximum length of the interarrival times of observations in* $[0, T]$.

The YUIMA package is equipped with the lead–lag estimator. We obtained lead–lag (s) and correlation between each pair of stock prices as follows.

ba-cc	1.4751087	0.2348809
ba-ge	−18.1460249	0.1311659
ba-gm	−4.1453611	0.1692068
cc-ge	−27.4679106	0.1760048
cc-gm	120.3912058	0.2170557
ge-gm	1.7497747	0.1282431

An extension to a multi-lag model is considered by Kato *et al.* (2011).

4.5 YUIMA II FOR STATISTICAL ANALYSIS AND SIMULATION FOR STOCHASTIC DIFFERENTIAL EQUATIONS

In modern finance, most of the theoretical results rely on the assumption that the underlying dynamics of asset prices, currencies exchange rates, interest rates, etc., are continuous time stochastic processes described by stochastic differential equations. Continuous time models are also at the basis of option pricing and this problem often requires Monte Carlo methods. Moreover, any computational method requires identification of a model by estimation or calibration in any case empirically from the real data. Most ready-to-use tools in computational finance rely on pure discrete time models, like ARCH, GARCH, etc., and very few examples of software handling continuous time processes in a general fashion are available also in the R community. There still exists a gap between what is going on in mathematical finance and applied finance. The YUIMA package is intended to fill this gap.

The Yuima II Project is an open source and collaborative effort of several mathematicians and statisticians aimed at developing the R package named YUIMA for inference and simulation of stochastic differential equations. The YUIMA package is an environment that follows the paradigm of methods and classes of the S4 system for the R language. The package can treat stochastic differential equations in a very general type, e.g., one or multidimensional, driven by Wiener process, fractional Brownian motion, and processes with or without jumps specified through Lévy processes.

The YUIMA package offers the infrastructure on which complex models and inference procedures can be built. In particular, the basic set of functions includes:

1. Simulation schemes for various types of stochastic differential equations driven by noises such as Wiener, fractional Brownian, and Lévy.
2. Various types of subsampling schemes including irregular and random samplings.
3. Asymptotic expansion formulas for precise approximation of the expected value of a general irregular functional of diffusion processes that can apply option pricing.
4. Efficient quasi-likelihood inference for diffusion processes and diffusion processes with jumps.

Proof-of-concept (but fully operational) examples of statistical procedures have been implemented, like change point analysis in volatility of stochastic differential equations, nonsynchronous covariance estimation, lead–lag estimation, various test statistics, and model selection. A preliminary version of YUIMA by Project YUIMA II is now available at R-forge https://r-forge.r-project.org/projects/yuima/.

A systematically constructed GUI facilitates data analysis and simulation for stochastic processes. NS Solutions Corporation and The Graduate School of Mathematical Sciences, University of Tokyo, are conducting a joint study (Azzurro Project) on "The Application of Advanced Mathematical Statistics Theories in the Financial Industry". NS

Solutions Corporation is developing financial software using a result of this study.

4.6 HIGHER ORDER ASYMPTOTICS AND FINANCE

4.6.1 Martingale expansion

For a process $X = (X_t)$ defined by the stochastic integral equation

$$X_t = X_0 + \int_0^t b(X_s)\mathrm{d}s + \int_0^t \sigma(X_s)\mathrm{d}w_s$$

we consider a quadratic form of the increments of X with a strongly predictable kernel:

$$U_n = \sum_{j=1}^{n} c(X_{t_{j-1}})(\Delta_j X)^2$$

where $\Delta_j X = X_{t_j} - X_{t_{j-1}}$ and $t_j = j/n$.

The asymptotic property is of interest as the realized volatility takes this form. For the normalized error

$$Z_n = \sqrt{n}(U_n - U_\infty)$$

where $U_\infty = \int_0^1 c(X_s)\sigma(X_s)^2\mathrm{d}s$, the limit theorem of mixed normal type is well known. Here we are interested in the second-order approximation of the distribution of Z_n.

Z_n admits the stochastic expansion

$$Z_n = M_1^n + \frac{1}{\sqrt{n}}N_n \qquad (4.14)$$

where

$$M_t^n = \sqrt{n}\sum_{j=1}^{n} 2c_{t_{j-1}}\sigma_{t_{j-1}}^2 \int_{t_{j-1}}^{t}\int_{t_{j-1}}^{s} \mathrm{d}w_r\mathrm{d}w_s$$

The expression of N_n is involved and omitted.

For a reference variable, we will consider the d_1-dimensional random variable

$$F_n = \frac{1}{n}\sum_{j=1}^{n}\beta(X_{t_{j-1}}) \quad \text{or} \quad F_n = F_\infty := \int_0^1 \beta(X_t)\mathrm{d}t$$

Asymptotic expansion of the distribution was presented by Yoshida (1997) for the variable (Z_n, F_n) having the stochastic expansion (4.14) when $\langle M^n \rangle_1 \to^p 1$. Joint distribution is inevitable in statistical applications. Related works are Mykland (1992, 1993). The expansion of Yoshida (1997) was applied to derive asymptotic expansion for an estimator of the linearly parameterized volatility. A distributional expansion was presented in Yoshida (2001) for martingales with jumps.

As mentioned above, the limit distribution of the realized volatility is mixed normal in general. This means that the statistics becomes "nonergodic". The higher order inference theory in nonergodic statistics was not developed by lack of probabilistic devices. The classical methods for convergence to a process with independent increments do not work. Recently asymptotic expansion for a martingale with a mixed normal limit was obtained (Yoshida, 2008, 2010a).

Two random symbols $\underline{\sigma}$ and $\bar{\sigma}$ are used to describe the second order terms of asymptotic expansion. The *adaptive random symbol* $\underline{\sigma}$ corresponds to the classical second order term given in Yoshida (1997). The *anticipative random symbol* $\bar{\sigma}$ is new and it has a representation in terms of the Malliavin calculus. See Yoshida (2010a) or the site of Yoshida (2009, 2010b) for details. The full random symbol is given by

$$\sigma = \underline{\sigma} + \bar{\sigma} \tag{4.15}$$

With this random symbol, the expansion formula is written by a certain adjoint operation:

$$p_n(z, x) = E\left[\phi(z; W_\infty, C_\infty)\delta_x(F_\infty) \right]$$
$$+ r_n E\left[\sigma(z, \partial_z, \partial_x)^* \left\{ \phi(z; W_\infty, C_\infty)\delta_x(F_\infty) \right\} \right] \tag{4.16}$$

where $\delta_x(F_\infty)$ is Watanabe's delta function and $r_n = n^{-1/2}$ in the present case.

Theorem 6 *Assume a certain nondegeneracy condition for (Z_n, F_n). Then for any positive numbers M and γ,*

$$\sup_{f \in \mathcal{E}(M, \gamma)} \left| E\left[f(Z_n, F_n) \right] - \int_{\mathbb{R}^{1+d_1}} f(z, x)p_n(z, x)\mathrm{d}z\mathrm{d}x \right| = o\left(\frac{1}{\sqrt{n}} \right)$$

as $n \to \infty$, where $\mathcal{E}(M, \gamma)$ is the set of measurable functions $f : \mathbb{R}^{1+d_1} \to \mathbb{R}$ satisfying $|f(z, x)| \leq M(1 + |z| + |x|)^\gamma$ for all $(z, x) \in \mathbb{R} \times \mathbb{R}^{d_1}$.

While the formula (4.16) is general, the function $p_n(z, x)$ is very explicitly written in the present problem we started this section with. See the above mentioned papers.

It is possible to give the asymptotic expansion of the conditional law $\mathcal{L}\{Z_n | F_n\}$ in the same framework we applied for the expansion of the joint law $\mathcal{L}\{(Z_n, F_n)\}$.

Statistical applications by the martingale expansion were presented in Yoshida (1997) and Sakamoto and Yoshida (1998a). Also see Fuka-sawa (2011) for finance. The martingale expansion is purely distributional; that is, the first order limit has a relationship to Z_n only through distribution.

Another efficient but classical expansion of purely distributional type is mixing expansion in the central limit. There the underlying process is assumed to bear a mixing property. In this direction, see Kusuoka and Yoshida (2000) and Yoshida (2004) for asymptotic expansion of a functional of semimartingales. There are studies on this line (Sakamoto and Yoshida, 1998b, 2003, 2004, 2008, 2009, 2010; Uchida and Yoshida, 2001, 2006; Kutoyants and Yoshida, 2007). Masuda and Yoshida (2005) treated a stochastic volatility model.

4.6.2 Small σ expansion

Watanabe's theory (1987) was applied to statistical estimation problems for a stochastic differential equation with small perturbations (Yoshida, 1992b). Related studies are Yoshida (1993), Dermoune and Kutoyants (1995), Sakamoto and Yoshida (1996), Uchida and Yoshida (2004b), and Masuda and Yoshida (2004).

As for finance, this method was applied to option pricing in Yoshida (1992a) as a by-product of statistical applications. In this direction, there are many studies: Kunitomo and Takahashi (2001); Uchida and Yoshida (2004a); Takahashi and Yoshida (2004, 2005); Osajima (2006); Taka-hashi and Takehara (2009); Anderson and Hutchings (2009); Antonov and Misirpashaev (2009); Li (2010). A general asymptotic expansion formula for a functional of diffusion process is now available on YUIMA.

ACKNOWLEDGMENTS

This work was in part supported by Grants-in-Aid for Scientific Research No. 19340021; the Global COE program "The Research and Training Center for New Development in Mathematics" of the Graduate

School of Mathematical Sciences, University of Tokyo; JST Basic Research Programs PRESTO; and by a Cooperative Research Program of the Institute of Statistical Mathematics. This chapter is a report for the author's talk at Asymptotic Statistics, Risk and Computation in Finance and Insurance, December 15, 2010. The author thanks the organizers of the conference for the opportunity to present the talk.

REFERENCES

Andersen, L.B.G. and N.A. Hutchings (2009) Parameter Averaging of Quadratic SDES with Stochastic Volatility, *Social Science Research Network*.

Antonov, A. and T. Misirpashaev (2009) Projection on a Quadratic Model by Asymptotic Expansion with an Application to LMM Swaption, *Social Science Research Network*.

Bandi, F.M. and J.R. Russell (2005) Microstructure Noise, Realized Volatility, and Optimal Sampling.

Bandi, F.M., J.R. Russell and C. Yang (2008) Realized Volatility Forecasting and Option Pricing, *Journal of Econometrics* **147**, 34–46.

Barndorff-Nielsen, O.E. and N. Shephard (2004) Power and Bipower Variation with Stochastic Volatility and Jumps, *Journal of Financial Econometrics* **2**, 1–48.

Barndorff-Nielsen, O.E., S.E. Graversen, J. Jacod, M. Podolskij and N. Shephard (2006) A Central Limit Theorem for Realised Power and Bipower Variations of Continuous Semimartingales. In *From Stochastic Calculus to Mathematical Finance*, Springer, Berlin, pp. 33–68.

Bergomi, L. (2010) Correlations in Asynchronous Markets, *Social Science Research Network*, http://ssrn.com/abstract=1635866.

Bibinger, M. (2011a) Efficient Covariance Estimation for Asynchronous Noisy High-Frequency Data, *Scandinavian Journal of Statistics* **38**, 23–45. DOI: 10.1111/j.1467-9469.2010.00712.x.

Bibinger, M. (2011b) An Estimator for the Quadratic Covariation of Asynchronously Observed Itô Processes with Noise: Asymptotic Distribution Theory, preprint.

Dalalyan A. and N. Yoshida (2011) Second-Order Asymptotic Expansion for a Nonsynchronous Covariation Estimator, *Annales de l'Institut Henri Poincaré, Probabilités et Statistiques* **47**(3), 748–789.

Dermoune, A. and Y. Kutoyants (1995) Expansion of Distribution of Maximum Likelihood Estimate for Misspecified Diffusion Type Observation, *Stochastics Report* **52**(1–2), 121–145.

Dohnal, G. (1987) On Estimating the Diffusion Coefficient, *Journal of Applied Probability* **24**(1), 105–114.

Fukasawa, M. (2011) Asymptotic Analysis for Stochastic Volatility: Martingale Expansion, *Finance and Stochastics*, **15**(14), 635–654.

Genon-Catalot, V. and J. Jacod (1993) On the Estimation of the Diffusion Coefficient for Multidimensional Diffusion Processes. *Annales de l'Institut Henri Poincaré, Probabilités et Statistiques* **29**(1), 119–151.

Genon-Catalot, V. and J. Jacod (1994) Estimation of the Diffusion Coefficient for Diffusion Processes: Random Sampling, *Scandinavian Journal of Statistics* **21**(3), 193–221.

Hansen, P.R. and A. Lunde (2006) Realized Variance and Market Microstructure Noise, *Journal of Business and Economic Statistics* **24**, 127–161.

Hayashi, T. and S. Kusuoka (2008) Consistent Estimation of Covariation Under Non-synchronicity, *Statistical Inference for Stochastic Processes* **11**, 93–106.

Hayashi, T. and N. Yoshida (2005) On Covariance Estimation of Non-synchronously Observed Diffusion Processes, *Bernoulli Official Journal of the Bernoulli Society for Mathematical Statistics and Probability* **11**(2), 359–379.

Hayashi, T. and N. Yoshida (2008a) Asymptotic Normality of a Covariance Estimator for Nonsynchronously Observed Diffusion Processes, *Annals of the Institute of Statistical Mathematics* **60**(2), 367–406.

Hayashi, T. and N. Yoshida (2008b) Nonsynchronous Covariance Estimator and Limit Theorem II, Institute of Statistical Mathematics, Research Memorandum 1067.

Hayashi, T. and N. Yoshida (2011) Nonsynchronous Covariance Process and Limit Theorems, *Stochastic Processes and their Applications* **121**(10), 2416–2454.

Hayashi, T., J. Jacod and N. Yoshida (2008) Irregular Sampling and Central Limit Theorems for Power Variations: The Continuous Case, Preprint.

Hoffmann, M., M. Rosenbaum and N. Yoshida (2010) Estimation of the Lead–Lag Parameter From Non-Synchronous Data, to appear in *Bernoulli*.

Hoshikawa, T., K. Nagai, T. Kanatani and Y. Nishiyama (2008) Nonparametric Estimation Methods of Integrated Multivariate Volatilities, *Econometric Reviews* **27**(1–3), 112–138.

Ibragimov, I.A. and R.Z. Has'minskii (1972) The asymptotic behavior of certain statistical estimates in the smooth case, I. Investigation of the likelihood ratio, *Teor. Verojatnost. i Primenen* **17**, 469–486.

Ibragimov, I.A. and R.Z. Has'minskii (1973) Asymptotic behavior of certain statistical estimates, II. Limit theorems for a posteriori density and for Bayesian estimates, *Teor. Verojatnost. i Primenen* **18**, 78–93.

Ibragimov, I.A. and R.Z. Has'minskii (1981) Statistical estimates, *Applications of Mathematics*, **16** (asymptotic theory, translated from the Russian by Samuel Kotz).

Kato, H., S. Sato and N. Yoshida (2011) Analysis of Foreign Exchange Data with the Lead–Lag Estimator (in Japanese), The 2011 Japanese Joint Statistical Meeting, 4–7 September 2011, Fukuoka.

Kessler, M. (1997) Estimation of an Ergodic Diffusion from Discrete Observations, *Scandinavian Journal of Statistics* **24**(2), 211–229.

Kunitomo, N. and A. Takahashi (2001) The Asymptotic Expansion Approach to the Valuation of Interest Rate Contingent Claims, *Mathematical Finance* **11**(1), 117–151.

Kusuoka, S. and N. Yoshida (2000) Malliavin Calculus, Geometric Mixing, and Expansion of Diffusion Functionals, *Probabability Theory and Related Fields* **116**(4), 457–484.

Kutoyants, Y. (1994) Identification of dynamical systems with small noise, *Mathematics and its Applications* **300**.

Kutoyants, Y.A. (1984) Parameter estimation for stochastic processes, *Research and Exposition in Mathematics* **6** (translated from the Russian and edited by B.L.S. Prakasa Rao).

Kutoyants, Y.A. (1998) Statistical inference for spatial Poisson processes, *Lecture Notes in Statistics* **134**.

Kutoyants, Y.A. (2004) Statistical inference for ergodic diffusion processes, *Springer Series in Statistics*.

Kutoyants, Y.A. and N. Yoshida (2007) Moment estimation for ergodic diffusion processes, *Bernoulli* **13**(4), 933–951.

Li, C. (2010) Managing Volatility Risk: Innovation of Financial Derivatives, Stochastic Models and Their Analytical Implementation, Columbia University.

Malliavin, P. and M.E. Mancino (2002) Fourier Series Method for Measurement of Multivariate Volatilities, *Finance and Stochastics* **6**(1), 49–61.

Masuda, H. (2010) Approximate Self-Weighted LAD Estimation of Discretely Observed Ergodic Ornstein-Uhlenbeck Processes, *Electronic Journal of Statistics* **4**, 525–565.

Masuda, H. and N. Yoshida (2004) An Application of the Double Edgeworth Expansion to a Filtering Model with Gaussian Limit, *Statistical Probability Letters* **70**(1), 37–48.

Masuda, H. and N. Yoshida (2005) Asymptotic Expansion for Barndorff–Nielsen and Shephard's Stochastic Volatility Model, *Stochastic Processes Application* **115**(7), 1167–1186.

Mykland, P. (2010) A Gaussian Calculus for Inference from High Frequency Data, *Annals of Finance*.

Mykland, P.A. (1992) Asymptotic Expansions and Bootstrapping Distributions for Dependent Variables: A Martingale Approach, *Annals of Statistics* **20**(2), 623–654.

Mykland, P.A. (1993) Asymptotic Expansions for Martingales, *Annals of Probability* **21**(2), 800–818.

Ogihara, T. and N. Yoshida (2011) Quasi-likelihood Analysis for the Stochastic Differential Equation with Jumps, *Statistical Inference for Stochastic Processes* **14**, 189–229.

Osajima, Y. (2006) The Asymptotic Expansion Formula of Implied Volatility for Dynamic SABR Model and FX Hybrid Model, UTMS 2006-29.

Podolskij, M. and M. Vetter (2009) Estimation of Volatility Functionals in the Simultaneous Presence of Microstructure Noise and Jumps, *Bernoulli Official Journal of the Bernoulli Society for Mathematical Statistics and Probability* **15**(3), 634–658.

Prakasa Rao, B.L.S. (1983) Asymptotic Theory for Nonlinear Least Squares Estimator for Diffusion Processes, *Mathematische Operationsforschung und Statistik Series Statistics* **14**(2), 195–209.

Prakasa Rao, B.L.S. (1988) Statistical Inference from Sampled Data for Stochastic Processes. In *Statistical Inference from Stochastic Processes,* Ithaca, New York, 1987, American Mathematical Society, Providence, Rhode Island; also *Contemporary Mathematics* **80**, 249–284.

Robert, C.Y. and M. Rosenbaum (2010a) A New Approach for the Dynamics of Ultra-High-Frequency Data: The Model With Uncertainty Zones, *Journal of Financial Econometrics Advance Access* 1–23.

Robert, C.Y. and M. Rosenbaum (2010b) Volatility and Covariation Estimation When Microstructure Noise and Trading Times are Endogenous, *Mathematical Finance*, DOI: 10.1111/j.1467-9965.2010.00454.x.

Sakamoto, Y. and N. Yoshida (1996) Expansion of Perturbed Random Variables Based on Generalized Wiener Functionals, *Journal of Multivariate Analysis* **59**(1), 34–59.

Sakamoto, Y. and N. Yoshida (1998a) Asymptotic Expansion of M-Estimator Over Wiener Space, *Statistical Inference of Stochastic Processes* **1**(1), 85–103.

Sakamoto, Y. and N. Yoshida (1998b) Third Order Asymptotic Expansion for Diffusion Process, *Theory of Statistical Analysis and Its Applications* **107**, 53–60.

Sakamoto, Y. and N. Yoshida (2003) Asymptotic expansion under degeneracy, *Journal of Japan Statistical Society* **33**(2), 145–156.

Sakamoto, Y. and N. Yoshida (2004) Asymptotic Expansion Formulas for Functionals of ϵ-Markov Processes with a Mixing Property, *Annals of the Institute of Statistical Mathematics* **56**(3), 545–597.

Sakamoto, Y. and N. Yoshida (2008) Asymptotic Expansion for Stochastic Processes: An Overview and Examples, *Journal of Japan Statistical Society* **38**(1), 173–185.

Sakamoto, Y. and N. Yoshida (2009) Third-Order Asymptotic Expansion of *M*-Estimators for Diffusion Processes, *Annals of the Institute of Statistical Mathematics* **61**(3), 629–661.

Sakamoto, Y. and N. Yoshida (2010) Asymptotic Expansion for Functionals of a Marked Point Process, *Communications in Statistics – Theory and Methods* **39**(8,9), 1449–1465.

Takahashi, A. and K. Takehara (2009) Asymptotic Expansion Approaches in Finance: Applications to Currency Options, Discussion Paper F Series, URL http://repository.dl.itc.u-tokyo.ac.jp/dspace/handle/2261/26663.

Takahashi, A. and N. Yoshida (2004) An Asymptotic Expansion Scheme for Optimal Investment Problems, *Statistical Inference for Stochastic Processes* **7**, 153–188.

Takahashi, A. and N. Yoshida (2005) Monte Carlo Simulation with Asymptotic Method, *Journal of Japan Statistical Society* **35**, 171–203.

Ubukata, M. and K. Oya (2008) A Test for Dependence and Covariance Estimator of Market Microstructure Noise, Discussion Papers In Economics and Business, 07-03, February 2007.

Uchida, M. (2010a) Adaptative Estimation of an Ergodic Diffusion Process Based on Sampled Data. In Proceedings of DYNSTOCH Meeting 2010, Angers, France, June 16–19, 2010.

Uchida, M. (2010b) Contrast-Based Information Criterion for Ergodic Diffusion Processes from Discrete Observations, *Annals of the Institute of Statistical Mathematics* **62**(1), 161–187.

Uchida, M. and N. Yoshida (2001) Information Criteria in Model Selection for Mixing Processes, *Statistical Inference for Stochastic Processes* **4**(1), 73–98.

Uchida, M. and N. Yoshida (2004a) Asymptotic Expansion for Small Diffusions Applied to Option Pricing, *Statistical Inference for Stochastic Processes* **7**(3), 189–223.

Uchida, M. and N. Yoshida (2004b) Information Criteria for Small Diffusions via the Theory of Malliavin–Watanabe, *Statistical Inference for Stochastic Processes* **7**(1), 35–67.

Uchida, M. and N. Yoshida (2006) Asymptotic Expansion and Information Criteria, *SUT Journal of Mathematics* **42**(1), 31–58.

Uchida, M. and N. Yoshida (2009) Estimation of the Volatility for Stochastic Differential Equations. In Asymptotical Statistics of Stochastic Processes VII, LeMans, March 16–19, 2009.

Uchida, M. and N. Yoshida (2010) Adaptive Estimation of an Ergodic Diffusion Process Based on Sampled Data, Preprint.

Uchida, M. and N. Yoshida (2011) Nondegeneracy of Statistical Random Field and Quasi Likelihood Analysis for Diffusion, Institute of Statistical Mathematics, Research Memorandum 1149.

Watanabe, S. (1987) Analysis of Wiener Functionals (Malliavin Calculus) and Its Applications to Heat Kernels, *Annals of Probability* **15**(1), 1–39.

Yoshida, N. (1992a) Asymptotic Expansion for Statistics Related to Small Diffusions, *Journal of Japan Statistical Society* **22**(2), 139–159, URL http://www2.ms.u-tokyo.ac.jp/probstat/?page id=23.

Yoshida, N. (1992b) Asymptotic Expansions of Maximum Likelihood Estimators for Small Diffusions Via the Theory of Malliavin–Watanabe, *Probability Theory and Related Fields* **92**(3), 275–311.

Yoshida, N. (1992c) Estimation for Diffusion Processes from Discrete Observation, *Journal of Multivariate Analysis* **41**(2), 220–242.

Yoshida, N. (1993) Asymptotic Expansion of Bayes Estimators for Small Diffusions, *Probability Theory and Related Fields* **95**(4), 429–450.

Yoshida, N. (1997) Malliavin Calculus and Asymptotic Expansion for Martingales, *Probability Theory and Related Fields* **109**(3), 301–342.

Yoshida, N. (2001) Malliavin Calculus and Martingale Expansion, *Bulletin of Scientific Mathematics* **125**(6–7), 431–456; also *Rencontre Franco-Japonaise de Probabilités*, Paris, 2000.

Yoshida, N. (2004) Partial Mixing and Conditional Edgeworth Expansion for Diffusions with Jumps, *Probability Theory and Related Fields* **129**, 559–624.

Yoshida, N. (2005) Polynomial Type Large Deviation Inequality and Its Applications, Preprint.

Yoshida, N. (2006) Polynomial Type Large Deviation Inequalities and Convergence of Statistical Random Fields, The Institute of Statistical Mathematics Research Memorandum 1021.

Yoshida, N. (2008) Expansion of Asymptotically Conditionally Normal Law. In Finace and Related Mathematical and Statistical Issues, Kyoto Research Park, Kyoto, September 3–6, 2008.

Yoshida, N. (2009) Asymptotic Expansion for the Asymptotically Conditionally Normal Law. SAPS VII, March 16–19, 2009.

Yoshida, N. (2010a) Expansion of the Asymptotically Conditionally Normal Law, The Institute of Statistical Mathematics Research Memorandum 1125.

Yoshida, N. (2010b) Quasi-likelihood Analysis and Limit Theorems for Stochastic Differential Equations. In Market Microstructure, Confronting Many Viewpoints, Institut Louis Bachelier, Paris.

Zhang, L., P.A. Mykland and Y. Aät-Sahalia (2005) A Tale of Two Time Scales: Determining Integrated Volatility with Noisy High-Frequency Data, *Journal of the American Statistical Association* **100**(472), 1394–1411.

Zhou, B. (1996) High-Frequency Data and Volatility in Foreign-Exchange Rates, *Journal of Business and Economic Statistics* **14**, 45–52.

Part III
Market Impact

5

Models for the Impact of All Order Book Events

Zoltán Eisler, Jean-Philippe Bouchaud, and Julien Kockelkoren

5.1 INTRODUCTION

The relation between order flow and price changes has attracted considerable attention in recent years (see Hasbrouck, 2007; Mike and Farmer, 2008; Bouchaud *et al.*, 2004, 2006, 2009; Lyons, 2006). Most empirical studies to date have focused on the impact of (buy/sell) market orders. Many interesting results have been obtained, such as the very weak dependence of impact on the volume of the market order, the long-range nature of the *sign* of the trades, and the resulting nonpermanent, power-law decay of market order impact with time (see Bouchaud *et al.*, 2009). However, this representation of impact is incomplete in at least two ways. First, the impact of all market orders is usually treated on the same footing, or with a weak dependence on volume, whereas some market orders are "aggressive" and immediately change the price, while others are more passive and only have a delayed impact on the price. Second, other types of order book events (limit orders, cancellations) must also directly impact prices: adding a buy limit order induces extra upwards pressure and cancelling a buy limit order decreases this pressure. Within a description based on market orders only, the impact of limit orders and cancellations is included in an indirect way, in fact as an effectively decaying impact of market orders. This decay reflects the "liquidity refill" mechanism explained in detail by Bouchaud *et al.* (2006, 2009), Weber and Rosenow (2005), Gerig (2008), and Farmer *et al.* (2006), whereby market orders trigger a counterbalancing flow of limit orders.

Market Microstructure: Confronting Many Viewpoints. Edited by F. Abergel, J.-P. Bouchaud,
T. Foucault, C.-A. Lehalle and M. Rosenbaum.
© 2012 John Wiley & Sons, Ltd.

A framework allowing one to analyze the impact of all order book events and to understand in detail the statistical properties of price time series is clearly desirable. Surprisingly, however, there are only very few quantitative studies of the impact of limit orders and cancellations (Hautsch and Huang, 2009; Eisler *et al.*, 2011) – partly due to the fact that more detailed data, beyond trades and quotes, is often needed to conduct such studies. The aim of the present paper is to provide a theoretical framework for the impact of all order book events, which allows one to build statistical models with intuitive and transparent interpretations (Eisler *et al.*, 2011).

5.2   A SHORT SUMMARY OF MARKET ORDER IMPACT MODELS

A simple model relating prices to trades posits that the mid-point price p_t just before trade t can be written as a linear superposition of the impact of all past trades (Bouchaud *et al.*, 2004, 2006):

$$p_t = \sum_{t' < t} \left[G(t - t')\xi_{t'} + \eta_{t'} \right] + p_{-\infty}, \qquad \xi_t \equiv \epsilon_t v_t^\theta \tag{5.1}$$

where v_t is the volume of the trade at time t, ϵ_t the sign of that trade ($+$ for a buy, $-$ for a sell), and η_t is an independent noise term that models any price change not induced by trades (e.g., jumps due to news). The exponent θ is found to be small. The most important object in the above equation is the function $G(\ell)$ describing the temporal evolution of the impact of a single trade, which can be called a "propagator": how does the impact of the trade at time $t' = t - \ell$ propagate, on average, up to time t? Because the signs of trades are strongly autocorrelated, $G(\ell)$ must decay with time in a very specific way, in order to maintain the (statistical) efficiency of prices. Clearly, if $G(\ell)$ did not decay at all, the returns[1] $r_t = p_{t+1} - p_t$ would simply be proportional to the sign of the trades, and therefore would themselves be strongly autocorrelated in time. The resulting price dynamics would then be highly predictable, which is not realistic. The result of Bouchaud *et al.* (2004) is that if the correlation of signs $C(\ell) = \langle \epsilon_t \epsilon_{t+\ell} \rangle$ decays at large ℓ as $\ell^{-\gamma}$ with $\gamma < 1$ (as found empirically), then $G(\ell)$ must decay as $\ell^{-\beta}$ with $\beta = (1 - \gamma)/2$ for the price to be exactly diffusive at long times. The impact of single

---

[1] In the following, we only focus on price changes over small periods of time, so that an additive model is adequate.

trades is therefore predicted to decay as a power-law (at least up to a certain time scale).

The above model can be rewritten in a completely equivalent way in terms of returns, with a slightly different interpretation (Gerig, 2008; Farmer *et al.*, 2006):

$$r_t = G(1)\xi_t + \sum_{t' < t} \kappa(t - t')\xi_{t'} + \eta_t; \qquad \kappa(\ell) \equiv G(\ell + 1) - G(\ell).$$

$$(5.2)$$

This can be read as saying that the tth trade has a permanent impact on the price, but this impact is history dependent and depends on the sequence of past trades. The fact that G decays with ℓ implies that the kernel κ is negative, and therefore that a past sequence of buy trades ($\xi_{t' < t} > 0$) tends to *reduce* the impact of a further buy trade but increase the impact of a sell trade. This is again a consequence of the dynamic nature of liquidity: when trades persist in a given direction, opposing limit orders tend to pile up and reduce the average impact of the next trade in the same direction. For the price to be an exact martingale, the quantity $\widehat{\xi}_t = - \sum_{t' < t} \kappa(t - t')\xi_{t'}$ must be equal to the conditional expectation of ξ_t at time t^-, such that $\xi_t - \widehat{\xi}_t$ is the surprise part of ξ_t. This condition allows one to recover the above mentioned decay of $G(\ell)$ at large ℓ.

In order to calibrate the model, one can use the empirically observable impact function $\mathcal{R}(\ell)$, defined as

$$\mathcal{R}(\ell) = \langle (p_{t+\ell} - p_t) \cdot \xi_t \rangle.$$

$$(5.3)$$

and the time correlation function $C(\ell)$ of the variable $\xi_t = \epsilon_t v_t^\theta$ to map out, numerically, the complete shape of $G(\ell)$. This was done by Bouchaud *et al.* (2006), using the exact relation

$$\mathcal{R}(\ell) = \sum_{0 < n \leq \ell} G(n)C(\ell - n) + \sum_{n > 0}[G(n + \ell) - G(n)]C(n).$$

$$(5.4)$$

Alternatively, one can use the "return" version of the model, Equation (5.2), which gives

$$\mathcal{S}(\ell) = \langle r_{t+\ell} \cdot \xi_t \rangle,$$

$$(5.5)$$

which in turn leads to

$$\mathcal{S}(\ell) = G(1)C(\ell) + \sum_{n > -\ell} \kappa(\ell + n)C(n).$$

$$(5.6)$$

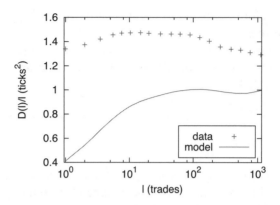

Figure 5.1 $D(\ell)/\ell$ and its approximation with the transient impact model (TIM) with only trades as events, with $\eta_t = 0$ and for small tick stocks. Results are shown when assuming that all trades have the same, nonfluctuating impact $G(\ell)$, calibrated to reproduce $\mathcal{R}(\ell)$. This simple model accounts for $\sim 2/3$ of the long-term volatility. Other events and/or the fluctuations of $G(\ell)$ must therefore contribute to the market volatility as well.

As noted in Sérié (2010), this second implementation is in fact much less sensitive to finite size effects and therefore more adapted to data analysis.[2]

The above model, regardless of the type of fitting, is approximate and incomplete in two interrelated ways. First, Equations (5.1) and (5.2) neglect the fluctuations of the impact: one expects in general that G and κ should depend both on t and t' and not only on $\ell = t - t'$. Impact can indeed be quite different depending on the state of the order book and the market conditions at t'. As a consequence, if one blindly uses Equations (5.1) and (5.2) to compute the second moment of the price difference, $D(\ell) = \langle (p_{t+\ell} - p_t)^2 \rangle$, with a nonfluctuating $G(\ell)$ calibrated to reproduce the impact function $\mathcal{R}(\ell)$, the result clearly underestimates the empirical price variance (see Figure 5.1).

Adding a diffusive noise $\eta_t \neq 0$ would only shift $D(\ell)/\ell$ upwards, but this is insufficient to reproduce the empirical data. Second, as noted in the introduction, other events of the order book can also change the mid-price, such as limit orders placed inside the bid-ask spread, or

---

[2] The key difference is that a numerical solution necessarily truncates $G(\ell)$ in Equation (5.4) and $\kappa(\ell)$ in Equation (5.6) at some arbitrary ℓ_{max}. This truncation in the former case corresponds to the boundary condition of $\kappa(\ell > \ell_{max}) \equiv 0$, and hence a fully temporary impact at long times, while in the latter case to $\kappa(\ell > \ell_{max}) \equiv G(\ell_{max})$, and hence a partially permanent impact. The latter solution is smoother and consequently it is better behaved numerically.

cancellations of all the volume at the bid or the ask. These events do indeed contribute to the price volatility and should be explicitly included in the description. A simplified description of price changes in terms of market orders only attempts to describe other events of the order book in an effective way, through the nontrivial time dependence of $G(\ell)$.

In the following, we will generalize the above model to account for the impact of other types of events, beyond market orders. In this case, however, it will become apparent that the two versions of the above model *are no longer equivalent*, and lead to different quantitative results. Our main objective will be to come up with a simple, intuitive model that (i) can be easily calibrated on data, (ii) reproduces as closely as possible the second moment of the price difference $D(\ell)$, (iii) can be generalized to richer and richer data sets, where more and more events are observable, and (iv) can in principle be systematically improved.

5.3   MANY-EVENT IMPACT MODELS

5.3.1   Notation and definitions

The dynamics of the order book is rich and complex, and involves the intertwined arrival of many types of events. These events can be categorized in different, more or less natural types. In the empirical analysis presented below, we have considered the following six types of events:

- market orders that do not change the best price (noted MO^0) or that do change the price (noted MO');
- limit orders at the current bid or ask (LO^0) or inside the bid-ask spread so that they change the price (LO'); and
- cancellations at the bid or ask that do not remove all the volume quoted there (CA^0) or that do (CA').

Of course, events deeper in the order book could also be added, as well as any extra division of the above types into subtypes, if more information is available. For example, if the identity code of each order is available, one can classify each event according to its origin, as was done in Tóth *et al.* (2011). The generic notation for an event type occurring at event time t will be π_t. The upper index $'$ ("prime") will denote that the event changed any of the best prices, and the upper index 0 that it did not. Abbreviations without the upper index (MO, CA, LO) refer to both the price changing and the price non-changing event type. Every event is

Table 5.1 Summary of the six possible event types and the corresponding definitions of the event signs and gaps

π	Event definition	Event sign definition	Gap definition ($\Delta_{\pi,\epsilon}$)
$\pi = \mathrm{MO}^0$	Market order, volume < outstanding volume at the best	$\epsilon = \pm 1$ for buy/sell market orders	0
$\pi = \mathrm{MO}'$	Market order, volume $\geq$ outstanding volume at the best	$\epsilon = \pm 1$ for buy/sell market orders	Half of first gap behind the ask ($\epsilon = 1$) or bid ($\epsilon = -1$)
$\pi = \mathrm{CA}^0$	Partial cancellation of the bid/ask queue	$\epsilon = \mp 1$ for buy/sell side cancellation	0
$\pi = \mathrm{LO}^0$	Limit order at the current best bid/ask	$\epsilon = \pm 1$ for buy/sell limit orders	0
$\pi = \mathrm{CA}'$	Complete cancellation of the best bid/ask	$\epsilon = \mp 1$ for buy/sell side cancellation	Half of first gap behind the ask ($\epsilon = 1$) or bid ($\epsilon = -1$)
$\pi = \mathrm{LO}'$	Limit order inside the spread	$\epsilon = \pm 1$ for buy/sell limit order	Half distance of limit order from the earlier best quote on the same side

given a sign ϵ_t according to its expected long-term effect on the price – the precise definitions are summarized in Table 5.1. Note that the table also defines the gaps $\Delta_{\pi,\epsilon}$, which will be used later. We will rely on indicator variables denoted as $I(\pi_t = \pi)$. This expression is equal to 1 if the event at t is of type π and zero otherwise. We also use the notation $\langle \cdot \rangle$ to denote the time average of the quantity between the brackets.

Let us now define the response of the price to different types of orders. The average behavior of price after events of a particular type π defines the corresponding *response function* (or the average impact function):

$$\mathcal{R}_\pi(\ell) = \langle (p_{t+\ell} - p_t) \cdot \epsilon_t | \pi_t = \pi \rangle . \tag{5.7}$$

Where the right-hand side of the bracket indicates a conditional average over t's where $\pi_t = \pi$. This is equivalent to a correlation function between $\epsilon_t I(\pi_t = \pi)$ at time t and the price change from t to $t + \ell$, normalized by the stationary probability of the event π, denoted as $P(\pi) = \langle I(\pi_t = \pi) \rangle$. This normalized response function gives the expected directional price change after an event π. Its behavior for all π's is shown on the left of Figure 5.2. Tautologically, $\mathcal{R}_\pi(\ell = 1) > 0$ for price changing events and $\mathcal{R}_\pi(\ell = 1) = 0$ for the others. Empirically,

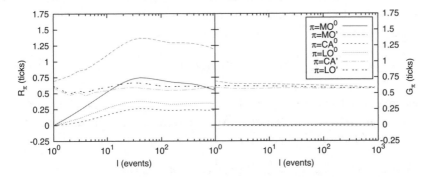

Figure 5.2 (left) The response function $\mathcal{R}_\pi(\ell)$ and (right) the bare impact function $G_\pi(\ell)$ for the TIM, for the data described in Section 5.4.1. The curves are labeled according to π in the legend. Note that $G_\pi(\ell)$ is to a first approximation independent of ℓ for all π's. However, the small variations are real and important to reproduce the correct price diffusion curve $D(\ell)$.

all types of events lead, on average, to a price change in the expected direction, i.e., $\mathcal{R}_\pi(\ell) > 0$.

We will also need the "return" response function, upgrading the quantity $\mathcal{S}(\ell)$ defined above to a matrix:

$$\mathcal{S}_{\pi_1,\pi_2}(\ell) = \langle I(\pi_{t+\ell} = \pi_2) \cdot r_{t+\ell} \cdot \epsilon_t | \pi_t = \pi_1 \rangle . \tag{5.8}$$

Clearly, as an exact identity,

$$\mathcal{R}_\pi(\ell) = \sum_{n=0}^{\ell-1} \sum_{\pi'} \mathcal{S}_{\pi,\pi'}(n). \tag{5.9}$$

Similarly, the signed-event correlation function is defined as

$$C_{\pi_1,\pi_2}(\ell) = \frac{\langle I(\pi_t = \pi_1)\epsilon_t I(\pi_{t+\ell} = \pi_2)\epsilon_{t+\ell}\rangle}{P(\pi_1)P(\pi_2)} . \tag{5.10}$$

Our convention is that the first index corresponds to the first event in chronological order. Note that, in general, there are no reasons to expect time reversal symmetry, which would impose $C_{\pi_1,\pi_2}(\ell) = C_{\pi_2,\pi_1}(\ell)$. If one has N event types, altogether there are N^2 of these event–event correlations and return response functions.

5.3.2   The transient impact model (TIM)

Let us write down the natural generalization of the above transient impact model (TIM), embodied by Equation (5.1), to the many-event case.

We now envisage that each event type π has a "bare" time dependent impact given by $G_\pi(\ell)$, such that the price reads

$$p_t = \sum_{t' < t} \left[G_{\pi_{t'}}(t - t') \epsilon_{t'} + \eta_{t'} \right] + p_{-\infty}, \tag{5.11}$$

where one selects, for each t', the propagator $G_{\pi_{t'}}$ corresponding to the particular event type at that time. After straightforward calculations, the response function (5.7) can be expressed as

$$\mathcal{R}_{\pi_1}(\ell + 1) - \mathcal{R}_{\pi_1}(\ell) = \sum_{\pi_2} P(\pi_2) \Big[G_{\pi_2}(1) C_{\pi_1, \pi_2}(\ell)$$

$$+ \sum_{n > -\ell} \left[G_{\pi_2}(\ell + n + 1) - G_{\pi_2}(\ell + n) \right] C_{\pi_1, \pi_2}(n) \Big]. \tag{5.12}$$

This is a direct extension of Equation (5.4). One can invert the system of Equations (5.12) to evaluate the unobservable G_π's in terms of the observable R_π's and C_{π_1, π_2}'s – see Figure 5.2 (right). Note that we formulate the problem here in terms of the "derivatives" of the G_π's since, as mentioned above, it is numerically much more stable to introduce new variables for the increments of $\mathcal{R}$ and G and solve (5.12) in terms of those.

Once this is known, one can explicitly compute the lag dependent diffusion constant $D(\ell) = \langle (p_{t+\ell} - p_t)^2 \rangle$ in terms of the G's and the C's, generalizing the corresponding result obtained by Bouchaud et al. (2004) (see the Appendix).

5.3.3   The history dependent impact model (HDIM)

Now, if one wants to generalize the history dependent impact model (HDIM), Equation (5.2), to the many-event case, one immediately realizes that the impact at time t depends on the type of event one is considering. For one thing, the instantaneous impact of price nonchanging events is trivially zero. For price changing events, $\pi' = \text{MO}', \text{LO}', \text{CA}'$, the instantaneous impact is given by

$$r_t = \epsilon_t \Delta_t. \tag{5.13}$$

Here Δ depends on the type of price changing event π' that happens then, and possibly also on the sign of that event. For example, if $\pi_t = \text{MO}'$ and $\epsilon_t = -1$ this means that a sell market order executed the total volume at the bid. The mid-quote price change is $-\Delta_t$, which usually means that the second best level was at $b_t - 2\Delta_t$, where b_t is the bid price before the event. The factor 2 is necessary, because the ask did not change, and the impact is defined by the change of the mid-quote. Hence Δ's for MO''s (and similarly CA''s) correspond to half of the gap between the first and the second best quote *just before* the level was removed (see also Farmer *et al.*, 2004). Another example is when $\pi = \text{LO}'$ and $\epsilon_t = -1$. This means that at t a sell limit order was placed inside the spread. The mid-quote price change is $-\Delta$, which means that the limit order was placed at $a_t - 2\Delta_t$, where a_t is the ask price. Thus Δ for LO''s correspond to half of the gap between the first and the second best quote *right after* the limit order was placed. In the following we will call the Δ's *gaps*. For large tick stocks, these nonzero Δ's are most of the time equal to half a tick, and only very weakly fluctuating. For small tick stocks, substantial fluctuations of the spread and of the gaps behind the best quotes can take place. The generalization of Equation (5.2) precisely attempts to capture these gap fluctuations, which are affected by the flow of past events. If we assume that the whole dynamical process is statistically invariant under exchanging buy orders with sell orders ($\epsilon \Rightarrow -\epsilon$) and bids with asks, the dependence on the current nonzero gaps on the past order flow can only include an even number of ϵ's. Therefore the lowest order model for nonzero gaps (including a constant term and a term quadratic in ϵ's) is

$$\Delta_t|_{\pi_t=\pi';\epsilon_t=\epsilon} = \Delta_{\pi'}^R + \sum_{t_1<t} \kappa_{\pi_1,\pi'}(t - t_1)\left[\epsilon_{t_1}\epsilon - C_{\pi_1,\pi'}(t - t_1)\right] + \eta_t'.$$

(5.14)

where $\kappa_{\pi_1,\pi'}$ are kernels that model the dependence of the gaps on the past order flow (note that $\kappa_{\pi_1,\pi'}$ is a 6×3 matrix) and $\Delta_{\pi'}^R$ are the average realized gaps, defined as $\langle\Delta_t|\pi_t = \pi'\rangle$, since the average of the second term in the right-hand side is identically zero. Note that the last term, equal to $\sum_{n>0}\sum_\pi P(\pi)\kappa_{\pi,\pi'}(n)C_{\pi,\pi'}(n)$, was not explicitly included in our previous analysis (Eisler *et al.*, 2011). However, typical values are less than 1 % of the average realized gap, and therefore negligible in practice. We set it to zero in the following.

Equation (5.14), combined with the definition of the return at time t, Equation (5.13), leads to our generalization of the HDIM, Equation (5.2):

$$r_t = \Delta_{\pi_t}^R\epsilon_t + \sum_{t_1<t}\kappa_{\pi_{t_1},\pi_t}(t - t_1)\epsilon_{t_1} + \eta_t.$$

(5.15)

It is interesting to compare the above equation with its analog for the transient impact model, which reads (after Equation (5.11))

$$r_t = G_{\pi_t}(1)\epsilon_t + \sum_{t_1 < t} \left[G_{\pi_{t_1}}(t - t_1 + 1) - G_{\pi_{t_1}}(t - t_1) \right] \epsilon_{t_1} + \eta_t.$$

$$(5.16)$$

The two models can only be equivalent if

$$\kappa_{\pi_{t_1},\pi}(\ell) \equiv G_{\pi_{t_1}}(\ell + 1) - G_{\pi_{t_1}}(\ell), \qquad \forall \pi, \qquad (5.17)$$

which means that the "influence matrix" $\kappa_{\pi_1,\pi}$ has a much constrained structure, which has no reason to be optimal. It is also a priori inconsistent since the TIM leads to a nonzero price move even if π is a price nonchanging event, since Equation (5.17) is valid for all event types π. This is a major conceptual drawback of the TIM framework (although, as we will see below, the model fares quite well at reproducing the price diffusion curve).

The matrix κ_{π_1,π_2} can in principle be determined from the empirical knowledge of the response matrices $\mathcal{S}_{\pi_1,\pi_2}$, since

$$\frac{1}{P(\pi_2)}\mathcal{S}_{\pi_1,\pi_2}(\ell) = \frac{1}{P(\pi_2)}\langle I(\pi_{t+\ell} = \pi_2) \cdot r_{t+\ell} \cdot \epsilon_t | \pi_t = \pi_1 \rangle$$

$$= \Delta_{\pi_2}^{R} C_{\pi_1,\pi_2}(\ell) + \sum_{t' < t+\ell} \sum_{\pi} \kappa_{\pi,\pi_2}(t + \ell - t')$$

$$\times \langle I(\pi_{t'} = \pi)\epsilon_{t'} I(\pi_t = \pi_1)\epsilon_t | \pi_{t+\ell} = \pi_2 \rangle. \quad (5.18)$$

Note, however, that the last term includes a three-body correlation function that is not very convenient to estimate. At this stage and below, we need to make some approximation to estimate higher order correlations. We assume that all three- and four-body correlation functions can be factorized in terms of two-body correlation functions, as if the variables were Gaussian. This allows us to extract κ_{π_1,π_2} from a numerically convenient expression, used in Eisler *et al.* (2011):

$$\frac{1}{P(\pi_2)}\mathcal{S}_{\pi_1,\pi_2}(\ell) = \Delta_{\pi_2}^{R} C_{\pi_1,\pi_2}(\ell) + \sum_{n > -\ell} \sum_{\pi} \kappa_{\pi,\pi_2}(n + \ell)C_{\pi_1,\pi}(n).$$

$$(5.19)$$

Knowing the κ_{π_1,π_2}'s and using the same factorization approximation, one can finally estimate the price diffusion constant, given in the Appendix. Although the factorization approximation used to obtain the diffusion constant looks somewhat arbitrary, we find that it is extremely precise when applied to the diffusion curve.

For large tick stocks, the gaps hardly vary with time and are all equal to one tick. In other words, $\kappa_{\pi_1,\pi} \approx 0$ and the model simplifies enormously, since now $G_\pi(\ell) \equiv \Delta_\pi^R$. In this limit, one therefore finds

$$R_\pi(\ell) = \langle (p_{t+\ell} - p_t) \cdot \epsilon_t | \pi_t = \pi \rangle \approx \Delta_\pi^R$$
$$+ \sum_{0 < t' < \ell} \sum_{\pi_1} \Delta_{\pi_1}^R P(\pi_1) C_{\pi,\pi_1}(t'), \qquad (5.20)$$

which means that the total price response to some event can be understood as its own impact (lag zero), plus the sum of the biases in the course of future events, conditional to this initial event. These biases are multiplied by the average price change Δ^R that these induced future events cause. Within the same model, the volatility reads

$$D(\ell) = \langle (p_{t+\ell} - p_t)^2 \rangle$$
$$\approx \sum_{0 \leq t',t'' < \ell} \sum_{\pi_1} \sum_{\pi_2} P(\pi_1) P(\pi_2) C_{\pi_1,\pi_2}(t' - t'') \Delta_{\pi_1}^R \Delta_{\pi_2}^R. \qquad (5.21)$$

For small ticks, on the other hand, gaps do fluctuate and react to the past order flow; the influence matrix $\kappa_{\pi_1,\pi'}$ describes how the past order flow affects the current gaps. If $\kappa_{\pi_1,\pi'}(\ell)$ is positive, it means that an event of type π_1 (price changing or not) tends to *increase* the gaps (i.e. reduce the liquidity) for a later price changing event π' in the same direction and decrease the gap if the sign of the event π' is opposite to that of π_1.

5.4   MODEL CALIBRATION AND EMPIRICAL TESTS

5.4.1   Data

We have tested the above ideas on a set of data made of 14 randomly selected liquid stocks traded on the NASDAQ during the period 03/03/2008 to 19/05/2008, a total of 53 trading days (see Eisler *et al.*, 2011, for a detailed presentation of these stocks and summary statistics). In order to reduce the effects of the intraday spread and liquidity variations we exclude the first 30 and the last 40 minutes of the trading days. The particular choice of market is not very important; many of our results were also verified on other markets, such as CME Futures, US Treasury Bonds, and stocks traded at the London Stock Exchange.

Our sample of stocks can be divided into two groups: large tick and small tick stocks. Large tick stocks are such that the bid-ask spread is almost always equal to one tick, whereas small tick stocks have spreads that are typically a few ticks. The behavior of the two groups is quite different; for example, the events that change the best price have a relatively low probability for large tick stocks (about 3 % altogether), but not for small tick stocks (up to 40 %). Note that there is a number of stocks with intermediate tick sizes, which to some extent possess the characteristics of both groups. Technically, they can be treated in exactly the same way as small tick stocks, and all our results remain valid. However, for the clarity of presentation, we will not consider them explicitly.

As explained above, we restrict ourselves to events that modify the bid or ask price, or the volume quoted at these prices. Events deeper in the order book are unobserved and will not be described: although they do not have an immediate effect on the best quotes, our description is still incomplete. Furthermore, we note that the stocks we are dealing with are traded on multiple platforms. This may account for some of the residual discrepancies reported below.

Since we consider six types of events, there are six response functions $\mathcal{R}_\pi$ and propagators G_π, and 36 correlation functions C_{π_1,π_2}. However, since the return response functions $\mathcal{S}_{\pi_1,\pi_2}$ and the influence kernels κ_{π_2,π_1} are nonzero only when the second event π_2 is a price changing event, there are only $3 \times 6 = 18$ of them.

5.4.2 The case of large ticks

As explained in the previous section, the case of large ticks is quite simple since the gap fluctuation term of HDIM can be neglected altogether. As shown in Eisler *et al.* (2011), the predictions given by Equations (5.20) and (5.21) are in very good agreement with the empirical determination of the $\mathcal{R}_\pi(\ell)$ and the price diffusion $D(\ell)$. Small remaining discrepancies can indeed be accounted for by adding the gap fluctuation contribution, of the order of a few percent.

The temporary impact model, on the other hand, is not well adapted to describe large tick stocks, for the following reason: when Equation (5.12) is used to extract $G_\pi(\ell)$ from the data, small numerical errors may lead to some spurious time dependence. However, as far as $D(\ell)$ is concerned, any small variation of G_π is amplified through the second term of Equation (5.24) in the Appendix, which is an infinite sum of positive terms. As noted in Eisler *et al.* (2011), this leads to large discrepancies between the predicted $D(\ell)$ and its empirical determination. At any rate, one should clearly favor the calibration of $G_\pi(\ell)$ using Equation (5.12) rather than the analog of Equation (5.4).

5.4.3   The case of small ticks

The case of small ticks is much more interesting, since in this case the role of gap fluctuations is crucial and is a priori a stringent test for the two models on stage.

5.4.3.1   TIM

Within the temporary impact model, the response functions $\mathcal{R}_\pi(\ell)$ are tautologically accounted for, since they are used to calibrate the propagators $G_\pi(\ell)$ using Equation (5.12). Once the $G_\pi(\ell)$'s are known (see Figure 5.2, where $\mathcal{R}_\pi(\ell)$ and $G_\pi(\ell)$ are shown for small tick stocks), one can compute the time dependent diffusion coefficient $D(\ell)/\ell$ and compare it with empirical data. This is shown in Figure 5.3 (left). Note that we calibrate the $G_\pi(\ell)$ for each stock separately, compute $D(\ell)/\ell$ in each case, and then average the results over all stocks. The agreement is surprisingly good for long times, while for shorter times the model underestimates price fluctuations, which is expected since the model does not allow for high frequency fluctuations. We also show the prediction based on the constant gap approximation, $\kappa_{\pi_1,\pi_2} \equiv 0$. Although Figure 5.2 suggests that this is an acceptable assumption, we see that $D(\ell)$ is overestimated. As will be argued below, gaps do adapt to past order flow, and the net effect of the gap dynamics is to reduce the price

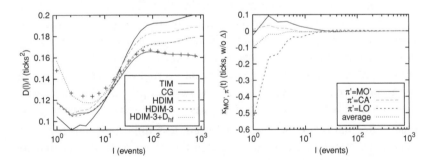

Figure 5.3 (left) $D(\ell)/\ell$ and its approximations. Crosses correspond to the data. The constant gap (CG) model corresponds to $G_\pi(\ell) \equiv G_\pi(1)$. TIM corresponds to the temporary impact model calibrated on returns. The curve for HDIM uses the approximate calibration of κ's, where HDIM-3 is taking 3 times the κ's as from the calibration. We also indicate HDIM-3 by adding the constant $D_{hf} = 0.04$. Note that the vertical scale is different from Figure 5.1, since the time clock is different in the two cases (all events versus trades in Figure 5.1). (right) Comparison of the three nonzero $\kappa_{MO',\pi'}(\ell)$ with their average over π'. Note that $\kappa_{MO',MO'} < 0$: after an MO' event, gaps on the same side are on average smaller.

volatility. We finally note that calibrating the $G_\pi(\ell)$ on the response functions directly (and not on their derivatives), as was done in Eisler *et al.* (2011), leads to much poorer results for the diffusion coefficient $D(\ell)/\ell$.

5.4.3.2   HDIM

We now turn to the history dependent impact model. As explained above, we determine the influence kernels $\kappa_{\pi_1,\pi_2}(\ell)$ using Equation (5.19). We plot in Figure 5.4 the resulting "integrated impact" on the future gaps of all six π_1 events, which we define as[3]

$$\delta G_\pi^*(\ell) = \sum_{n=1}^{\ell-1} \sum_{\pi'} P(\pi')\kappa_{\pi,\pi'}(n), \qquad (5.22)$$

As explained in Eisler *et al.* (2011), $\delta G_\pi^*(\ell)$ captures the contribution of the gap "compressibility" to the impact of an event of type π up to a time lag ℓ, leaving the sequence of events unchanged. If $\kappa_{\pi,\pi'}(n)$ were independent of π', as postulated in the TIM, one would have $\delta G_\pi^*(\ell) = G_\pi(\ell) - G_\pi(1)$ as an identity. The agreement turns out to be excellent (see Figure 5.4), which was not guaranteed a priori since the HDIM is calibrated on a much larger set of correlation functions.

However, this does not mean that $\kappa_{\pi,\pi'}(n)$'s are necessarily independent of π'. To illustrate the point that Equation (5.17) is too restrictive, Figure 5.3 (right) compares the three $\kappa_{MO',\pi'}$'s, which are clearly different from one another. Note that the average over π' is negative, meaning that MO' events tend to "harden" the book (i.e. after an MO' event, gaps on the same side are on average smaller). This is true for all price changing events, while (perhaps surprisingly) small market orders MO^0 "soften" the book: $\delta G_{MO^0}^*$ is positive and gaps tend to grow. Queue fluctuations (CA^0 and LO^0) seem less important, but for small ticks these types of events also harden the book. Note finally that for large ticks δG^*'s are found to be about two orders of magnitude smaller, which confirms that gap fluctuations can be neglected in that case.

Now, Equation (5.19) relies on the factorization of a three-point correlation function and is not exact, so there is no guarantee that the response functions $\mathcal{R}_\pi(\ell)$ are exactly reproduced using this calibration method.

---

[3] Note that this definition is compatible with the one given in Eisler *et al.* (2011), because of a slight change in the interpretation in the κ kernels here.

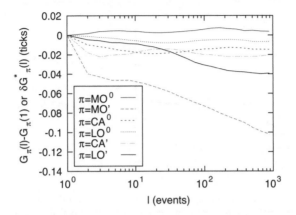

Figure 5.4 The integrated impact on the future gaps $\delta G_\pi^*(\ell)$ in the HDIM estimated via Equation (5.17). The results are indistinguishable from $G_\pi(\ell) - G_\pi(1)$ calculated for the TIM. The curves are labeled according to π in the legend.

In order to check this approximation, we have simulated an artificial market dynamics where the price evolves according to Equation (5.15), with the true (historical) sequence of signs and events and $\eta_t = 0$. The kernels κ_{π_1,π_2} are calibrated using Equation (5.19). This leads to the predictions shown as dashed lines in Figure 5.5. The agreement can be much improved by simply multiplying all κ's by a factor 3 (see Figure 5.5). Of course, some discrepancies remain and one should use the historical simulation systematically to determine the optimal κ's. This is, however, numerically much more difficult and an improved analytical approximation of the three-point correlation function, which would allow a more accurate workable calibration, would be welcome.

Finally, we computed $D(\ell)$ for the HDIM using (5.25) in the Appendix. Here again, we have tested the quality of the factorization approximation using the same historical simulation. In this case, the $D(\ell)$ curve is indistinguishable from its approximation, so any discrepancy between the data and formula (5.25) cannot be blamed on its approximate nature, but rather on an inadequate calibration of the κ's.

The result is given in Figure 5.3 (left) together with the previous theoretical predictions and the empirical data.[4] With the naïve calibration the HDIM turns out to be worse than the TIM for large lags: it overestimates $D(\ell)$ by 15 % or so. Increasing the κ's by a factor of 3 again

---

[4] The $D(\ell)$-HDIM shown here is indistinguishable from the one appearing in Figure 16 of Eisler *et al.* (2011).

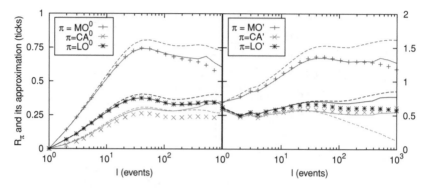

Figure 5.5 $\mathcal{R}_\pi(\ell)$ and their approximation with the HDIM. Symbols correspond to data: they are perfectly in line with the model prediction under the assumption that approximation (5.19) is correct. The dashed lines correspond to the response function of an actual simulation of the model with the κ's calibrated via Equation (5.19). The solid lines correspond to the simulation if we increase all calibrated κ's by a factor 3 (HDIM-3). The lines vary according to π, as shown in the legend.

greatly improves the fit but part of the discrepancy remains. For small lags, one needs to add a constant contribution $D_{\mathrm{hf}} \approx 0.04$ ticks squared to match the data.[5] The HDIM produces a significant improvement over the constant gap model, because it explicitly includes the effect of gap fluctuations. However, since the calibration procedure relies on an approximation, we do not reproduce the response functions exactly. Hence the better founded model (HDIM) fares worse in practice than a model with theoretical inconsistencies (TIM). As noted above, a better calibration procedure for the κ's could improve the situation.

At any rate, numerical discrepancies should be expected regardless of the fitting procedure, since we have neglected several effects, which must be present. These include (i) all volume dependence, (ii) unobserved events deeper in the book and on other platforms, and (iii) higher order, nonlinear contributions to model history dependence. On the last point, we note that based on symmetry arguments, the gap fluctuation term may include higher order terms of the form

$$\sum_{t_1, t_2, t_3 < t'} \kappa_{\pi_{t_1}, \pi_{t_2}, \pi_{t_3}; \pi_{t'}}(t' - t_1, t' - t_2, t' - t_3)\epsilon_{t_1}\epsilon_{t_2}\epsilon_{t_3}\epsilon_{t'}, \qquad (5.23)$$

---

[5] This contribution accounts for high frequency "noise" in the data that the model is not able to reproduce, as, for example, sequences of placement and cancellation of the same limit order inside the gap.

or with a larger (even) number of ϵ's. The presence of a four ϵ term is in fact suggested by the data shown in Figure 13 of Eisler *et al.* (2011), and also by more recent analysis (Tóth, 2011). It would be interesting to study these effects in detail, and understand their impact on price diffusion.

5.5 CONCLUSION

Let us summarize what we have tried to accomplish in the present paper. Our aim was to provide a general framework to describe the impact of different events in the order book, in a way that is flexible enough to deal with any classification of these events (provided this classification makes sense).[6] We have specifically considered market orders, limit orders, and cancellation at the best quotes, further subdividing each category into price changing and price nonchanging events, giving a total of six types. In trying to generalize previous work, which focused on the impact of market orders only, we have discovered that two different models can be envisaged. These are equivalent when only a single event type, market orders regardless of their aggressivity, are taken into account. One model posits that each event type has a temporary impact (TIM), whereas the other assumes that only price changing events have a direct impact, which is itself modulated by the past history of all events, a model we called "history dependent impact" (HDIM).

The TIM is a natural extension of Hasbrouck's VAR model to a multi-event setting: one writes a vector autoregression model for the return at time t in terms of *all* signed past events, but neglects the direct influence of past returns themselves (although these would be easy to include if needed). We have discussed the fact that TIMs are, strictly speaking, inconsistent since they assign a nonzero immediate impact to price non-changing events. Still, provided the model is correctly calibrated using returns (see Equation (5.12)), we find that the TIM framework allows one to reproduce the price diffusion pattern surprisingly accurately.

The HDIM family can also be thought of as a VAR model, although one now distinguishes between different types of event-induced returns before regressing them on past events. The HDIM is interesting because it gives a very appealing interpretation of the price changing process in terms of history dependent "gaps", which determine the amplitude of the price jump if a certain type of price changing event takes place.

---

[6] See Tóth *et al.* (2011) for an application of this method to orders with brokerage codes.

We have in particular defined a lag dependent, 6×3 "influence matrix" (called $\kappa_{\pi,\pi'}$ in the text), which tells us how much, on average, an event of type π affects the immediate impact of a π' price changing event of the same sign in the future.

The HDIM therefore envisages the dynamics of prices as consisting of three processes: instantaneous jumps due to events, events inducing further events and thereby affecting the future jump *probabilities* (described by the correlation between events), and events exerting pressure on the gaps behind the best price and thereby affecting the future jump *sizes* (described by the κ's). By describing this third effect with a linear regression process, we came up with the explicit model (5.15), which can be calibrated on empirical data provided some factorization approximation is made (which unfortunately turns out not to be very accurate, calling for further work on this matter). This allows one to measure the influence matrix κ and its lag dependence. We find in particular that price changing events, such as aggressive market orders MO', tend to reduce the impact of later events of the same sign (i.e. a buy MO' following a buy MO') but increase the impact of later events of the opposite sign. As stressed in Bouchaud *et al.* (2009), Gerig (2008), and Farmer *et al.* (2006), this history dependent asymmetric liquidity is the dominant effect that mitigates persistent trends in prices that would otherwise be induced by the long-ranged correlation in the sign of market orders.

In spite of these enticing features, we have found that the HDIM leads to a worse determination of the price diffusion properties than the TIM. The almost perfect agreement between the TIM prediction and empirical data is perhaps accidental, but it may also be that TIMs (which have fewer parameters) are numerically more robust than HDIMs. For HDIMs, a more accurate calibration procedure is needed. This could be achieved either by finding a better, workable approximation for the three-point correlation function or by using a purely numerical approach based on a historical simulation of the HDIM. On the other hand, some effects have been explicitly neglected, such as the role of unobserved events deeper in the book and on other platforms, or possible nonlinearities in the history dependence of gaps. It would be very interesting to investigate the relevance of these effects and to come up either with a fully consistent version of HDIM or with a convincing argument for why the TIM appears to be particularly successful.

In any case, we hope that the intuitive and versatile framework that we proposed above, together with operational calibration procedures, will help to make sense of the highly complex and intertwined sequences of events that take place in the order books, and allows one to build a comprehensive theory of price formation in electronic markets.

APPENDIX

Expression of the price diffusion for the TIM and HDIM

We give here the rather ugly looking explicit expressions for the diffusion curve $D(\ell)$ in both models. For the TIM, one gets as an exact expression:

$$
\begin{aligned}
D(\ell) = D_0\ell &+ \sum_{0 \le n < \ell} \sum_{\pi_1} G_{\pi_1}(\ell - n)^2 P(\pi_1) \\
&+ \sum_{n>0} \sum_{\pi_1} \left[G_{\pi_1}(\ell + n) - G_{\pi_1}(n) \right]^2 P(\pi_1) \\
&+ 2 \sum_{0 \le n < n' < \ell} \sum_{\pi_1, \pi_2} G_{\pi_1}(\ell - n) G_{\pi_2}(\ell - n') C_{\pi_1,\pi_2}(n' - n) \\
&+ 2 \sum_{0 < n < n' < \ell} \sum_{\pi_1, \pi_2} \left[G_{\pi_1}(\ell + n) - G_{\pi_1}(n) \right] \\
&\quad \times \left[G_{\pi_2}(\ell + n') - G_{\pi_2}(n') \right] C_{\pi_1,\pi_2}(n - n') \\
&+ 2 \sum_{0 \le n < \ell} \sum_{n' > 0} \sum_{\pi_1, \pi_2} G_{\pi_1}(\ell - n) \left[G_{\pi_2}(\ell + n') - G_{\pi_2}(n') \right] \\
&\quad \times C_{\pi_2,\pi_1}(n' + n).
\end{aligned}
\tag{5.24}
$$

where D_0 is the variance of the noise term η_t.

For the HDIM, on the other hand, one has to use a factorization approximation to compute three- and four-point correlation functions in terms of two-point correlations. One can finally estimate the price diffusion constant, which is given by the following approximate equation (Eisler *et al.*, 2011):

$$
\begin{aligned}
D(\ell) &= \left\langle (p_{t+\ell} - p_t)^2 \right\rangle \\
&\approx D_0\ell + \sum_{0 \le t', t'' < \ell} \sum_{\pi_1} \sum_{\pi_2} P(\pi_1) P(\pi_2) C_{\pi_1,\pi_2}(t' - t'') \Delta_{\pi_1}^{R} \Delta_{\pi_2}^{R} \\
&+ 2 \sum_{-\ell < t < \ell} \sum_{\pi_2,\pi_3} \sum_{\tau > 0} (\ell - |t|) \Delta_{\pi_3}^{R} \kappa_{\pi_2,\pi_3}^{+}(\tau, t) C_{\pi_2,\pi_3}(t + \tau) \\
&\times P(\pi_2) P(\pi_3) + \sum_{-\ell < t < \ell} \sum_{\pi_2,\pi_4} \sum_{\tau,\tau' > 0} (\ell - |t|) \kappa_{\pi_2,\pi_4}^{++}(\tau, \tau', t) \\
&\times C_{\pi_2,\pi_4}(\tau - \tau' + t) P(\pi_2) P(\pi_4).
\end{aligned}
\tag{5.25}
$$

where D_0 is again the variance of the noise η_t,

$$\kappa_{\pi_2,\pi_3}^{+}(\tau, t) = \sum_{\pi_1} \kappa_{\pi_2,\pi_1}(\tau)[I(t = 0)I(\pi_1 = \pi_3) + I(t \neq 0)P(\pi_1)$$
$$+ I(t = -\tau)P(\pi_1)\Pi_{\pi_2\pi_1}(\tau)], \qquad (5.26)$$

and, for $t \geq 0$,

$$\kappa_{\pi_2,\pi_4}^{++}(\tau, \tau', t) = \sum_{\pi_1,\pi_3} \kappa_{\pi_2,\pi_1}(\tau)\kappa_{\pi_4,\pi_3}(\tau')\{I(t = \tau')I(\pi_1 = \pi_4)P(\pi_3)$$
$$+ I(t \neq \tau')P(\pi_1)P(\pi_3)[\Pi_{\pi_1,\pi_3}(t) + 1]\}, \qquad (5.27)$$

whereas for $t < 0$, we use $\kappa_{\pi_2,\pi_4}^{++}(\tau, \tau', -t) = \kappa_{\pi_4,\pi_2}^{++}(\tau', \tau, t)$. We also introduced a correlation function between event types as (Eisler *et al.*, 2011):

$$\Pi_{\pi_1,\pi_2}(\ell) = \frac{P(\pi_{t+\ell} = \pi_2 | \pi_t = \pi_1)}{P(\pi_2)} - 1$$
$$\equiv \frac{\langle I(\pi_t = \pi_1)I(\pi_{t+\ell} = \pi_2)\rangle}{P(\pi_1)P(\pi_2)} - 1. \qquad (5.28)$$

ACKNOWLEDGMENTS

The authors are grateful to Emmanuel Sérié for his ideas on fitting impact kernels. They also thank Bence Tóth for his critical reading and comments.

REFERENCES

Bouchaud, J.-P., Y. Gefen, M. Potters and M. Wyart (2004) Fluctuations and Response in Financial Markets: The Subtle Nature of "Random" Price Changes, *Quantitative Finance* 4, 176.

Bouchaud, J.-P., J.D. Farmer and F. Lillo (2009) How Markets Slowly Digest Changes in Supply and Demand, in *Handbook of Financial Markets: Dynamics and Evolution*, T. Hens and K.R. Schenk-Hoppe (Eds), North-Holland, Elsevier.

Bouchaud, J.-P., J. Kockelkoren and M. Potters (2006) Random Walks, Liquidity Molasses and Critical Response in Financial Markets, *Quantitative Finance* 6, 115.

Eisler, Z., J.-P. Bouchaud and J. Kockelkoren (2011) The Price Impact of Order Book Events: Market Orders, Limit Orders and Cancellations, arXiv:0904.0900, to appear in *Quantitative Finance*.

Farmer, J.D., L. Gillemot, F. Lillo, S. Mike and A. Sen (2004) What Really Causes Large Price Changes? *Quantitative Finance* 4, 383.

Farmer, J.D., A. Gerig, F. Lillo and S. Mike (2006) Market Efficiency and the Long-Memory of Supply and Demand: Is Price Impact Variable and Permanent or Fixed and Temporary?, *Quantitative Finance* 6, 107.

Gerig, A. (2008) A Theory for Market Impact: How Order Flow Affects Stock Price, PhD Thesis, arXiv:0804.3818.

Hasbrouck, J. (2007) *Empirical Market Microstructure: The Institutions, Economics, and Econometrics of Securities Trading,* Oxford University Press.

Hautsch, N. and R. Huang (2009) The Market Impact of a Limit Order, Working Paper.

Lyons, R.K. (2006) *The Microstructure Approach to Exchange Rates,* MIT Press.

Mike, S. and J.D. Farmer (2008) An Empirical Behavioral Model of Liquidity and Volatility, *Journal of Economic Dynamics and Control* **32**, 200.

Sérié, E. (2010) unpublished report, Capital Fund Management, Paris, France.

Tóth, B. (2011) In preparation.

Tóth, B., Z. Eisler, F. Lillo, J.-P. Bouchaud, J. Kockelkoren and J. Farmer (2011) How Does the Market React to Your Order Flow?, arXiv:1104.0587.

Weber, P. and B. Rosenow (2005) Order Book Approach to Price Impact, *Quantitative Finance* **5**, 357.

6

Limit Order Flow, Market Impact, and Optimal Order Sizes: Evidence from NASDAQ TotalView-ITCH Data

Nikolaus Hautsch and Ruihong Huang

6.1 INTRODUCTION

Electronic limit order book (LOB) systems are the dominant trading form of most financial markets worldwide, including leading exchanges like NASDAQ, NYSE, BATS, and Euronext, various Alternative Trading Systems (ATSs), and Electronic Communication Networks (ECNs). The recent decade witnesses substantial technological progress in trading systems as well as trade recording and an increasing importance of intraday trading. Transparency, low latency, high liquidity, and low trading costs attract an increasing number of intraday traders, long-horizon traders as well as institutional investors. Though electronic limit order book trading has already existed for many years, further developments in trading systems and structures are ongoing and are faster than ever before. The successive automatization of order management and execution by computer algorithms, the growing importance of smart order routing as well as changes of market structures and trading forms challenge empirical and theoretical market microstructure research.

The objective of this chapter is to provide new empirical evidence on order activities and market dynamics at NASDAQ – the largest electronic market for equities in the US By employing TotalView-ITCH data containing information directly stemming from the NASDAQ data feed, our study sheds some light on recent order arrival rates, execution rates,

Market Microstructure: Confronting Many Viewpoints. Edited by F. Abergel, J.-P. Bouchaud,
T. Foucault, C.-A. Lehalle and M. Rosenbaum.
© 2012 John Wiley & Sons, Ltd.

cancellation rates, and the price impact of incoming quotes. Particularly, the market impact of a limit order is a key parameter for trading decisions and plays a crucial role for (algorithmic) trading strategies. Also theoretical studies, such as, for example, Harris (1997), Parlour and Seppi (2008), Boulatov and George (2008), or Roşu (2010), predict that the revelation of a trading intention by limit order placements can indeed adversely affect asset prices. Despite its importance, empirical evidence on the influence of incoming limit orders is still limited. Only very recently, Hautsch and Huang (2012), Eisler *et al.* (2011) and Cont *et al.* (2011) analyzed the price impact of limit orders and found significant effects. In this study, we employ Hautsch and Huang's (2012) framework, which extends the approach by Engle and Patton (2004) and provides deeper insights into the market impact of limit orders in recent NASDAQ trading. Of particular interest is whether the magnitudes of price impacts identified in other markets are also found in the extremely liquid NASDAQ market and which limit order sizes can be ultimately posted without significantly moving the market.

TotalView-ITCH data contains all order messages and thus allows us to reconstruct the NASDAQ limit order book in a very precise way, particularly accounting for all high-frequency limit order activities including also so-called fleeting orders. The latter are present for only a few seconds and have the purpose of testing for hidden orders placed in the bid-ask spread. A detailed analysis of the NASDAQ order flow in October 2010 provides the following major results. First, the number of limit order submissions is twenty to forty higher than the number of trades. Second, limit order sizes are typically small and clustered at round lot sizes of a hundred shares. Third, more than 95 % of all limit orders are cancelled without getting executed, with most of them being cancelled nearly instantaneously (less than one second) after their submission, reflecting the proliferation of algorithmic trading at NASDAQ. Fourth, volume-weighted execution times are significantly greater than average execution times, indicating that large orders face more execution risk than small ones.

The market impact of limit orders is quantified by modeling ask and bid quotes and several levels of depth in terms of a cointegrated vector-autoregressive (VAR) system, which is updated in event time. Short-run and long-run quote reactions are quantified by impulse-response functions. As proposed by Hautsch and Huang (2012), this framework allows us to estimate the impact of specific limit order activities including limit order submissions, cancellations, and executions (corresponding to trades), which are represented as shocks to the system. Our empirical results show that the short-run and long-run quote reaction patterns after the arrival of a limit order are indeed quite similar to those, for example, found for Euronext Amsterdam (see Hautsch and Huang, 2012). Buy (sell) limit orders cause permanent quote increases (decreases) and a temporary decline of the spread. Moreover, we find that the permanent impact of a limit order posted at the best quote is in most cases approximately 25 % of that of a trade of similar size. However, this magnitude can be much smaller when hidden orders are placed inside of the spread. As on other liquid markets, only aggressive limit orders posted on the first or second order level induce significant price impacts whereas orders posted with greater distance to the market have virtually no effect.

Finally, using the estimates of market impacts, we suggest a way to compute the optimal size of a limit order given its expected price impact. The implied order size is calculated by inverting the closed form of the permanent impact, yielding a function of the current limit order book and the given market impact control level. This provides useful information to control risks in trading strategies.

The remainder of the chapter is organized in the following way. Section 6.2 briefly introduces the market environment and the data. Section 6.3 provides an explorative analysis of the order flow. The econometric framework is reviewed in Section 6.4. Section 6.5 gives empirical evidence of short-run and long-run quote reactions on order activities. In Section 6.6, we propose a method to compute the optimal order size subject to its position in the book and the expected market impact. Finally, Section 6.7 concludes.

6.2   MARKET ENVIRONMENT AND DATA

The NASDAQ stock market is the largest electronic stock market (in terms of trading volume) in the world. In 2006, its traditional market center, Brut and INET electronic communication networks (ECNs), were integrated into a single system. This system offers a single execution algorithm based on price and time order precedence for both market makers and participants of ECNs. During the continuous trading period between 9:30 and 16:00 EST, limit orders are submitted to a centralized computer system where they are matched to prevailing limit or hidden orders on the opposite side. If there is no match or the standing volume in the system is insufficient to execute the incoming order fully, the remaining order volume is placed in the order book. NASDAQ supports various order types like pure market orders (immediate order execution without a price limit), stop orders (automatic issuing of limit orders or market orders when a given price is reached), immediate-or-cancel (IOC) orders, reserve orders, and nondisplay orders, among others.

In this study, we use TotalView-ITCH data containing rich information on order activities. The database includes limit order submissions, cancellations, executions, and hidden order executions for every trading day since 7:00 a.m. EST when the system starts accepting incoming limit orders. The system is initialized by an empty order book where all overnight limit orders are resubmitted automatically at the beginning of each day. Therefore, we can exactly reconstruct the order book at any time by aggregating the existing visible limit orders according to their limit prices. Furthermore, NASDAQ TotalView, surpassing NASDAQ Level 2, is the standard NASDAQ data feed for displaying the full order book depth for market participants. Hence, the reconstructed order book exactly represents historical real-time-disseminated order book states. Trades are identified via the records of limit orders and hidden order executions. Since the trading direction of limit orders and hidden orders is recorded, we can exactly identify whether a trade is buyer-initiated or seller-initiated. Finally, TotalView-ITCH data record a unique identification of any limit order, which allows it to track the order and to compute, for instance, its lifetime.[1]

Note that a market order, especially when its order size is comparably large, is likely to be filled by several pending limit orders. This results in multiple limit order executions corresponding to a sequence of same-type (sub)trades within a short time interval. We identify transactions as subtrades if they occur in less than half a second after the previous trade and have the same initiation types. All corresponding subtrades are consolidated to a single trade representing a market order. Furthermore, to avoid erratic effects during the market opening and closure, our sample period covers only the continuous trading periods between 9:45 and 15:45.

We select ten assets out of the 200 biggest stocks listed at NASDAQ according to their market capitalization on 1 October 2010. To obtain a representative cross-section, we first divide the 200 stocks into twenty blocks and then randomly select one stock from each category. Table 6.1 summarizes fundamental characteristics of these stocks extracted from the Center for Research in Security Prices (CRSP) database.

---

[1] The limit order book reconstruction and limit order tracking is performed by the software "LOBSTER" (see Huang and Polak, 2011), which can be freely accessed at http://lobster.wiwi.hu-berlin.de.

Table 6.1   Summary statistics of selected stocks. The variables are calculated for each stock using data from the Center for Research in Security Prices (CRSP) database. The sample period covers October 2010, including 21 trading days. MktCap is the market capitalization by 1 October 2010. AvgVol denotes the average daily volume (in thousand shares). MedTurn is the median daily turnover. AvgPrc denotes the average daily closing price. StdRet gives the standard deviation of daily returns

	MktCap (billion $)	AvgVol (1000 shares)	MedTurn (%)	AvgPrc ($)	StdRet (%)
GOOG	130.13	4059.6	1.24	575.94	2.56
ADBE	13.66	15132	2.04	27.512	3.11
VRTX	7.02	1909.7	0.90	35.947	1.64
WFMI	6.38	3018.5	1.54	37.636	1.80
WCRX	5.66	2941.1	0.94	23.535	2.27
DISH	3.93	2486.5	1.12	19.412	1.38
UTHR	3.18	747.95	0.97	55.884	1.89
LKQX	2.99	430.38	0.26	21.465	1.21
PTEN	2.63	5445.5	3.26	18.536	2.35
STRA	2.37	514.49	2.55	145.42	4.24

6.3   MAJOR ORDER FLOW AND ORDER BOOK CHARACTERISTICS

Electronic limit order book markets are characterized by high transparency and low latency. They enable most market participants having a view on the current state of the market via real-time updated order books. Traders' instructions are transmitted to the trading platform and executed with extremely short time delays (usually only a few milliseconds).[2] As a consequence, sophisticated trading strategies minimizing trading costs and exploiting high-frequency price movements are performed using computer algorithms. Triggered by technological advances, systematic trading is highly sophisticated nowadays. For instance, in order to make a profit from high frequency price fluctuations and liquidity rebates, many high frequency trading algorithms post a huge number of limit orders, which are again cancelled almost immediately if they are not executed. As a consequence, enormous limit order activities on extremely high frequencies are observed.

Table 6.2 summarizes the limit order activities of selected stocks and Figure 6.1 shows the histograms of constructed variables for one

---

[2] There are indeed numerous brokers providing their clients direct market access (DMA).

Table 6.2 Limit order activities at NASDAQ. These are calculated for each stock using TotalView-ITCH messages. The sample period covers October 2010, including 21 trading days. NumLO is the average daily number of standing limit orders. AvgSZ denotes the average size of limit orders. NumALO is the average daily number of limit orders placed inside the spread ("aggressive" limit orders). NumALO (in %) gives the percentage of aggressive limit orders. NumExe is the number of limit orders being (possibly partially) executed. MedETim denotes the median execution time of limit orders. VWETim is the volume-weighted execution time. NumCanc (in %) is the percentage of limit orders that are cancelled without (partial) execution. MedCTim denotes the median cancellation time. NumACan (in %) is the cancellation rate of aggressive limit orders. MedACTim gives the median cancellation time of aggressive limit orders

	NumLO (×10³)	AvgSZ (100 shares)	NumALO (×10³)	NumALO (%)	NumExe (×10³)	MedETim (s)	VWETim (s)	NumCanc (%)	MedCTim (s)	NumACan (%)	MedACTim (s)
GOOG	220.55	1.28	23.50	10.65	5.45	2.77	118.79	97.52	0.42	89.35	0.011
ADBE	206.05	2.48	2.38	1.15	15.28	3.07	107.68	92.57	4.38	50.87	0.351
VRTX	51.59	1.26	3.11	6.03	3.18	6.82	65.67	93.82	8.12	72.49	0.192
WFMI	109.46	1.53	8.06	7.36	5.19	5.92	87.04	95.25	5.88	86.43	0
WCRX	54.50	1.65	1.78	3.27	3.84	10.19	83.87	92.93	10	57.23	0.873
DISH	71.42	1.69	0.91	1.27	3.88	14.35	104.25	94.56	5.55	52.90	0.353
UTHR	27.44	1.20	3.31	12.06	1.22	6.04	52.35	95.54	9.87	81.40	0.352
LKQX	22.92	1.44	1.76	7.68	0.77	12.97	71.15	96.62	14.76	84.37	2.096
PTEN	91.57	1.98	1.81	1.98	7.66	5.71	77.56	91.62	4.84	53.80	0.545
STRA	13.05	1.12	4.02	30.83	0.57	4.89	89.11	95.57	5.17	90.96	1.502

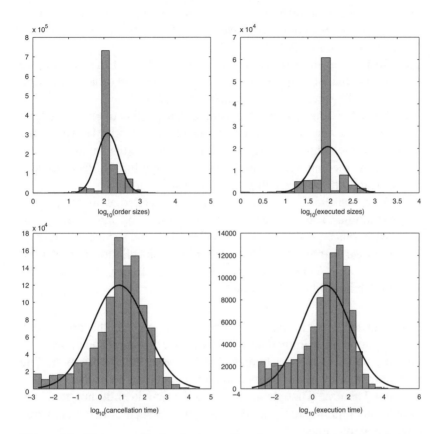

Figure 6.1 Histogram of order sizes, execution sizes, cancellation times, and execution times of limit orders. The black line denotes kernel density estimates. Zero cancellation times and execution times are discarded. Trading of WCRX on NASDAQ in October 2010.

illustrating stock, Warner Chilcott plc (ticker symbol WCRX).[3] The following main findings can be summarized:

(i) Market participants submit a huge number of limit orders with small sizes. The average limit order size is approximately 156 shares. The top left plot in Figure 6.1 shows that a large

---

[3] The corresponding histograms for the other nine stocks are provided on the companion website http://amor.cms.hu-berlin.de/huangrui/project/order_impact_nasdaq/. They confirm that our findings are quite consistent across the market.

proportion of limit orders have a size of 100 shares, corresponding to a round lot on NASDAQ.

(ii) Most of the limit orders are posted at or behind the market. We observe that only approximately 8.2 % of the limit orders are placed within the spread and thus update the best quotes.

(iii) Only a few limit orders are executed. The median of execution time across the ten stocks is approximately 7 seconds. However, the volume-weighted average execution time is substantially greater than its median, reflecting the fact that large limit orders face significantly higher execution risks than small orders.

(iv) More than 95 % of limit orders are cancelled without (partial) execution. The median cancellation time of aggressive limit orders placed inside the spread is less than one second. Hasbrouck and Saar (2009) argue that such a high cancellation rate of limit orders at NASDAQ mainly results from traders "pinging" for hidden liquidity in the market.

Note that the quickly cancelled limit orders change the order book but reverse it back immediately. This nearly instantaneous change is virtually unobservable for humans but can be captured only by trading algorithms run by high-speed computers connecting to exchanges with very low latency.[4] Though such limit order activities do not generally provide any liquidity to the market, they are indispensable for analyzing order book dynamics.

Table 6.3 gives summary statistics of market order activities. The number of market orders is substantially smaller than the number of (incoming) limit orders. Interestingly, most market orders are filled by standing limit or hidden orders pending at prices better than or equal to the best quote. Hence, we hardly find market orders walking through the order book.

Table 6.4 gives descriptive statistics of the order book data used in the chapter. We observe significantly more order book updates in the first three order levels than transactions. Moreover, on average, second level market depth is higher than the first level depth while it is lower than the depth on the third level.

---

[4] As a matter of fact, ITCH-TotalView has already reserved time stamps in nanosecond precision in order potentially to increase the time resolution in the near future.

Table 6.3 Market order activities. These are calculated for each stock using TotalView-ITCH messages. The sample period covers October 2010, including 21 trading days. NumMO is the average daily number of market orders. AvgSZ denotes the average size of market orders. NumIS (in %) is the percentage of market orders completely filled by hidden orders placed in the spread. NumL1 (in %) is the percentage of market orders filled at the best displayed quote. NumL2 (in %) is the percentage of market orders walking through the book up to the second level. NumL3 (in %) is the percentage of market orders walking through the book up to (or deeper than) the third level

	NumMO	AvgSZ (100 shares)	NumIS (%)	NumL1 (%)	NumL2 (%)	NumL3 (%)
GOOG	6226.4	1.66	43.3	53.8	2.10	0.42
ADBE	4169.1	6.93	4.8	94.9	0.24	0.01
VRTX	1730.0	2.68	13.0	86.4	0.43	0.02
WFMI	2285.7	3.27	7.2	92.2	0.38	0.04
WCRX	1977.0	3.15	8.5	91.0	0.44	0.01
DISH	1339.1	4.45	4.6	95.2	0.15	0
UTHR	857.1	2.16	26.3	72.9	0.67	0
LKQX	469.8	2.23	15.9	83.7	0.29	0.02
PTEN	2647.2	5.36	4.9	95.0	0.07	0
STRA	657.9	1.51	39.8	58.6	1.11	0.12

6.4   AN ECONOMETRIC MODEL FOR THE MARKET IMPACT OF LIMIT ORDERS

To estimate the market impact of limit orders, we apply the framework proposed by Hautsch and Huang (2012). The major idea is to model the limit order book in terms of a cointegrated VAR model for quotes and order book depth and to back out the price impact of specific types of limit orders based on impulse response functions.

6.4.1   A cointegrated VAR model for the limit order book

Denote t as a (business) time index, indicating all order book activities, i.e., incoming limit or market orders as well as limit order cancellations. Furthermore, p_t^a and p_t^b denote the best log ask and bid quotes instantaneously after the tth order activity and $v_t^{a,j}$ and $v_t^{b,j}$, $j = 1, \ldots, k$, define the log depth on the jth best observed quote level on the ask and bid side, respectively. Moreover, to capture dynamic interactions between limit order and market order activities, we define two dummy variables, BUY_t and $SELL_t$, indicating the occurrence of buy and sell trades. Then, the resulting $(4 + 2 \times k)$-dimensional vector of endogenous

Table 6.4 Summary of order books. The variables are calculated for each stock using reconstructed order book data. The sample period covers October 2010, including 21 trading days. AvgObs($\times 10^3$) is the average number of observations per day. AvgTrd is the average number of daily trades. AvgAsk is the average of the best ask quote in order books. AvgBid is the average of the best bid quote. AvgSpr ($\$$) is the average dollar spread in cents. AvgSpr (%) is the average relative spread. L1 to L3 denote the average pending volume on the best quote up to the third best quote

	AvgObs ($\times 10^3$)	AvgTrd ($\times 10^3$)	AvgAsk ($\$$)	AvgBid ($\$$)	AvgSpr (cents)	AvgSpr (%)	Depth on ask (100 shares)			Depth on bid (100 shares)		
							L1	L2	L3	L1	L2	L3
GOOG	96.97	3.66	572.45	572.17	28.74	0.051	2.05	1.70	1.56	2.01	1.70	1.58
ADBE	139.52	3.95	27.336	27.325	1.51	0.055	32.87	48.34	63.86	28.86	45.29	61.51
VRTX	39.79	1.51	35.913	35.895	2.25	0.063	4.48	5.19	7.764	4.12	5.13	7.80
WFMI	76.28	2.13	37.59	37.576	1.85	0.049	5.82	8.76	13.61	5.60	8.35	12.56
WCRX	43.32	1.81	23.57	23.558	1.81	0.076	9.22	11.71	15.95	8.31	10.95	15.40
DISH	62.70	1.26	19.396	19.385	1.52	0.078	15.36	18.85	27.88	16.18	18.68	26.54
PTEN	80.33	6.44	18.677	18.666	6.39	0.114	17.02	23.67	28.71	16.65	22.18	27.24
LKQX	19.17	4.01	21.464	21.441	2.70	0.126	3.39	3.96	5.02	3.36	4.18	5.44
UTHR	18.92	2.51	56.083	56.026	1.50	0.080	2.20	2.13	2.40	2.06	2.01	2.18
STRA	16.26	0.40	145.25	144.77	53.33	0.364	1.75	2.09	2.85	1.50	1.68	2.05

146

variables is given by

$$y_t := [p_t^a, p_t^b, v_t^{a,1}, \ldots, v_t^{a,k}, v_1^{b,1}, \ldots, v_t^{b,k}, BUY_t, SELL_t]' \qquad (6.1)$$

The quote levels associated with $v_t^{a,j}$ and $v_t^{b,j}$ are not observed on a *fixed* grid at and behind the best quotes. Consequently, their price distance to p_t^a and p_t^b is not necessarily exactly $j - 1$ ticks but might be higher if there are no limit orders on all possible intermediate price levels behind the market. However, Table 6.3 shows that trades "walking through the book", i.e., trades absorbing more than one price level in the limit order book, occur extremely rarely. Consequently, we expect that an augmentation of the system by the inclusion of level-specific limit prices does not provide significantly additional information but just increases the dimension and the complexity of the system.

Note that market depth enters the vector y_t in levels and thus is treated as a possibly nonstationary variable. Since market depth is highly persistent and (on very high frequencies) reveals features of a near-unit-root process, Hautsch and Huang (2012) recommend treating this variable as being possibly nonstationary. This guarantees consistency of estimates, even if market depth is truly stationary.

Following Hautsch and Huang (2012) we model the process in terms of a restricted cointegrated VAR model of the order p (VAR(p)) with the vector error correction (VEC) form for $\Delta y_t := y_t - y_{t-1}$:

$$\Delta y_t = \mu + \alpha\beta' y_{t-1} + \sum_{i=1}^{p-1} \gamma_i \Delta y_{t-i} + u_t \qquad (6.2)$$

where u_t is white noise with covariance matrix σ_u, μ is a constant, γ_i with $i = 1, \ldots, p - 1$ is a $k \times k$ parameter matrix, and α and β denote the $k \times r$ loading and cointegrating matrices with $r < k$. By treating the trading indicators BUY_t and $SELL_t$ as stationary variables, the two first columns of β are restricted to $\beta_1 = [0, \ldots, 0, 1, 0]'$ and $\beta_2 = [0, \ldots, 0, 0, 1]'$.

The corresponding reduced VAR representation in levels of y_t is given by

$$y_t = \mu + \sum_{i=1}^{p} a_i y_{t-i} + u_t \qquad (6.3)$$

where $a_1 := I_k + \alpha\beta' + \gamma_1$ with I_k denoting a $k \times k$ identity matrix, $a_i := \gamma_i - \gamma_{i-1}$ with $1 < i < p$, and $a_p := -\gamma_{p-1}$. As illustrated by

Table 6.5   Representative estimates of cointegrating vectors. The vectors are sorted according to their corresponding eigenvalues in Johansen's ML approach. Overall there are nine cointegrating vectors. Two of them are known, i.e., $\beta_1 = [0, \ldots, 0, 1, 0]$ and $\beta_2 = [0, \ldots, 0, 0, 1]$, representing the stationary trading indicators. Accordingly, the elements corresponding to *BUY* and *SELL* in $\hat{\beta}_3$ to $\hat{\beta}_9$ are set to zero and are omitted as well. Trading of WRCX at NASDAQ on 1 October 2010

Variable	$\hat{\beta}_3$	$\hat{\beta}_4$	$\hat{\beta}_5$	$\hat{\beta}_6$	$\hat{\beta}_7$	$\hat{\beta}_8$	$\hat{\beta}_9$
p^a	1.00	−1.00	1.00	1.00	0.99	−0.64	−0.97
p^b	−0.98	0.99	−0.99	−0.99	−1.00	1.00	1.00
$v^{a,1}$	0.00	−0.25	−0.01	−0.12	−0.03	−0.03	0.02
$v^{a,2}$	−0.00	0.26	0.06	−0.11	0.00	−0.34	0.03
$v^{a,3}$	0.00	−0.18	−0.04	0.19	0.09	−0.54	0.02
$v^{b,1}$	0.01	0.16	−0.03	0.02	−0.06	0.02	0.02
$v^{b,2}$	−0.01	−0.17	0.05	0.15	−0.07	0.37	0.01
$v^{b,3}$	0.01	0.11	−0.02	−0.10	0.13	0.73	−0.00

Hautsch and Huang (2012), the model (6.2) can be estimated by a full information maximum likelihood (FIML) according to Johansen (1991) and Johansen and Juselius (1990).

Table 6.5 shows the estimated cointegrating vectors for a representative trading day, where we omit the two known cointegrating vectors associated with the (stationary) trading indicators and all corresponding elements in the remaining cointegration vectors. The resulting vectors are ordered according to their corresponding eigenvalues, reflecting their likelihood contributions.

We observe that the first five and the last cointegration relations are mostly linear combinations of spreads and depths. Specifically, the first one is quite similar to a linear combination mimicking the bid-ask spread. The most interesting relationship is implied by the vector $\hat{\beta}_8$, revealing relatively large (and different) coefficients associated with the depth variables. This indicates that depth has a significant impact on the long-term relationship between quotes. Intuitively, the connection between ask and bid quotes becomes weaker (and thus deviates from the spread) if the depth is less balanced between both sides of the market. Hence, depth has a significant impact on quote dynamics and should be explicitly taken into account in a model for quotes. These results strongly confirm corresponding findings by Hautsch and Huang (2012) for trading at Euronext.

Finally, note that model (6.3) can be further rotated in order to represent dynamics in spreads, relative spread changes, midquotes, midquote returns as well as (ask-bid) depth imbalances. Hence, the model is sufficiently flexible to capture the high frequency dynamics of all relevant trading variables. In this sense, the approach complements dynamic models for order book curves such as proposed by Härdle *et al.* (2009) and Russell and Kim (2010).

6.4.2   Estimating market impact

The market impact of limit orders can be backed out by representing an incoming order as a shock to the dynamic order book system, as specified in Equation (6.3). Whenever an order enters the market, it (i) will change the depth in the book, (ii) may change the best quotes depending on which position in the queue it is placed, and (iii) will change the trading indicator dummy in case of a market order. Consequently, the direct effects of a limit order can be represented in terms of a "shock" vector $\delta_y := [\delta_p', \delta_v', \delta_d']'$, where δ_p denotes a 2×1 vector containing shocks in quotes, δ_v is a $2k \times 1$ vector representing shocks in depths, and δ_d denotes a 2×1 vector containing changes of the trading indicator dummy.

Following Hautsch and Huang (2012), we design the impulse response vectors associated with four scenarios commonly faced by market participants. As graphically illustrated by Figures 6.2 to 6.4, a three-level order book is initialized at the best ask $p_t^a = 1002$, best bid $p_t^b = 1000$, second best ask 1003, second best bid 999, and depth levels on the bid side $v_t^{b,1} = 1$, $v_t^{b,2} = 1.5$, $v_t^{b,3} = v_t^{b,4} = 1.4$. The following scenarios are considered:[5]

Scenario 1a (normal limit order). Arrival of a buy limit order with price 1000 and size 0.5 to be placed *at the market*. As shown in Figure 6.2, this order will be consolidated at the best bid without changing the prevailing quotes. Because the initial depth on the first level is 1.0, the change of the log depth is $\ln(1.5) \approx 0.4$. Correspondingly, the shock vectors are given by $\delta_v = [0, 0, 0, 0.4, 0, 0]'$, $\delta_p = \delta_d = [0, 0]'$.

Scenario 1b (passive limit order). Arrival of a buy limit order with price 999 and size 0.5 to be posted *behind the market*. As in the scenario above, it does not change the prevailing quotes and only affects the depth at the second best bid. We have $\delta_v = [0, 0, 0, 0, \ln(2) - \ln(1.5) \approx 0.29, 0]'$, $\delta_p = \delta_d = [0, 0]'$.

---

[5] For the sake of brevity, the scenarios are only characterized for buy orders. Sell orders are analyzed accordingly.

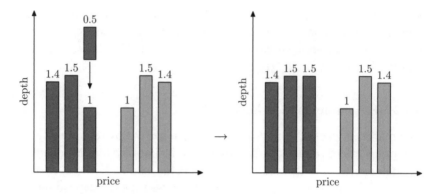

Figure 6.2 **(Scenario 1a (normal limit order))** An incoming buy limit order with price 1000 and size 0.5. It affects only the depth at the best bid without changing the prevailing quotes or resulting in a trade.
Source: Figure from Hautsch and Huang, 2012.

Scenario 2 (aggressive limit order). Arrival of a buy limit order with price 1001 and size 0.5 to be posted inside of the current spread. Figure 6.3 shows that it improves the best bid by 0.1 % and accordingly shifts all depth levels on the bid side. The resulting shock vector is given by $\delta_v = [0, 0, 0, (\ln(0.5) \approx -0.69), (\ln(1/1.5) \approx -0.4), (\ln(1.5/1.4) \approx 0.07)]'$, $\delta_p = [0, 0.001]'$, and $\delta_d = [0, 0]'$.

Scenario 3 (normal market order). Arrival of a buy order with price 1002 and size 0.5. This order will be immediately executed against

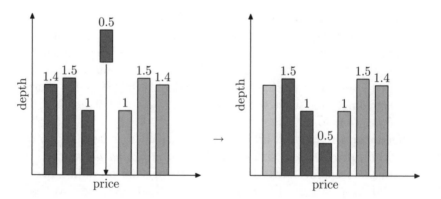

Figure 6.3 **(Scenario 2 (aggressive limit order))** An incoming buy limit order with price 1001 and size 0.5 improving the best bid and changing all depth levels on the bid side of the order book.
Source: Figure from Hautsch and Huang, 2012.

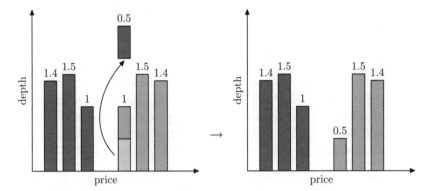

Figure 6.4 **(Scenario 3 (normal market order))** An incoming buy market order with price 1002 and size 0.5, which results in a buyer-initiated (buy) trade.
Source: Figure from Hautsch and Huang, 2012.

standing limit orders at the best ask quote. Because it absorbs liquidity from the book, it shocks the corresponding depth levels negatively. Figure 6.4 depicts the corresponding changes of the order book as represented by $\delta_v = [\ln(0.5) \approx -0.69, 0, 0, 0, 0, 0]'$, $\delta_p = [0, 0]'$ and $\delta_d = [1, 0]'$.

Table 6.6 summarizes the shock vectors implied by the illustrating scenarios.

The market reactions induced by incoming limit orders are captured by the impulse response function

$$f(h; \delta_y) = \mathbb{E}[y_{t+h}|y_t + \delta_y, y_{t-1}, \ldots] - \mathbb{E}[y_{t+h}|y_t, y_{t-1}, \ldots] \quad (6.4)$$

Table 6.6 Shock vectors implied by the underlying four scenarios. Initial order book: best ask $p_t^a = 1002$, best bid $p_t^b = 1000$, second best ask = 1003, second best bid = 999. Volumes on the ask/bid side: $v_t^{a/b,1} = 1$ at the best bid, $v_t^{a/b,2} = 1.5$ at the second best bid, and $v_t^{a/b,3} = v_t^{a/b,4} = 1.4$ at the third and fourth best bids, respectively. Notation: δ_v denotes changes in market depths; δ_p denotes changes of the best bid and best ask; δ_d denotes changes of the trading indicator variables.
Source: Table from Hautsch and Huang, 2012.

Scenario	Limit order (dir, price, size)	Shock vectors δ_v'	δ_p'	δ_d'
Normal limit order	(Bid, 1000, 0.5)	[0, 0, 0, 0.4, 0, 0]	[0, 0]	[0, 0]
Passive limit order	(Bid, 999, 0.5)	[0, 0, 0, 0, 0.29, 0]	[0, 0]	[0, 0]
Aggressive limit order	(Bid, 1001, 0.5)	[0, 0, 0, −0.69, −0.4, 0.07]	[0, 0.001]	[0, 0]
Normal market order	(Bid, 1002, 0.5)	[−0.69, 0, 0, 0, 0, 0]	[0, 0]	[1, 0]

where the shock on quotes, depths, and trading indicators is denoted by $\delta_y := [\delta'_p, \delta'_v, \delta'_d]'$ and h is the number of periods (measured in "order event time").

Note that the impulse responses do not need to be orthogonalized as contemporaneous relationships between quotes and depths are captured by construction of the shock vector. Moreover, our data are based on the arrival time of orders avoiding time aggregation as another source of mutual dependence in high-frequency order book data. The impulse-response function according to Equation (6.4) can be written as

$$f(h; \delta_y) = J\mathbf{A}^h J' \delta_y \tag{6.5}$$

where

$$\mathbf{A} := \underbrace{\begin{bmatrix} A_1 & \cdots & A_{p-1} & A_p \\ I_K & & 0 & 0 \\ & \ddots & \vdots & \vdots \\ 0 & \cdots & I_K & 0 \end{bmatrix}}_{K_p \times -K_p}$$

Given the consistent estimator $\widehat{a}$ for $a := \text{vec}(A_1, \ldots, A_p)$ in (6.3) we have

$$\sqrt{T}(\widehat{a} - a) \xrightarrow{d} \mathcal{N}(0, \Sigma_{\widehat{a}})$$

Lütkepohl (1990) shows that the asymptotic distribution of the impulse-response function is given by

$$\sqrt{T}(\hat{f} - f) \xrightarrow{d} \mathcal{N}(0, G_h \Sigma_{\widehat{a}} G'_h) \tag{6.6}$$

where $G_h := \partial \text{vec}(f)/\partial \text{vec}(A_1, \ldots, A_p)'$. This expression can be explicitly written as

$$G_h = \sum_{i=0}^{h-1} \left(\delta'_y J(\mathbf{A}')^{h-1-i} \otimes J\mathbf{A}^i J' \right) \tag{6.7}$$

The permanent impact of limit order can be deduced from Ganger's representation of the cointegrated VAR as

$$\bar{f}(\delta_y) := \lim_{h \to \infty} f(h; \delta_y) = C\delta_y \tag{6.8}$$

where

$$C = \beta_\perp \left(\alpha'_\perp \left(I_K - \sum_{i=1}^{p-1} \Gamma_i \right) \beta_\perp \right)^{-1} \alpha'_\perp \qquad (6.9)$$

6.5 MARKET IMPACT AT NASDAQ

We model the best quotes and market depths up to the third level. The computational burden is reduced by separately estimating the model for each of the 21 trading days. The market impact is then computed as the monthly average of individual (daily) impulse responses. Likewise, confidence intervals are computed based on daily averages. For the sake of brevity we refrain from presenting all individual results for the ten stocks. We rather illustrate representative evidence based on Warner Chilcott plc (ticker symbol WCRX) using a cointegrated VAR(10) model. The results for the remaining stocks are provided in a web appendix on http://amor.cms.hu-berlin.de/~huangrui/project/order_impact_nasdaq/.

Figure 6.5 depicts the market impact of buy and sell limit orders posted at the best quotes as shown in Scenario 1 in Section 6.4.2.[6] The

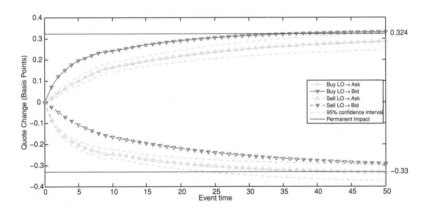

Figure 6.5 Changes of ask and bid quotes induced by buy/sell limit orders placed at the market (level one) with a size equal to half of the depth on the first level. The marked number on the vertical axes indicates the magnitude of the permanent impact. The dashed lines indicate the corresponding 95 % confidence intervals. Trading of WCRX at NASDAQ in October 2010. LO: limit order.

---

[6] In all figures in this section, the notation "A → B" is interpreted as "the impact on B induced by A".

impact starts at zero since such a limit order does not *directly* change quotes. As expected, both ask and bid quotes significantly rise (decline) after the arrival of a buy (sell) limit order. In the long run, both quotes converge to a permanent level at which the information content of the incoming limit order is completely incorporated. We observe that the long-run price change is approximately 0.3 basis points. In the short run, ask and bid quotes adjust in an asymmetric way, where bid (ask) quotes tend to react more quickly than ask (bid) quotes after the arrival of a buy (sell) limit order. This adjustment induces a one-sided and temporary decrease of the bid-ask spread.

The significant permanent impact induced by an incoming limit order indicates that it contributes to price discovery. Thus, market participants perceive that limit orders carry private information, which is in contrast to the common assumption in theoretical literature that informed traders only take liquidity but do not provide it. On the other hand, it is supported by the experiment by Bloomfield *et al.* (2005) showing that informed traders use order strategies involving both market orders and limit orders optimally to capitalize their informational advantage.

To explore the role of the order's position in the book, Figure 6.6 depicts the impact on the bid quote induced by a buy limit order placed at the market (level one) and behind the market (levels two and three).

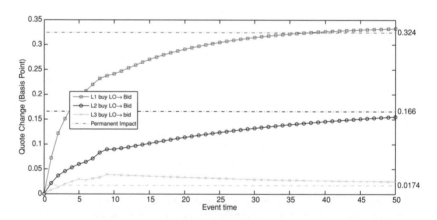

Figure 6.6 Changes of bid quotes induced by buy limit orders placed at the market (level one) and behind the market (levels two and three). The order size equals half of that at the best bid. The initial order book equals the corresponding monthly average shown in Table 6.4. The marked number on the vertical axes indicates the magnitude of the permanent impact. Trading of WCRX at NASDAQ in October 2010. L1: level one; L2: level two; L3: level three; LO: limit order.

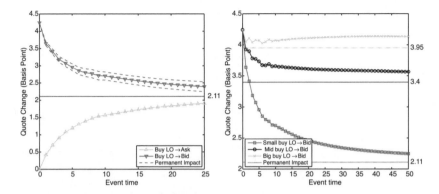

Figure 6.7 (left) Changes of quotes induced by buy limit orders placed inside of the spread with a size equal to the depth at the bid. (right) Changes of bid quote induced by buy limit orders placed inside the spread with different sizes. The initial order book equals the corresponding monthly average shown in Table 6.4. Small size: depth at the bid. Mid size: 7 times the depth at the bid. Big size: 15 times the depth at the bid. Trading of WCRX at NASDAQ in October 2010. LO: limit order.

We observe that the magnitude and speed of the quote reaction are negatively correlated with the order's distance from the spread. Specifically, for orders posted deeper than the third level in the order book, virtually no market impacts can be identified.

Limit orders placed inside the spread perturb the order book dynamics in a more complex way, as shown in Scenario 2 in Section 6.4.2. They directly improve the ask or bid, resulting in an immediate narrowing of the spread and a shift of one side of the order book. Hence, the system seeks the new equilibrium on a path recovering from an immediate quote change and a simultaneous rebalancing of liquidity. Figure 6.7 shows the reactions of bid and ask quotes induced by an aggressive buy limit order. Given our setting, a buy limit order induces a 4.3 basis point increase of the bid quote (corresponding to approximately one cent). However, the long-run price change is just 2.11 basis points. The immediate quote reversal is induced either by sell trades picking up the volume or by cancellations on the bid side. Likewise, the ask quote shifts upward. We hence observe an asymmetric rebalancing of quotes and a corresponding rewidening of the spread.

The right plot of Figure 6.7 shows how the size of incoming aggressive limit orders affects quote reactions. In the case of a comparably small order, the posted volume is likely to be quickly picked up or cancelled, shifting back the bid quote. In contrast, large volumes

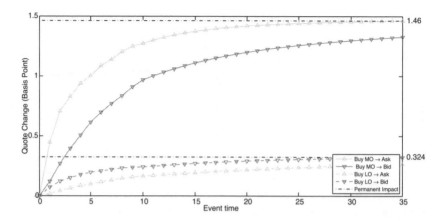

Figure 6.8 Changes of ask and bid quotes induced by a buy market order and a buy limit order of similar size placed at the market. The order size is half of the depth at the best bid. The initial order book equals the corresponding monthly average shown in Table 6.4. Trading of WCRX at NASDAQ in October 2010. LO: limit order; MO: market order.

over-bid the prevailing quote, causing a significant long-run impact. This confirms findings by Hautsch and Huang (2012) for Euronext Amsterdam and shows that aggressive limit orders with large order sizes carry information and serve as pricing signals.

Figure 6.8 compares the market impact induced by a buy market order and a similar buy limit order posted at the bid. We observe that both bid and ask quotes sharply increase after the arrival of a buy market order. The permanent shift of quotes induced by a market order is approximately 4 times greater than that by an incoming limit order. This finding supports theoretical predictions by Roşu (2010). Moreover, in the case of a market order, the ask reacts more quickly than the bid. Hence, we observe an asymmetric adjustment of the two sides of the market, resulting in a temporary widening of spreads.

Since the market impact of limit orders depends not only on the market microstructure but also on the characteristics of the individual stock, an ultimate comparison of estimated market impacts on NASDAQ with those on Euronext (see Hautsch and Huang, 2012) is rather difficult. Nevertheless, we do find a significant difference when comparing the market impact of trades to that of limit orders. While on Euronext Hautsch and Huang (2012) find robust evidence for the market impact of trades trading at best quotes being approximately four times the market impact of a limit order of similar size, this does not necessarily hold for all stocks at NASDAQ, such as, for example, GOOG, STRA, and UTHR. We explain this finding by the existence of hidden liquidity inside bid-ask spreads, as shown in Table 6.3. When the market participant expects a better price than the best quote to be available inside the spread, he or she would naturally interpret a market order placed at the best quotes as being comparably more aggressive as it walks through the (hidden) price levels. As a consequence, the reaction to an incoming market order becomes stronger. Similarly, an incoming limit order is interpreted as being comparably more passive. Consequently, the market impact of limit orders decreases.

6.6   OPTIMAL ORDER SIZE

The expected price impact induced by a limit order placement is a key parameter in trading decisions. Therefore, in trading strategies, it might be of particular interest explicitly to control the expected market impact. The estimates of the price impact provided in the previous section can be used to back out the size of an order (given its position in the queue), which is necessary to cause a given expected price impact.

In fact, due to the discreteness of prices, the magnitude of a price impact can be interpreted in a probabilistic context. Given a minimum tick size at equity markets like NASDAQ, a practitioner who prefers not to shift the price with probability ξ must design the order such that the expected price shift, i.e., the magnitude of the impact, is less than $1 - \xi$ ticks. This is straightforwardly seen by noticing that when the probability is exactly ξ, the minimum level of the market impact is

$$
\begin{aligned}
\text{Permanent market impact} &= \mathbb{E}[\text{long-run price shift}] \\
&= \xi \times (0 \text{ ticks}) + (1 - \xi) \times (1 \text{ ticks}) \\
&= 1 - \xi \quad (\text{ticks})
\end{aligned}
\tag{6.10}
$$

In the following we shall illustrate how to compute explicitly the optimal order size subject to the given control level ξ. For ease of illustration, consider a bid limit order with size m placed at the second best bid. In our setting based on a three-level order book, it is represented as a ten-dimensional shock vector with only one nonzero element at the ninth row according to the order of variables in Equation (6.1):

$$
\delta_9 = \log \left(\frac{m}{\text{depth at second best bid}} + 1 \right)
$$

By Equation (6.8), the corresponding permanent impact on the bid is given by

$$c_{29} \times \log \left(\frac{m}{\text{depth at second best bid}} + 1 \right) \times \left[\frac{\text{bid}}{\text{tick size}} \right] \qquad (6.11)$$

where c_{29} is the ninth element in the second row of matrix C in (6.9). Plugging (6.11) into (6.10) and solving for m gives

$$m = \left(\exp \left[\frac{(1 - \xi) \times \text{tick size}}{\text{bid} \times c_{29}} \right] - 1 \right) \times (\text{depth at second best bid})$$

$$(6.12)$$

Figure 6.9 depicts the permanent impact on bid prices against order sizes for the ten selected stocks. Each curve in the subplots presents the permanent impact induced by the particular type of bid limit order, i.e., "limit orders placed at the second best bid", "limit orders placed at the best bid", and "limit orders placed inside the spread". The order book is initialized at its average. For the sake of clarity, we change the unit of impacts (on the y axis) from basis points of bid prices to the number of ticks. Furthermore, the control level ξ is set to 0.9 (corresponding to a permanent market impact of 0.1 ticks), represented by the horizontal dashed line. The intersections S_1 and S_2 correspond to optimal sizes of limit orders placed on the best bid and second best bid, respectively. For instance, for WCRX and subject to the condition that the market impact is less than 0.1 cent, the optimal size for a limit order placed at the best bid is around 600 shares. Likewise, the optimal size for a limit order placed at the second bid is around 1400 shares.

For the stocks GOOG, UTHR, and STRA, we observe that the market impact is so large that the intersection S_1 corresponds to an order size of less than 100 shares. We explain this phenomenon in three reasons. First, the depth at the best bid is comparably small. Therefore, a 100 share order is a relatively large order given the available liquidity at the market. Second, as shown in Table 6.1, prices of these stocks are relatively high. Consequently, the relative minimum tick size is comparably small, implying lower costs of front-running strategies. Hence, the high market impact reflects a high probability of being affected by front-running. Third, the average absolute spread in ticks is large. Consequently, there is more room for other market participants to improve their quotes.

Finally, for some stocks, we observe zero or even negative permanent impacts of small orders placed inside the spread, as, for example, GOOG, ADBE, DISH, PTEN, and STRA. This is caused by the effect that small

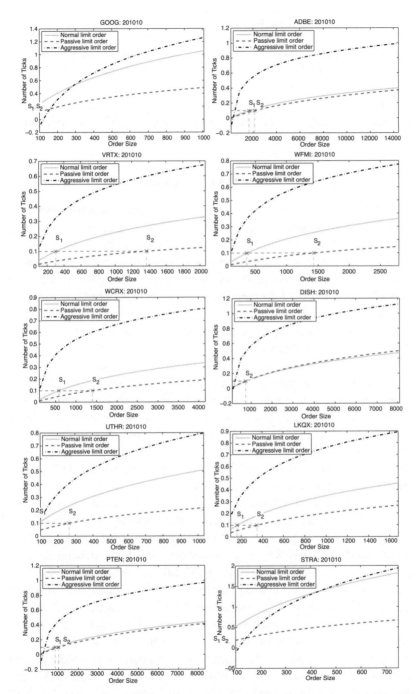

Figure 6.9 Permanent impacts against order sizes. The impacts are induced by bid orders. The initial order book is set to its monthly average. The order sizes at the x axis range from 100 shares to 5 times the depth at the best bid in the initial order book. The aggressive (in-the-spread) limit orders improve the bid price by 1 cent. The horizontal dashed line presents a subject control level corresponding to a permanent market impact of 0.1 cents. Trading of ten selected stocks at NASDAQ in October 2010.

limit orders placed inside the spread are mainly submitted by trading algorithms and tend to be cancelled very quickly if not being executed. In other situations, they might be quickly picked up and trigger other algorithms issuing market orders and/or cancelling existing limit orders on their own side.

6.7 CONCLUSIONS

In this chapter, we provide new empirical evidence on limit order submissions and market impacts in NASDAQ trading. Employing TotalView-ITCH data, we can summarize the following major findings. First, we observe huge numbers of order submissions per day with order sizes clustering around round lots. Second, most of the limit orders are cancelled before being executed. Cancellation times are hardly greater than one second. Third, the volume-weighted execution time of limit orders is substantially greater than its median, indicating that big limit orders face clearly more execution risk. Finally, we observe that only very few market orders tend to "walk through the book".

We find the short-run and long-run price reactions induced by limit order placements to be consistent with those found by Hautsch and Huang (2012) for data stemming from the Euronext Amsterdam. This implies that these effects are quite stable across markets, despite differences in market settings. In particular, we find that incoming limit orders have significant short-run and long-run effects on ask and bid quotes. Buy (sell) limit orders increase (decrease) both ask and bid quotes while temporarily decreasing bid-ask spreads. Similar but stronger effects are found after arrivals of market orders with temporary increases of bid-ask spreads. For aggressive limit orders posted in the spread we find different effects depending on the order size. While the new quote level caused by a large aggressive order also holds in the long run, this is not true for small orders. Their direct effect on quotes tends to be reversed after a while as the order is picked up. Moreover, it turns out that only limit orders posted up to the second order level have significant market impacts. Orders that are placed even deeper in the book have virtually no effect on the market. Interestingly, we find that small orders placed inside the spread cause zero or even negative long-run impacts. We explain this finding by the existence of trading algorithms, which cancel such orders very quickly if they do not get executed.

Finally, we illustrate how to use the setup to compute optimal sizes of limit orders given a certain intended price impact. This might be helpful in controlling the risk in trading strategies.

ACKNOWLEDGMENT

This research is supported by the Deutsche Forschungsgemeinschaft (DFG) via the Collaborative Research Center 649 'Economic Risk'.

REFERENCES

Bloomfield, R., M. O'Hara and G. Saar (2005) The "Make or Take" Decision in an Electronic Market: Evidence on the Evolution of Liquidity, *Journal of Financial Economics* **75**, 165–199.

Boulatov, A. and T.J. George (2008) Securities Trading when Liquidity Providers are Informed, Working Paper, University of Houston.

Cont, R., A. Kukanov and S. Stoikov (2011) The Price Impact of Order Book Events, *Quantitative Finance*, forthcoming doi:10.1080/14697688.2010.528444.

Eisler, Z., J. Bouchaud and J. Kockelkoren (2011) The Price Impact of Order Book Events: Market Orders, Limit Orders and Cancellations, *Quantitative Finance*, forthcoming doi: 10.1080/1469768832010.528444.

Engle, R.F. and A.J. Patton (2004) Impact of trades in an error-correction model of quote prices, *Journal of Financial Markets* **7**, 1–25.

Härdle, W.K., N. Hautsch and A. Mihoci (2009) Modelling and Forecasting Liquidity Supply Using Semiparametric Factor Dynamics, Discussion Paper 2009/18, Collaborative Research Center 649 "Economic Risk", Humboldt-Universität zu Berlin.

Harris, L. (1997) Order Exposure and Parasitic Traders, Working Paper, Marshall School of Business, University of Southern California.

Hasbrouck, J. and G. Saar (2009) Technology and Liquidity Provision: The Blurring of Traditional Definitions, *Journal of Financial Markets* **12**, 143–172.

Hautsch, N. and R. Huang (2012) The Market Impact of a Limit Order, *Journal of Economic Dynamics and Control* **36**, 502–522.

Huang, R. and T. Polak (2011) LOBSTER: The Limit Order Book Reconstructor, Discussion Paper, School of Business and Economics, Humboldt Universität zu Berlin, http://lobster.wiwi.hu-berlin.de/Lobster/LobsterReport.pdf.

Johansen, S. (1991) Estimation and Hypothesis Testing of Cointegration Vectors in Gaussian Vector Autoregressive Models, *Econometrica* **59**, 1551–1580.

Johansen, S. and K. Juselius (1990) Maximum Likelihood Estimation and Inference on Cointegration – With Applications to the Demand for Money, *Oxford Bulletin of Economics and Statistics* **52**, 169–210.

Lütkepohl, H. (1990) Asymptotic Distributions of Impulse Response Functions and Forecast Error Variance Decompositions of Vector Autoregressive Models, *Review of Economics and Statistics* **72**, 116–125.

Parlour, C. and D. Seppi (2008) Limit Order Markets: A Survey, in *Handbook of Financial Intermediation and Banking*, A.W.A. Boot and A.V. Thakor (Eds), Elsevier.

Roşu, I. (2010) Liquidity and Information in Order Driven Markets, Working paper HEC Paris, Available at SSRN:http://ssrn.com/abstract=1286193.

Russell, J. and T. Kim (2010) A New Model for Limit Order Book Dynamics, in *Volatility and Time Series Econometrics, Essays in Honor of Robert Engle*, T. Bollerslev, J. Russell and M. Watson (Eds), Oxford University Press.

Part IV
Optimal Trading

Introduction: Trading and Market Micro-structure

Charles-Albert Lehalle

An on-going increase of computer-driven trading

The last few years have seen dramatic changes in trading practices: the use of computers to buy and sell financial products went from zero to 25 % (depending on the asset class) in 2004 to 10 to 60 % in 2010 (see Figure 1 and Hendershott *et al.*, 2011).

To be more accurate: "algorithmic trading" encompasses only the orders that are explicitly sent by an investor (pension fund, hedge fund, investment bank, etc.) to a server hosting trading algorithms. Three other activities should be added to these figures: "program trading" (orders that are sent as portfolios to servers), "high frequency market making" (proprietary traders providing electronic quotes in publicly available order books), and orders sent to human intermediaries who are themselves using trading algorithms to access the order books. Adding all those numbers together, at least 70 % of the trades on equity markets in the US (50 % in Europe, 35 % in Japan) are said to have a computer-operated counterpart.

The main factors of these on-going changes are:

- A preference by policy-makers and regulators for transactions on electronic market transactions rather than over-the-counter ones. The main reason is that they have the feeling that the monitoring and controlling of systemic risk is easier when supported by large data centers storing the history of positions of all market participants.
- The decline of margins and increase of competition in the trading in-dustry encouraging more automated approaches to guarantee reliable performances.

Market Microstructure: Confronting Many Viewpoints. Edited by F. Abergel, J.-P. Bouchaud, T. Foucault, C.-A. Lehalle and M. Rosenbaum.

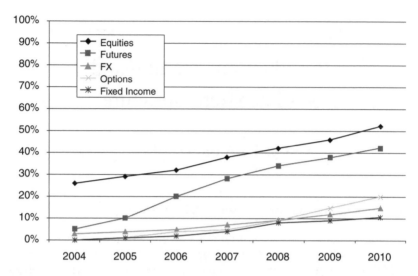

Figure 1 Evolution of the use of algorithmic trading from 2004 to 2010 on US markets.

Source: Aite Group.

- A broader access to fast hardware solutions allowing data capture, storage and processing that were previously only used by the defense and aerospace industries (mainly for artificial vision; see Granado and Garda, 1997).

Besides, the financial crisis put the emphasis on liquidity issues and short-term proprietary trading strategies (to reduce inventory exposure to market risk).

The competition between market operators increased during the same period: the mergers of NYSE with Euronext, the one of the London Stock Exchange and Turquoise, or between Chi-X and BATS Europe are side effects of this competition. In Asia the convergence operates at a slower rate; the alignment of trading hours and some mergers are nevertheless ongoing.

Early academic answers and old practices

The academic literature slowly addressed this change of trading practices. While market micro-structure has been addressed long ago by economists (see Ho and Stoll, 1981; Mendelson, 1982; Garman, 1976; Glosten and Milgrom, 1985; Kyle, 1985), theoretical frameworks to optimize the point of view of a trader trying to optimize his trading process have been proposed only recently (mainly from the viewpoint of "optimal trade scheduling"; see Almgren and Chriss, 2000; Bertsimas and Lo, 1998). On their side, econophysicists studied empirically the market impact of trades on any scales (Bouchaud *et al.*, 2002; Lillo *et al.*, 2003). More recently statistical and econometric studies focused on the cost of trading (Dufour and Engle, 2000). Last but not least, probabilists developed an interest for rounded diffusion processes that could be considered as a model of the diffusion of the price on a discretized price grid (Jacod, 1996).

From the practitioner's viewpoint, the topics of interest at the end of the 1990s were mainly:

- To understand the "slippage" of the trading process, with respect to explanatory variables mixing the market context (volatility, momentum, traded volume, etc.) and the liquidity of the traded instrument (bid-ask spread, average trade size, imbalance, etc.).
- To control the risk of a large buy or sell order using "trading curves" to avoid trading too fast (to avoid market impact and adverse selection) or too slow (to minimize the exposure to market risk).

Two regulation changes, Reg NMS in the US (2005) and MiFID in Europe (2007), promoted the fragmentation of markets. The financial crisis reduced the margin of almost all market participants and increased the intraday and extra day volatility, putting more emphasis on the trading costs and intraday risk control. The complexity of buying or selling a large amount of lots increased because of two major effects:

- The liquidity was now spread over four to seven trading destinations, demanding to split each already small order before sending it to the trading venues.
- The latency became an issue: first to capture instantaneous crossing of the best bid and ask on two different venues, then to be aware of the availability of liquidity on a trading venue before other participants.

New practical needs and academic recent advances

Optimal trading or quantitative trading is now an area of quantitative finance, combining and refining results enhancing the understanding of the price formation process, such as:

- *Statistical methods* to use high frequency data emerged, aiming to decompose the price moves between randomness and micro-structural effects (Zhang *et al.*, 2005; Hayashi and Yoshida, 2005; Robert and Rosenbaum, 2010; Bacry *et al.*, 2011).

- *Market impact* has been studied more intensively with respect to its interactions with a trading process (Gatheral, 2010).
- The effect of *market design* choices and the nature of market participants on the efficiency of the price formation process have been tested empirically and theoretically (Foucault *et al.*, 2005; Menkveld, 2011).

These results provide the tools to put in place more sophisticated trading techniques as follows:

- The mean-variance framework that gave birth to the first optimal trading curves can now be replaced by *stochastic control* approaches (Bouchard *et al.*, 2011), and the high frequency market-making problem has also been formalized (Guéant *et al.*, 2011).
- *Forward optimizing methods*, inspired by statistical learning, have been proposed to take into account very short time scale statistical properties of the order flow (Pagès *et al.*, 2009; Laruelle *et al.*, 2011).

This field is now expanding fast, offering practitioners a wide toolbox to choose from . All aspects of optimal trading have nevertheless not yet been investigated, especially:

- *Performance analysis*: once a trading algorithm is implemented, its efficiency and its performance are periodically reviewed: first from the point of view of a trader confronting variations of the same algorithm to different market conditions and then from the point of view of a large investor using different (unknown) algorithms hosted by different execution providers to buy or sell instruments according to different investment motivations (alpha extraction, hedging, risk reduction, etc.).
- *Stress testing*: before putting a trading algorithm on real markets, there is a need to understand its exposure to different market conditions, from volatility or momentum to bid-ask spread or trading frequency. The study of "Greeks" of the payoff of a trading algorithm is not straightforward since it is inside a closed loop of liquidity: its "psi" should be its derivative with respect to the bid-ask spread, its "phi" with respect to the trading frequency, and its "lambda" with respect to the liquidity available in the order book.

Let us hope that events such as this International Conference help in mixing mathematical, economic, and physicist cultures to continue to bring better answers to the needs of practitioners and regulators.

REFERENCES

Almgren, R.F. and N. Chriss (2000) Optimal Execution of Portfolio Transactions, *Journal of Risk* **3**(2), 5–39.

Bacry, E., S. Delattre, M. Hoffmann and J.F. Muzy (2011) Modeling microstructure noise with mutually exciting point processes.

Bertsimas, D. and A.W. Lo (1998) Optimal Control of Execution Costs, *Journal of Financial Markets* **1**(1), 1–50.

Bouchard, B., N.-M. Dang and C.-A. Lehalle (2011) Optimal Control of Trading Algorithms: A General Impulse Control Approach, *SIAM Journal of Financial Mathematics*.

Bouchaud, J.-P., M. Mezard and M. Potters (2002) Statistical Properties of Stock Order Books: Empirical Results and Models, *Quantitative Finance* **2**, 251–256.

Dufour, A. and R.F. Engle (2000) Time and the Price Impact of a Trade, *Journal of Finance* **55**(6), 2467–2498.

Foucault, T., O. Kadan and E. Kandel (2005) Limit Order Book as a Market for Liquidity, *Review of Financial Studies* **18**(4), 1171–1217.

Garman, M.B. (1976) Market Microstructure, *Journal of Financial Economics* **3**(3), 257–275.

Gatheral, J. (2010) No-Dynamic-Arbitrage and Market Impact, *Quantitative Finance* **10**(7), 749–759.

Glosten, L.R. and P.R. Milgrom (1985) Bid, Ask and Transaction Prices in a Specialist Market with Heterogeneously Informed Traders, *Journal of Financial Economics* **14**(1), 71–100.

Granado, B. and P. Garda (1997) Evaluation of the CNAPS Neuro-computer for the Simulation of MLPS with Receptive Fields, in *Biological and Artificial Computation: From Neuroscience to Technology*, J. Mira, R. Moreno-Diíz and K. Cabestany, (Eds), Vol. 1240 of *Lecture Notes in Computer Science*, Chapter 84, Springer, Berlin/Heidelberg, pp. 817–824.

Guéant, O., C.-A. Lehalle and J. Fernandez-Tapia (2011) Dealing with the Inventory Risk, forthcoming in *SIAM Journal on Financial Mathematics*.

Hayashi, T. and N. Yoshida (2005) On Covariance Estimation of Non-synchronously Observed Diffusion Processes, *Bernoulli* **11**(2), 359–379.

Hendershott, T.J., C.M. Jones and A.J. Menkveld (2011) Does Algorithmic Trading Improve Liquidity? *Journal of Finance* **66**(1), 1–33.

Ho, T. and H.R. Stoll (1981) Optimal Dealer Pricing Under Transactions and Return Uncertainty, *Journal of Financial Economics* **9**(1), 47–73.

Jacod, J. (1996) La Variation Quadratique Moyenne du Brownien en Présence d'Erreurs d'Arrondi. In *Hommage a P.A. Meyer et J. Neveu*, Vol. 236. Asterisque.

Kyle, A.P. (1985), Continuous Auctions and Insider Trading, *Econometrica* **53**(6), 1315–1335.

Laruelle, S., C.-A. Lehalle and G. Pagès (2011) Optimal Posting Distance of Limit Orders: A Stochastic Algorithm Approach.

Lillo, F., J.D. Farmer and R.N. Mantegna (2003) Econophysics – Master Curve for Price – Impact Function, *Nature* **421**(6919), 129.

Mendelson, H. (1982) Market Behavior in a Clearing House, *Econometrica* **50**(6), 1505–1524.

Menkveld, A.J. (2011) High Frequency Trading and the New-Market Makers, Working Paper.

Pagès, G., S. Laruelle and C.-A. Lehalle (2009) Optimal split of orders across liquidity pools: a stochatic algorithm approach, forthcoming in *SIAM Journal of Financial Mathematics*.

Robert, C.Y. and M. Rosenbaum (2010) On the Microstructural Hedging Error, *SIAM Journal on Financial Mathematics* **1**, 427–453.

Zhang, L., P.A. Mykland and Y.A. Sahalia (2005) A Tale of Two Time Scales: Determining Integrated Volatility with Noisy High-Frequency Data, *Journal of the American Statistical Association*, **100**(472).

7

Collective Portfolio Optimization in Brokerage Data: The Role of Transaction Cost Structure

Damien Challet and David Morton de Lachapelle

7.1 INTRODUCTION

Regarding financial market behavior as a result of the interaction between many traders, i.e., as collective phenomena, opens the way to applying concepts and tools of statistical physics. In the last few decades, the latter has developed a powerful mathematical machinery that is able to solve the macroscopic dynamics resulting from the non-linear microscopic interaction of fully heterogeneous adaptive complex agents, no less. One usually starts from known microscopic behavior and interaction and then study and possibly solve the resulting collective dynamics. In the case of financial markets, the lack of knowledge about the agents themselves hinders progress in this field. On the one hand, experimental psychology and behavioral finance put forward a picture of trader minds and actions that does not resemble many rational agents. On the other hand, the actual behavior of traders is seldom studied. Thus, one attempts to reverse engineer markets with agent-based models, trying painstakingly to guess what microscopic mechanism is necessary to reproduce a set of macroscopic stylized facts one observed in available data.

There has been some notable progress so far from statistical physicists. A quite important one is about volatility clustering. In game theory, giving the players the ability not to take part in a given game gives rise

Market Microstructure: Confronting Many Viewpoints. Edited by F. Abergel, J.-P. Bouchaud,
T. Foucault, C.-A. Lehalle and M. Rosenbaum.
© 2012 John Wiley & Sons, Ltd.

to much richer phenomenology (Szabó and Hauert, 2002). In the context of financial market models, letting the traders be active or inactive according to an indicator that fluctuates is enough to give rise to a long-term memory of the collective activity, and thus of volatility (Bouchaud *et al.*, 2001). In other words, including this ingredient in an agent-based model guarantees the production of clustered volatility (see, for example, Johnson *et al.*, 2000; Giardina and Bouchaud, 2003; Challet, 2007; Challet *et al.*, 2005a). Another contribution is to relate the onset of large fluctuations to a phase transition between unpredictable and predictable price dynamics (Challet *et al.*, 2005b).

The problem with this approach is that simple mechanisms may not be sufficient to understand and replicate the full complexity of financial markets, as some part of it may lie instead in the heterogeneity of the agents themselves. While the need for heterogeneous agents in this context is intuitive (see, for example, Arthur, 1994), there is no easily available data against which to test or to validate microscopically an agent-based model. Even if it is relatively easy to design agent-based models that reproduce some of the stylized facts of financial markets (see, for example, Challet *et al.*, 2005b; Lux and Marchesi 1999; Caldarelli *et al.*, 1997; Brock and Hommes, 1997; Alfarano and Lux, 2003), one never knows if this is achieved for good reasons. In addition, it is to be expected that real traders behave sometimes at odds with one's intuition.

Hence the need for data on trader behavior, which are usually hard to obtain; brokers of course have some data, but these are not easily accessible. Quite tellingly, this lack of data is not entirely to blame for the current ignorance of real-trader dynamics: researchers, even when given access to broker data, tend to focus on trading gains and behavioral biases (see, for example, Barber *et al.*, 2004; Bauer *et al.*, 2007; Dea *et al.*, 2010).

The aim of this contribution is to show that a simple law of collective (read average) behavior of a population of traders, with large individual fluctuations, can be found when plotting the average transaction value against the average portfolio value of each agent, for the whole population of traders. The collective behavior we report here reflects to a large extent mean-variance portfolio optimization with transaction cost.

7.2 DESCRIPTION OF THE DATA

Our dataset is extracted from the database of the largest Swiss on-line broker, Swissquote Bank SA (further referred to as Swissquote). The sample contains comprehensive details about all 19 million electronic orders sent by 120 000 professional and nonprofessional on-line traders from January 2003 to March 2009. Of these orders, 65 % have been cancelled or have expired and 30 % have been filled; the remaining 5 % were still valid as of the 31 March 2009. Since this study focuses on the transaction value as a function of the account value, we chose to exclude orders for products that allow traders to leverage their investments, i.e., orders to margin-calls markets such as the foreign exchange market (FOREX) and the derivative exchange (EUREX). The resulting sample contains 540 % of orders for derivatives, 420 % for stocks, and 4 % for bonds and funds. Finally, 70 % of these orders were sent to the Swiss market, 20 % to the German market, and about 10 % to the US market.

Swissquote clients consist of three main groups: *individuals* (or *retail clients*), *companies*, and *asset managers*. Individual traders are mainly nonprofessional traders acting for their own account. The account of a company is usually managed by an individual trading on its behalf and, as we shall see, behaves very much like retail clients, albeit with a larger typical account value. Finally, asset managers manage accounts of individuals and/or companies, some of them dealing with more than a thousand clients.

7.3 RESULTS

For each trader i, we determine the days of trading activity t_k, $k = 1$, $\ldots, T_i$ and define the average portfolio value on the days before the transactions took place, i.e., $P_v = (1/T_i) \sum_k P_v(t_k - 1)$. The average transaction value, denoted by T_i, is defined as the price paid times the volume of the transaction and does not include transaction fees. We have excluded the traders who have leveraged positions on stocks, and hence $T_i \leq P_v$.

We first produce a scatter plot of $\langle \log T \rangle$ versus $\langle \log P_v \rangle$ (Figure 7.1). In a log-log scale plot, it shows a cloud of points that is roughly increasing. A density plot is, however, clearer for retail clients as there are many more points (Figure 7.2).

These plots make it clear that the average relationship between $\log T$ and $\log P_v$ is rather simple. A robust nonparametric regression method (Cleveland and Devlin, 1988) reveals a double linear relationship between $\langle \log T \rangle$ and $\langle \log P_v \rangle$ (see Figures 7.1 and 7.2) that can be formalized as

$$\langle \log T \rangle = \beta_x \langle \log P_v \rangle + a_x \tag{7.1}$$

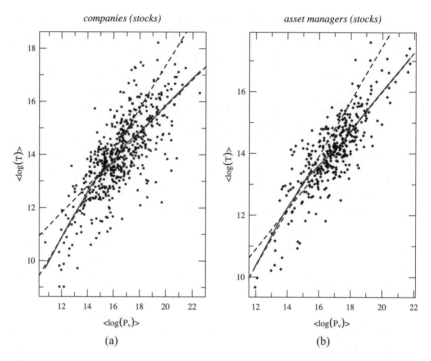

Figure 7.1 Scatter plot of the average $\log T$ versus the average $\log P_v$, robust non-parametric fit (solid line) and linear fits (dashed lines).

where $x = 1$ when $\langle \log P_v \rangle < \Theta_1$ and $x = 2$ when $\langle \log P_v \rangle > \Theta_2$. Fitted values with confidence intervals are reported in Table 7.1.

Remarkably, the transition occurs at roughly the same values of $\langle \log P_v \rangle$ for the three categories of traders; in addition, the slopes of these lines are very similar. This begs for a generic explanation, which, we argue below, is to be found in the collective tendency of Swissquote on-line traders to hold mean-variance portfolios that take into account the effective broker transaction fee structure of Swissquote, which has also two regions.

The relationships above only applies to local averages over all the agents. Regression residuals are for the most part (i.e. more than 95 %) normally distributed with constant standard deviations ξ_x, without fat tails. This directly suggests the following simple relation for individual traders

$$T^i = e^{a_x + \delta^i a_x}(P_v^i)^{\beta_x} \qquad (7.2)$$

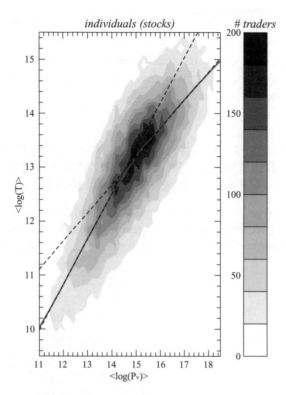

Figure 7.2 Density plot of the average $\log T$ versus the average $\log P_v$, robust non-parametric fit (solid line) and linear fits (dashed lines).

Table 7.1 Parameter values and 95 % confidence intervals for the double linear model (7.2). For each category of investors, the first and second rows correspond respectively to $\langle \log P_v \rangle \leq \Theta_1$ and $\langle \log P_v \rangle \geq \Theta_2$. For confidentiality reasons, we have multiplied P_v and T by a random number. This only affects the true values of a_x and Θ in the table

	β_x	a_x	ξ	Θ	R^2
Individuals	0.84 ± 0.02	0.73 ± 1.25	0.71	14	0.52
	0.54 ± 0.01	5.07 ± 0.15	0.77	14.5	0.40
Companies	0.81 ± 0.13	1.12 ± 8.17	0.88	15.5	0.47
	0.50 ± 0.07	5.82 ± 1.65	1.00	15.6	0.33
Asset managers	0.89 ± 0.20	-0.31 ± 0.76	0.62	15.5	0.52
	0.63 ± 0.08	3.28 ± 5.78	0.62	16.5	0.46

where T^i and P_v^i are respectively the turnover and portfolio value of investor i and $\delta^i a_x$ are i.i.d. $N(0, \xi_x^2)$ idiosyncratic variations independent from P_v that mirror the heterogeneity of the agents. As we shall see, portfolio optimization with heterogeneous parameters yields this precise relationship.

7.4   THE INFLUENCE OF TRANSACTION COSTS ON TRADING BEHAVIOR FROM OPTIMAL MEAN-VARIANCE PORTFOLIOS

As hinted above, we will argue that the origin lies in the Swissquote fee structure, which is shown in Figure 7.3; it is a piecewise constant, nonlinear looking function and flat for transactions larger than some

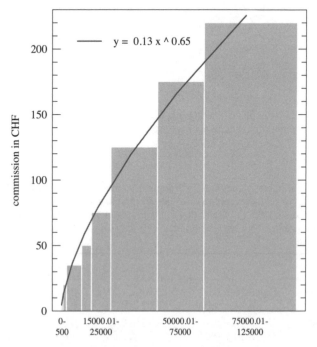

Figure 7.3   Swissquote fee curve for the Swiss stock market. Commissions based on a sliding scale of costs are common practice in the world of on-line finance. The solid line results from a nonlinear fit to Equation (7.4). Parameter values are $C = 0.13 \in [0.05, 0.5]_{95}$ and $\delta = 0.63 \in [0.5, 0.74]_{95}$, where the 95 % confidence intervals are obtained from the BC_a bootstrap method of Efron and Tibshirani (1993).

given value. Fitting all increasing segments to Equation (7.4) gives $\delta = 0.63 \in [0.5, 0.74]_{95}$.

In order to understand the influence of this peculiar transaction cost structure not accounted for in the literature, we need to derive simple portfolio optimization results. The simplest setting is found in Brennan (1975): it is a one-shot portfolio mean-variance optimization. The function to minimize is

$$L_\lambda(R) = \lambda E(R) - \text{Var}(R) \qquad (7.3)$$

where R is the stochastic return of the portfolio over the investment time horizon and λ is the relative importance of return with respect to risk. The return of the portfolio can be decomposed into contributions from risky assets, the interests of the amount kept in cash, and the total relative cost of broker commission, which we denote as $R = R^{risky} + R^{cash} - R^{cost}$. More precisely.

- $R^{risky} = \Sigma_{i=1}^{N} x_i R_i$, where R_i is the return of stock i over this horizon, x_i is the fraction of the total wealth invested in this stock, and N is the total number of investable assets; we shall denote the total fraction of wealth invested in risky assets by $x = \Sigma_{i=1}^{N} x_i$.
- $R^{cash} = (1 - x)r$, where r is the interest rate.
- $R^{cost} = (\Sigma_{i=1}^{N} F(x_i P_v)/P_v)(1 + r)$, where $F(x)$ is the amount charged by a broker to exchange an amount x of cash into shares or vice versa.

The fees structure of Swissquote is approximated by a power function law until up to $F = F_{\max}$ and then a constant value. We hence choose

$$F(x_i P_v) = \min\left(C(x_i P_v)^\delta, F_{\max}\right) \qquad (7.4)$$

where δ interpolates between a flat-fee ($\delta = 0$), as in Brennan (1975), and a proportional scheme ($\delta = 1$) via a power function law, and C is a constant. We assume that the return of asset i follows a one-factor model (Sharpe, 1964)

$$R_i = \beta_i(R_M - r) + r + \varepsilon_i \qquad (7.5)$$

where ε_i is an uncorrelated white noise $E(\varepsilon_i) = E(\varepsilon_i \varepsilon_j) = E(R_M \varepsilon_i) = 0$ and β_i the factor associated to asset i. This is a surprisingly good approximation to Swiss securities price dynamics.

Assuming an equally weighted portfolio, $x_i = x/N$ is constant for all i and we are left with only four parameters x, N, δ, and λ; since all the transactions have the same value, there is no risk to hit the two regions of Swissquote fee structure within a single portfolio, and hence

δ is constant. We are mostly interested in N as a function of x. The technical details can be found in Morton de Lachapelle and Challet (2010). One finally finds that

$$N^{2-\delta} \left(1 + \frac{\delta}{1-\delta} \frac{K}{N} \right) = K \frac{\bar{\beta}(E(R_M) - r)}{(1-\delta)C(1+r)} (xP_v)^{1-\delta} \qquad (7.6)$$

where K is the ratio of residual risk to market risk, defined as

$$K = 2 \left(\frac{\bar{\beta}^2 \text{Var}(R_M)}{\overline{\text{Var}(\varepsilon)}} + \frac{1}{N} \right)^{-1} \underset{N \gg 1}{\approx} 2 \frac{\overline{\text{Var}(\varepsilon)}}{\bar{\beta}^2 \text{Var}(R_M)} \qquad (7.7)$$

Given the desired level of investment x, (7.6) can be solved for N numerically in an actual portfolio optimization. Further insight is gained by considering the high diversification limit $N \gg 1$ (or, equivalently, the high portfolio value limit), which yields $1 + [\delta/(1-\delta)](K/N) \approx 1$ in (7.6) and thus

$$N = \left(K \frac{\bar{\beta}(E(R_M) - r)}{(1-\delta)C(1+r)} \right)^{1/(2-\delta)} (xP_v)^{(1-\delta)/(2-\delta)} \qquad (7.8)$$

where K is given by the right-hand side of (7.7). The latter equation generalizes (Brennan, 1975) to the case of a varying cost impact, represented here by the parameter δ (i.e. the result of Brennan, 1975, is recovered by setting $\delta = 0$ and $\beta_i = 1$ in (7.8)). These results can be to some extent generalized to nonequally weighted portfolios.

In essence, (7.8) says that the number of securities held in an equally weighted mean-variance portfolio with Sharpe-like returns is related to the amount invested as

$$\log(N) = \frac{1-\delta}{2-\delta} \log(xP_v) + \kappa \qquad (7.9)$$

in the high diversification limit, where κ is the pre-factor of $(xP_v)^{(1-\delta)/(2-\delta)}$ in (7.8). The last equation gives N as a function of P_v for a pre-defined x in the optimal portfolio. The heterogeneity of the traders, beyond their account value, is not apparent yet, but may occur both in x and κ: first each trader may have his own preference regarding the fraction of this account to invest in risky assets, x; therefore one should replace x by x^i; next, κ includes both a term related to transaction costs, which does vary from trader to trader, and some measures and expectation of market returns and variance; each trader may have his own perception or way of measuring them, and hence

κ should also be replaced by κ^i. Finally, both terms can be merged in the same constant term $\zeta^i = (1 - \delta)/(2 - \delta)\log(x^i) + \kappa^i$. This explains how the heterogeneity of the traders is a cause of fluctuations in the kind of relationships we are interested in.

The result above only links the number of securities in a portfolio N with its value P_v, but one of course wishes to obtain relationships that involve the turnover per transaction, T, in order to compare Equation (7.9) with the empirical results of Section 7.3. One problem we face is that the portfolio optimization setup rests on the assumption that the agents build their portfolio by selecting a group of assets and stick to them over a period of time. This, obviously, does not include the possibility of speculating by a series of buy and sell trades on even a single asset, nor portfolio re-balancing, which consists in adjusting the relative proportions of some assets, all of which are in the data we have used in Section 7.3.

We have found a simple and effective method to select portfolio-building transactions: it consists in assuming that the latter include only the very first transaction of assets not traded previously; sell orders are ignored as Swissquote clients cannot short sell easily. In other words, if trader i owns some shares of assets A, B, and C and then buys some shares of asset D, this last transaction is deemed to contribute to his portfolio building process; the set of such transactions is denoted by Φ_i, while the full set of transactions is denoted by Ω_i. Subsequent transactions of shares of assets A, B, C, or D do not belong to Φ_i. The number of different assets that trader i owns is supposed to be $N_i \simeq |\Phi_i|$, where $|X|$ is the cardinal of set X; this approach assumes that a trader always owns shares in all the assets ever traded; surprisingly, this is the most common case.

Let us drop the index i and now focus on $T_\Phi = \sum_{k \in \Phi} T_k$, the total transaction value that helped build his portfolio. We should first check how it is related to the total portfolio value P_v. Let us define $\langle P_v \rangle_\Phi$, the account value of this trader averaged at the times at which he trades a new asset. Plotting $\log \langle P_v \rangle_\Phi$ against $\log T_\Phi$ gives a cloudy relationship, as usual, but fitting it with $\log \langle P_v \rangle_\Phi = \chi \log T_\Phi$ gives $\chi = 1.03 \pm 0.02$ for individuals, $\chi = 0.99 \pm 0.02$ for asset managers, and $\chi = 1.00 \pm 0.01$ for companies with an adjusted $R^2 = 0.99$ in all cases. This relationship trivially holds with $\chi = 1$ for the traders who buy all their assets at once, as assumed in the portfolio model. The traders who do not lie on this line either hold positions in cash (this line is then a lower bound) or do not build their portfolio in a single day: they pile up positions in derivative products or stocks whose price fluctuations are one cause of the deviations from the line. However, the fact that the slope is close to 1 means that the average fluctuation is zero and hence that on average traders do not make money from the positions taken on new stocks. The consequence of this is that $\log P_v$ can be safely replaced by $\log T_\Phi$ in (7.9); thus, setting $x = 1$,

$$\log N = \frac{1 - \delta}{2 - \delta} \log T_\Phi + \kappa \qquad (7.10)$$

The $x = 1$ assumption is in fact quite reasonable. Most Swissquote traders do not use their trading account as savings accounts and are fully invested; we do not know what amount they keep on their other bank accounts.

A robust nonparametric fit does reveal a linear relationship between $\log N$ and $\log T_\Phi$ in a given region $(N, T_\Phi) \in \Gamma$ (Figure 7.4 overleaf). In this region, we have

$$\log N = \alpha \log T_\Phi + \beta \qquad (7.11)$$

which gives

$$\alpha = \frac{1 - \delta}{2 - \delta} \qquad (7.12)$$

The fitted values are reported in Table 7.2. We still need to link $\langle T \rangle_\Phi$ and $\langle P_v \rangle_\Phi^\beta$. While Section 7.3 showed that the unconditional averages lead to $\langle T \rangle \sim \langle P_v \rangle^\beta$, one still finds that $\langle T \rangle_\Phi \sim \langle P_v \rangle_\Phi^\beta$. Therefore, one can write

$$\log \langle T \rangle_\Phi = \beta \log \langle P_v \rangle_\Phi + \text{cst} \qquad (7.13)$$

Table 7.3 contains the fitted parameters. Thus, one is finally rewarded with the needed link

$$\beta = \frac{1}{2 - \delta} \qquad (7.14)$$

which directly involves the transaction cost structure in the relationship between turnover and portfolio value, as argued in Section 7.3.[1] This

---

[1] Note that this relationship can be obtained directly by assuming that all the transactions happen at the same time, and hence that $T = (xP_v)/N$, which leads straightforwardly to (7.14).

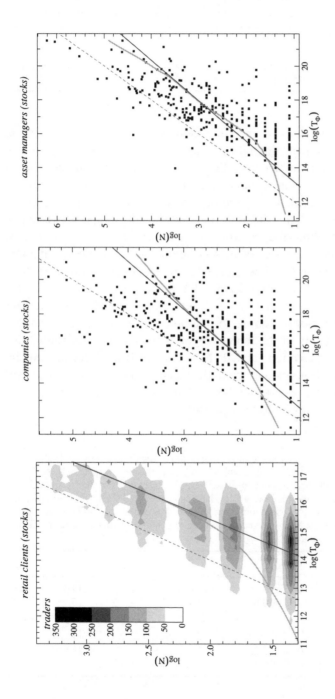

Figure 7.4 Turnover of transactions contributing to the building of a portfolio T_Φ versus the number N of assets held by a given trader at the time of the transaction. Light grey lines: nonparametric fit; dark grey lines: fits of the linear part of the nonparametric fit. From left to right: companies, asset managers, and individuals.

181

Table 7.2   Slope α linking $\log T_\Phi$ and $\log N$ for the three trader categories

	Individuals	Companies	Asset managers
α	0.52 ± 0.02	0.36 ± 0.14	0.44 ± 0.13
$\log T_\Phi \in$	[16,19]	[17,19.8]	[15.8,18]

relationship allows us to close the loop as we are now able to relate directly the exponents linking T, N, and P_v. Going back to Section 7.3, this justifies the claim that the bilinear relationship between log turnover per transaction and log account value is linked to two values of δ.

The surprise comes from the precise value at which the transition occurs. Let us recall that the transitions between the standard Swissquote and an effective flat-fee structure occur *at the same average value* of T for the three categories of traders (idem for T_Φ). However, the real transition value of T is lower than 125 000 CHF (we cannot be more precise for confidentiality reasons). We propose two main reasons for this: first traders with a large account value negotiate a flat fee for all their transactions, leading to a simple and plausible explanation: most of the traders of the three categories who have a portfolio value larger than the transition value do have effectively a flat fee agreement. The other possibility is that the traders tend to either neglect, or regard as constant, transaction fees whose relative value is smaller than some threshold when they build their portfolio.

Table 7.3   Results of the double linear regression of $\log \langle T \rangle_\Phi$ versus $\log \langle P_v \rangle_\Phi$. For each category of investors, the first and second row correspond respectively to $\log \langle P_v \rangle_\Phi \leq \Theta_1$ and $\log \langle P_v \rangle_\Phi \geq \Theta_2$, where $\Theta_{1,2}$ have been determined graphically using the nonparametric method of Cleveland and Devlin (1988), as in Section 7.3. Parameters are as in the double linear model (7.2). For confidentiality reasons, we have multiplied P_v and T by a random number, which only affects the true values of $\Theta_{1,2}$ and of the ordinate a_x

	β_x	a_x	ξ	Θ	R^2
Individuals	0.85 ± 0.02	0.71 ± 0.16	0.65	14.5	0.59
	0.51 ± 0.01	5.62 ± 0.17	0.76	15	0.31
Companies	0.83 ± 0.17	1.03 ± 2.47	0.86	15.5	0.42
	0.62 ± 0.14	3.99 ± 2.55	0.93	17	0.32
Asset managers	0.84 ± 0.25	0.45 ± 3.77	0.79	15.95	0.50
	0.73 ± 0.17	1.72 ± 3.23	0.72	18	0.41

Table 7.4 Table summarizing the empirical and theoretical relationships between α, β, and δ

Small T_ϕ	Individuals	Companies	Asset managers
β	0.85 ± 0.02	0.83 ± 0.17	0.84 ± 0.25
$\log T_\Phi <$	14.5	17	18
$\delta_{eff} = 2 - \frac{1}{\beta}$	0.82 ± 0.02	0.80 ± 0.20	0.81 ± 0.30
δ_{SQ}	$0.63 \in [0.50, 0.74]$	$0.63 \in [0.50, 0.74]$	$0.63 \in [0.50, 0.74]$
δ'_{SQ}	$0.74 \in [0.43, 0.79]$	$0.74 \in [0.43, 0.79]$	$0.74 \in [0.43, 0.79]$
$\tilde{\beta} = \frac{1}{2-\delta_{SQ}}$	$0.73 \in [0.66, 0.74]$	$0.73 \in [0.66, 0.74]$	$0.73 \in [0.66, 0.74]$

Large T_ϕ	Individuals	Companies	Asset managers
β	0.51 ± 0.01	0.62 ± 0.14	0.73 ± 0.17
$\log T_\Phi >$	15	17	18
$\delta_{eff} = 2 - \frac{1}{\beta}$	0.04 ± 0.02	0.39 ± 0.23	0.63 ± 0.23
$\alpha_{eff} = \frac{1-\delta_{eff}}{2-\delta_{eff}}$	0.49 ± 0.01	0.38 ± 0.09	0.27 ± 0.08
α	0.52 ± 0.02	0.36 ± 0.14	0.44 ± 0.13
$\log T_\Phi \in$	$[16,19]$	$[17,19.8]$	$[15.8,18]$

Let us finally discuss the empirical values of α, β, and δ against their theoretical counterparts, which are summarized in Table 7.4.

(i) *Small values of T_Φ.* It was impossible to measure α in that case since the nonparametric fit shows a nonlinear relationship in the log-log plot for retail clients, which we trust more since they have many more points than the graphs for the two other categories of clients. However, it may not make sense to expect a linear relationship since such a relationship is only expected for N large enough ($N \geq 10$ in practice) and a small T_Φ is related to a small N. Hence we can only test $\beta = 1/(2 - \delta)$. The reported value of β is consistent for all the clients. Retail clients have a larger $\delta_{eff} = 2 - 1/\beta$ than the estimated δ_{SQ}. Since the shape of the fee structure is not continuous, the values of these exponents can hardly be expected to match. However, fitting the whole curve structure may be problematic in this context: indeed, the traders with a typical small value of T_Φ see a more linear relationship in the region of a small transaction value, which, when considering the whole curve – for instance, removing the two largest segments from the fee structure – yields $\delta'_{SQ} = 0.74 \in [0.43, 0.79]$, which is not far from δ_{eff}.

(ii) *Large values of T_Φ*. The relationships between all the exponents are verified for the three categories of clients. While uncertainties make the match not very impressive for companies and asset managers, this result is much stronger in the case of retail clients as relative uncertainties are small (1–2 %). The value of β_{retail} is of particular interest as it corresponds to $\delta_{eff} = 0$ or, equivalently, to a flat fee structure. Going back to the fees structure of Swissquote, one finds that the transition happens when the relative transaction cost falls below some threshold (we cannot give its precise value for confidentiality reasons; it is smaller than 1 %). A possible explanation is that either some traders with a high enough average turnover have a flat-fee agreement with Swissquote or that the rest of them simply act as if they were not able to take correctly into account transaction costs. Since not all traders have a flat-fee agreement, one must conclude that some traders disregard small relative fees. The reported value of β for companies and asset managers is larger that β_{retail}, but it is more likely than not that the small sample size is responsible for this discrepancy, since these two categories of clients have a greater propensity to negotiate a flat-fee structure.

7.5   DISCUSSION AND OUTLOOK

We have been able to determine empirically a bilinear relationship between the average log-turnover per transaction and the average log-account value and have related it to the transaction fee structure of the broker and its perception by the agents. A theoretical derivation of optimal simple one-shot mean-variance portfolios with nonlinear transaction costs predicted relationships between turnover, number of different assets in the portfolio, and log-account values that could be verified empirically. This means that the populations of traders do take correctly *on average*, i.e., *collectively*, the transaction costs into account and act *collectively* as mean-variance equally weighted portfolio optimizers. This is not to say that each trader is a mean-variance optimizer, but that the population taken as a whole behaves as such – with differences across populations, as discussed in the previous section. This can be related to findings of Kirman's famous work on demand and offer average curves in Marseille's fish market (Härdle and Kirman, 1995) and more generally as what has become known as the wisdom of the crowds (see Surowiecki, 2005, for an easy-to-read account).

The fact that the turnover depends in a nonlinear way on the account value has important implications for agent-based models, which from now on must take into account the fact that the real traders do invest in a number of assets that depend nonlinearly on their wealth.

Future research will address the relationship between account value and trading frequency, which is of the utmost importance to understand if the many small trades of small investors have a comparable influence on the financial market than those of institutional investors. This will give an understanding of whom provides liquidity and what all the nonlinear relationships found above mean in this respect. This is also crucial in agent-based models, in which one often imposes such a relationship by hand, arbitrarily; conversely, one will be able to validate evolutionary mechanisms of an agent-based model according to the relationship between trading frequency, turnover, number of assets, and account value they achieve in their steady state.

ACKNOWLEDGMENTS

The authors thank the organizers of this stimulating conference. Swissquote Bank SA provided us with data and financial support to DMdL.

REFERENCES

Alfarano, S. and T. Lux (2003) A Minimal Noise Traders Model with Realistic Time Series Properties, in *Long Memory in Economics*, G. Teyssière and A.P. Kirman (Eds), Springer, Berlin.

Arthur, B.W. (1994) Inductive Reasoning and Bounded Rationality: The El Farol Problem, *American Economic Review* **84**, 406–411.

Barber, B.M., Y.T. Lee, Y.J. Liu and T. Odean (2009) Just how much do individual investors lose by trading? *Review of Financial Studies* **22**, 609.

Bauer, R., M. Cosemans and P. Eichholtz (2007) The Performance and Persistence of Individual Investors: Rational Agents or Tulip Maniacs?, http://papers.ssrn.com/sol3/papers.cfm?abstract_id=965810.

Bouchaud, J.-P., I. Giardina and M. Mézard (2001) On a universal mechanism for long ranged volatility correlations. *Quantitative Finance* **1**, 212, cond-mat/0012156.

Brennan, M.J. (1975) The Optimal Number of Securities in a Risky Asset Portfolio When There are Fixed Costs of Transacting: Theory and Some Empirical Results, *Journal of Financial and Quantitative Analysis* **10**(3), 483–496.

Brock, W.A. and C.H. Hommes (1997) A Rational Route to Randomness, *Econometrica* **65**, 1059–1095.

Caldarelli, G., M. Marsili and Y.-C. Zhang (1997) A Prototype Model of Stock Exchange, *Europhysics Letters* **50**, 479–484.

Challet, D. (2007) Inter-pattern Speculation: Beyond Minority, Majority and $-Games, *Journal of Economics, Dynamics and Control* (32), physics/0502140.

Challet, D., A. De Martino, M. Marsili and I.P. Castillo (2005a) Minority games with finite score memory, *Journal of Experiment and Theory*, P03004, cond-mat/0407595.

Challet, D., M. Marsili and Y.-C. Zhang (2005b) *Minority Games*, Oxford University Press, Oxford.

Cleveland, W.S. and S.J. Devlin (1988) Locally Weighted Regression: An Approach to Regression Analysis by Local Fitting, *Journal of the American Statistical Association* **83**(403), 596–610.

Dea, S., N.R. Gondhib, V. Manglac and B. Pochirajud (2010) Success/Failure of Past Trades and Trading Behavior of Investors.

Efron, B. and R.-J. Tibshirani (1993) *An Introduction to the Bootstrap*, Chapman & Hall, New York.

Giardina, I. and J.-Ph. Bouchaud (2003) Crashes and Intermittency in Agent Based Market Models, *European Physics Journal Series B*, **31**, 421–437.

Härdle, W. and A. Kirman (1995) Nonclassical Demand: A Model-Free Examination of Price-Quantity Relations in the Marseille Fish Market, *Journal of Econometrics* **67**(1), 227–257.

Johnson, N.F., M. Hart, P.M. Hui and D. Zheng (2000) Trader Dynamics in a Model Market, *ITJFA* **3**, cond-mat/9910072.

Lux, T. and M. Marchesi (1999) Scaling and Criticality in a Stochastic Multi-Agent Model of a Financial Market, *Nature* **397**, 498–500.

Morton de Lachapelle, D. and D. Challet (2010) Turnover, Account Value and Diversification of Real Traders: Evidence of Collective Portfolio Optimizing Behavior, *New Journal of Physics* **12**, 075039.

Sharpe, W.F. (1964) Capital Asset Prices: A Theory of Market Equilibrium Under Conditions of Risk, *Journal of Finance* **19**(3), 425–442.

Surowiecki, J. (2005) *The Wisdom of Crowds*, Anchor Books, New York.

Szabó, G. and C. Hauert (2002) Phase Transitions and Volunteering in Spatial Public Goods Games, *Physical Review Letters* **89**(11), 118101, August.

8

Optimal Execution of Portfolio Transactions with Short-Term Alpha

Adriana M. Criscuolo and Henri Waelbroeck

8.1 INTRODUCTION

In recent years, we have witnessed an increasing use of quantitative modeling tools and data processing infrastructure by high frequency trading firms and automated market makers. They monetize the value of the options written by institutional trade algorithms with every order placement on the market. This creates a challenge for institutional traders. The result for institutions is that trades with poor market timing typically execute too fast and those that have high urgency tend to execute too slowly and sometimes fail to complete. When the market controls the execution schedule, it is seldom to the advantage of the institutional trader.

To cope with this problem, the trader needs to perform three challenging tasks. First, develop an understanding of how urgent a trade is, i.e., when the benefits of speedier execution outweigh the additional impact costs. Second, map this urgency to an optimal execution schedule; and, third, implement the schedule efficiently in the presence of market noise – a stochastic optimization problem. The industry is increasingly working to solve each of these three problems.

Our purpose in this chapter is to address the second task: assign an optimal trade schedule given a view on short-term alpha. To this end, we propose an alternative framework to AC 2000 that is based on more

Market Microstructure: Confronting Many Viewpoints. Edited by F. Abergel, J.-P. Bouchaud, T. Foucault, C.-A. Lehalle and M. Rosenbaum.

realistic assumptions for market impact and explicitly considers the possibility of a directional bias, or "short-term alpha".

Our framework addresses the optimal execution of a large portfolio transaction that is split into smaller slices and executed incrementally over time. There are many dimensions to this problem that are potentially important to the institutional trader: liquidity fluctuations, the news stream, order flow imbalances, etc. In response to these variables, traders make decisions including the participation rate, limit price, and other strategy attributes. We limit the scope of the problem by adopting the definition of optimal execution from Almgren and Chriss (2000): optimal execution is the participation rate profile that minimizes the cost or risk-adjusted cost while completing the trade in a given amount of time.

To optimize the risk-adjusted cost, one must first specify a model for market impact. Market impact has been analyzed for different authors as a function of time and trade size. See, for example, Bertismas and Lo (1998), Almgren and Chriss (2000), Almgren et al. (2005), and Obizhaeva and Wang (2006).

Almgren and Chriss' landmark paper derived execution profiles that are optimal if certain simplifying assumptions hold true. These include the hypothesis that the market is driven by an arithmetic Brownian motion overlaid with a stationary market impact process. Impact is proposed to be the linear sum of permanent and temporary components, where the permanent impact depends linearly on the number of traded shares and the temporary impact is a linear function of the trading velocity. It follows that total permanent impact is independent of the trade schedule. The optimal participation rate profile requires trading fastest at the beginning and slowing down as the trade progresses according to a hyperbolic sine function.

This type of front-loaded participation rate profile is widely used by industry participants, yet it is also recognized that it is not always optimal. Some practitioners believe that the practice of front-loading executions bakes in permanent impact early in the trade (Ben Sylvester, personal communication), resulting in higher trading costs on average. A related concern is that liquidity exhaustion or increased signaling risk could also lead to a higher variance in trade results (Hora, 2006), defeating the main purpose of front-loading. In their theory paper, Almgren and Chriss acknowledge that the simplifying assumptions required to find closed-form optimal execution solutions are imperfect.

The nonlinearity of temporary impact in the trading velocity has been addressed previously in Almgren (2003) and Almgren *et al.* (2005); the optimization method has also been adjusted for nonlinear phe-nomenological models of temporary impact (Loeb, 1983; Lillo *et al.*, 2003). However, most studies share the common assumptions that short-term price formation in nonvolatile markets is driven by an arithmetic Brownian motion and that the effect of trading on price is stationary; i.e., the increment to permanent impact from one interval to the next is independent of time. In addition, the temporary impact is a correction that depends only on the current trading velocity but not on the amount of time that the strategy has been in operation. We find reasons to doubt the assumption of stationary impact. Practitioners find that reversion grows with the amount of time that an algorithm has been engaged; this suggests that temporary impact grows as a function of time. Phenomenological models of market impact consistently produce concave functions for total cost as a function of trade size; this is inconsistent with linear permanent impact.

In previous work (Farmer *et al.*, 2011) (FGLW) showed that it is possible to derive a concave shape for both temporary and permanent impact of a trade that is executed at a uniform participation rate. The basic assumption in this theory is that arbitrageurs are able to detect the existence of an algorithm and temporary impact represents expectations of further activity from this algorithm. The concave shape of market impact follows from two basic equations. The first is an arbitrage equation for traders who observe the amount of time an execution has been in progress. They use the distribution of hidden order sizes to estimate the probability that the hidden order will continue in the near future. The second is the assumption that institutional trades break even on average after reversion. In other words, the price paid to acquire a large position is on average equal to the price of the security after arbitrageurs have determined that the trade is finished. The model explains how temporary impact sets the fair price of the expected future demand or supply from the algorithmic trade. When the trade ends and these expectations fade away, the model predicts how price will revert to a level that incorporates only permanent impact. The shape of the impact function can be derived from knowledge of the hidden order size distribution. If one believes the hidden order size distribution to have a tail exponent of approximately 1.5, the predicted shape of the total impact function is a square root of trade size in agreement with phenomenological models including the Barra model (Torre, 1997). See also, Chan and Lakonishok (1993, 1995), Almgren *et al.* (2005), Bouchaud *et al.* (2009), and Moro *et al.* (2009).

Hidden order arbitrage theory has been extended to varying participation rate profiles by the authors (Criscuolo and Waelbroeck, 2010). They add the assumption that temporary impact depends only on the current trading speed and total number of shares acquired so far in the execution process.

This chapter is organized as follows. In Section 8.2, we use the extended hidden order arbitrage theory to derive the cost functions for two optimal execution problems. In Section 8.3.1, the minimization of trading cost is given a specific directional view on short-term alpha decay. In Section 8.3.2, the minimization of risk-adjusted cost in the absence of short-term alpha is discussed. It is of interest when risk is a consideration but one has no directional bias on the short-term price trends in the stock. In Section 8.4, we will derive numerical solutions in the cases of some relevance to institutional trading desks. In the concluding section, we discuss the implications of our results to the choice of benchmarks used at institutional trading desks to create incentives for traders.

8.2   SHORT-TERM ALPHA DECAY AND HIDDEN ORDER ARBITRAGE THEORY

The alpha coefficient (α) and beta coefficient (β) play an important role in the capital asset pricing model (CAPM). Both constants can be estimated for an individual asset or portfolio using regression analysis for the asset returns versus a benchmark. The excess return of the asset over the risk-free rate follows a linear relation with respect to the market return r_m as

$$r_a = \alpha_a + \beta_a r_m + \epsilon_a \tag{8.1}$$

where ϵ_a is the statistical noise with null expectation value. The variance of asset returns introduces idiosyncratic risk, which is minimized by building a balanced portfolio, and systematic risk, for which the investor is compensated through the multiplier beta. The same terminology is used to project future returns: a portfolio manager will assign α to desirable positions based on estimated target prices. It is common to borrow from this terminology in the trade execution arena. The expected market return over the execution horizon is generally assumed to be zero, so the term "short-term alpha" is used by different authors to denote either the expected return of a stock or the expected alpha after beta-adjustment, as given in (8.1). To address the optimal execution problem it is important to know not only the total short-term alpha to the end of the execution horizon but also the manner in which it decays over time. There are four cases of interest:

1. Urgent trades (on news or liquidity exhaustion events, for example) can be expected to have an exponential alpha decay with a short time constant, e.g., 10–60 minutes.
2. Other informed trades may be expected to have slower alpha decay, with an adverse trend persisting throughout the execution horizon – e.g., if multiple managers are competing to execute similar trades.
3. Some trades have no short-term market timing and no alpha decay is expected on the execution horizon.
4. Contrarian trades (exit trades or value buys aiming to take advantage of selling pressure on the market, for example) are expected to have slow negative alpha over the execution horizon.

All cases above are well modeled with an exponential alpha decay profile,

$$\alpha(t) = \alpha_\infty \left(1 - e^{\{t-t_0\}/\tau}\right) \tag{8.2}$$

with a magnitude α_∞ and decay constant τ. In the presence of a trade, the expected return will be

$$E(r, t) = \text{Impact}(t) + \alpha(t) \tag{8.3}$$

where we considered $E(r_m) \approx 0$, but we added a market impact component as the result of the intrinsic dynamics of the trade.

In recent work (Criscuolo and Waelbroeck, 2010), we proposed an impact model that assumes that market makers are able to observe imbalances caused by institutional trades. Below, we summarize the hypothesis used there for the description of market impact and we add the new components modeling the short-term alpha decay.

Hypothesis 1. Hidden order detection
A hidden order executed during a period Δt with an average rate π is detected at the end of intervals of $\tau(\pi) = 1/\pi^2$ market transactions.[1] We will use the term "detectable interval" below to mean

---

[1] If order flow were a random walk with a bias π between buy and sell transactions, the imbalance would be detected with t-stat=1 after $1/\pi^2$ transactions.

each set of $\tau(\pi_i) = 1/\pi_i^2$ market transactions, for each $i \in \mathbb{N}$, over which a hidden order is detected with a constant participation rate π_i. A detectable interval i contains $1/\pi_i$ hidden order transactions, with $0 < \pi_i < 1, \forall i$.

In addition, there exists a function $\tau_r(X, \pi_f)$ such that the end of a hidden order can be detected after a reversion time $\tau_r(X, \pi_f)$, where π_f is the most recently observed rate. Let $N^* = N^*(X) \in \mathbb{R}_{>0}$; then $N^* = q + [N^*]$, $[N^*] \stackrel{\text{def}}{=}$ Integer part $[N^*]$, $0 \leq q < 1$. We set $\tau_r(X, \pi_f) = q\pi_f^{-2}$. The number N^* will be determined by the trade size X and $[N^*]$ represents the last detectable interval.

Hypothesis 2. Linear superposition of alpha and impact

Considering the asset return as the difference between the initial price of a share S_0 and the price paid at the k-interval, $\tilde{S}_k$, we are able to write Equation (8.3) as

$$\tilde{S}_k - S_0 = \alpha_k + \text{Impact}_{[0,k]} \tag{8.4}$$

Here, α_k is a function of the transactional time t_k elapsed from the beginning of the trade to the interval k, and will be called the "short term alpha". $\text{Impact}_{[0,k]}$ is the impact of the security price from the beginning of the trade to the end of the interval k.

We will denote by $\tilde{S}_k$ the expected average price in the interval, where the expectation is over a Gaussian (G) function of an arithmetic random walk, with fixed $\{\pi_1, \pi_2, \ldots, \pi_k\}$.

Hypothesis 3. Impact model

Impact of the security price is related to price formation from the beginning of the trade to the end of the interval k, as

$$\text{Impact}_{[0,k]} = \mu \left\{ \pi_k^\beta \left(\sum_{i=1}^{k} \pi_i^{-1} \right)^{\alpha-1} + \sum_{i=1}^{k-1} \pi_i^{\beta-1} \left(\sum_{j=1}^{i} \pi_j^{-1} \right)^{\alpha-2} \right\},$$
$$2 \leq k \leq [N^*] \tag{8.5a}$$

$$\text{Impact}_{[0,1]} = \mu \pi_1^{\beta-\alpha+1} \tag{8.5b}$$

Here, $\alpha = 1.5$ (Gopikrishnan *et al.*, 2000; Gabaix *et al.*, 2006). Empirical observations from Aritas data suggest $\beta = 0.3$ (Gomes and

Waelbroeck, 2008), close to theoretical predictions of 0.25 (Bouchaud *et al.*, 2009). The constant $\mu > 0$ for a buy and $\mu < 0$ for a sell.

By Hypothesis 1, we consider the possibility that the total number of detectable steps N^* has a noninteger value, which means that the institution could finish at an "extra time" $q = N^* - [N^*]$, $0 \leq q < 1$ — that it is completed in less than π^{-2} market transactions.

In the case where $q \neq 0$, the total impact between the origin 0 and N^* will be

$$\text{Impact}_{[0,N^*]} = \mu \left\{ \pi_{N^*}^\beta \xi_{N^*}^{\alpha-1} + \sum_{i=1}^{[N^*]} \pi_i^{\beta-1} \left(\sum_{j=1}^{i} \pi_j^{-1} \right)^{\alpha-2} \right\} \tag{8.5c}$$

where ξ_{N^*} is the total number of transactions traded until the last detectable interval N^* and is by definition

$$\xi_{N^*} \overset{\text{def}}{=} \left(\sum_{i=1}^{[N^*]} \frac{1}{\pi_i} + q\pi_{N^*}^{-1} \right) \tag{8.6}$$

Hypothesis 4. Alpha decay model

$$\alpha_k = S_0 \alpha_\infty \left(1 - e^{(t_k + t_{k-1})/(2\kappa)} \right) \tag{8.7}$$

$$t_k = \sum_{i=1}^{k} \pi_i^{-2} \tag{8.8}$$

where κ is a typical time decay and α_∞ is a parameter associated with the information of a trade.

8.3   TOTAL COST DEFINITION AND CONSTRAINTS

8.3.1   Equations without the risk term

The expected total cost of the trade (over G) is

$$E(\pi, N^*) \overset{\text{def}}{=} n\xi_{N^*} S_0 - \sum_{i=1}^{[N^*]} n_i \tilde{S}_i - qn\pi_{N^*}^{-1} \tilde{S}_{N^*} \tag{8.9}$$

where $n_i = n\pi_i^{-1}$ is the number of shares traded in the i segment and n is the number of traded shares in each institutional transaction, with $n > 0$

for a sell and $n < 0$ for a buy. In addition, we suppose that there exists $N \in \mathbb{N}, N \leq N^*$, such that from $N + 1$ to N^* the institution participates with a constant rate π_f. Therefore, the variables $(\boldsymbol{\pi}, N^*)$ will be reduced to $(\{\pi_i\}_{i=1}^N, \pi_f, N^*)$. After a calculation, using the equations above, the expected total cost turns out to be

$$
E(\{\pi_i\}_{i=1}^N, \pi_f, N^*; \boldsymbol{p}) = |\mu n| \xi_{N^*} \left\{ \sum_{k=1}^{[N^*]} \pi_k^{\beta-1} \left(\sum_{i=1}^k \pi_i^{-1} \right)^{\alpha-2} \right.
$$
$$
\left. + q\pi_f^{\beta-1} \left(\sum_{i=1}^{[N^*]} \pi_i^{-1} + q\pi_f^{-1} \right)^{\alpha-2} \right\}
$$
$$
- nS_0\alpha_\infty \left\{ \xi_{N^*} - \sum_{i=1}^N \pi_i^{-1} e^{(t_i + t_{i-1})/2\kappa} \right.
$$
$$
- \pi_f^{-1} \left(\sum_{i=N+1}^{[N^*]} e^{\left(\sum_{j=1}^N \pi_j^{-2} + (i-N)\pi_f^{-2} - 0.5\pi_f^{-2} \right)/\kappa} \right.
$$
$$
\left. \left. + (N^* - [N^*])e^{\left(\sum_{j=1}^N \pi_j^{-2} + (N^*-N)\pi_f^{-2} \right)/\kappa} \right) \right\}
$$

$$(8.10)$$

with:

$$
N^* = q + [N^*], \quad [N^*] \stackrel{\text{def}}{=} \text{Integer part} [N^*], \quad 0 \leq q < 1
$$

$$
t_k = \sum_{i=1}^k \pi_i^{-2}, \quad 1 \leq k \leq N
$$

and the parameter vector

$$
\boldsymbol{p} = (\mu, n, N, \alpha, \beta, S_0, \alpha_\infty, \kappa)
$$

We set the constraints to be

$$
\frac{X}{n} = \xi_{N^*} \stackrel{\text{def}}{=} \left\{ \sum_{j=1}^N \pi_j^{-1} + (N^* - N) \pi_f^{-1} \right\}
$$

$$(8.11)$$

$$
T_M \geq t_{N^*} \stackrel{\text{def}}{=} \sum_{i=1}^N \pi_i^{-2} + (N^* - N) \pi_f^{-2}
$$

$$(8.12)$$

Here X is the total number of shares fixed to trade and T_M is the time horizon.

In Section 8.4.1, we will find optimal trajectories for the set of the expected trading rates $(\{\pi_i\}_{i=1}^N, \pi_f)$ and the total number of detectable steps N^*, which minimize the total cost. Using Mathematica 8, we will resolve by simulated annealing.

8.3.2 Equations including risk without the alpha term

Additionally, as in Almgren and Chriss (2000), we will evaluate the *variance of the cost* $V(\pi, N^*; \alpha_\infty = 0) \stackrel{\text{def}}{=} \langle (E(\pi, N^*; \alpha_\infty = 0) - \langle E(\pi, N^*; \alpha_\infty = 0)\rangle_G)^2\rangle_G$. For that, we will sum the term representing the volatility of the asset

$$\sigma \sum_{i=1}^{k} \pi_i^{-1} \varsigma_i \tag{8.13}$$

to Equations (8.5). The ς_{i+1} are random variables with zero Gaussian mean and unit variance and σ is a constant with units $[\sigma] = \$/\text{share} \times \sqrt{\text{transaction}}$. Therefore, the *variance* of $E(\pi, N^*; \alpha_\infty = 0)$ takes the form

$$V(\pi, N^*; \alpha_\infty = 0) = \sigma^2 n^2 \sum_{k=1}^{[N^*]} \pi_k^{-2} \left(\xi_{N^*} - \sum_{j=1}^{k} \pi_j^{-1} \right)^2 \tag{8.14}$$

We next write the *risk-adjusted cost function*

$$U(\pi, N^*; \lambda, \mu, n, \sigma, \alpha, \beta, N) \stackrel{\text{def}}{=} E(\pi, N^*; \alpha_{\infty=0}) + \lambda V(\pi, N^*; \alpha_{\infty=0}) \tag{8.15}$$

where λ is the *risk parameter* with units $[\lambda] = \$^{-1}$.

Applying the previous expressions, we obtain

$$U(\{\pi_i\}_{i=1}^N, \pi_f, N^*; \lambda, \mu, n, \sigma, \alpha, \beta, N)$$
$$= |\mu n| \xi_{N^*} \left\{ \sum_{k=1}^{[N^*]} \pi_k^{\beta-1} \left(\sum_{i=1}^{k} \pi_i^{-1} \right)^{\alpha-2} \right.$$

$$+ q\pi_f^{\beta-1} \left(\sum_{i=1}^{[N^*]} \pi_i^{-1} + q\pi_f^{-1} \right)^{\alpha-2} \Bigg\}$$

$$+ \lambda\sigma^2 n^2 \sum_{k=1}^{[N^*]} \pi_k^{-2} \left(\xi_{N^*} - \sum_{j=1}^{k} \pi_j^{-1} \right)^2 \qquad (8.16)$$

with the constraints set to be (8.11) and (8.12). In Section 8.4.2, we will
provide optimal trajectories.

8.4 TOTAL COST OPTIMIZATION

8.4.1 Results for λ = 0 and the arbitrary alpha term

Below we reproduce the results for $\lambda = 0$ and different values of the
parameter α_∞ and the decay parameter in time κ on a graph showing
the optimal participation rate π_k in a function of the transactional time
t_k. The parameters are set to be:

λ	μ	n	N	β	α	S_0	X	T_M
0	0.0315\$/ share	−250 shares (buy)	10 steps	0.3	1.5	50\$/ share	−25 000 shares (buy)	1000 transactions

8.4.1.1 Slow alpha decay

This is a case where alpha decay is slow and almost linear over the
execution horizon: $\kappa \gg T_M$. Unsurprisingly, when the outlook is for
the price to drift in the opposite direction of the trade ($\alpha_\infty < 0$), it is
optimal to push the execution schedule toward the end of the allowed
window as for a market-on-close strategy. In the neutral case ($\alpha_\infty = 0$),
the optimal strategy starts slowly to minimize information leakage early
in the trade and steadily increases the participation rate. In the presence
of adverse momentum ($\alpha_\infty > 0$), the optimal schedule has trading speed
reaching a maximum near the middle of the execution horizon or, for
very strong directional bias, ramping up quickly to a 20 % participation
rate to complete the trade early.

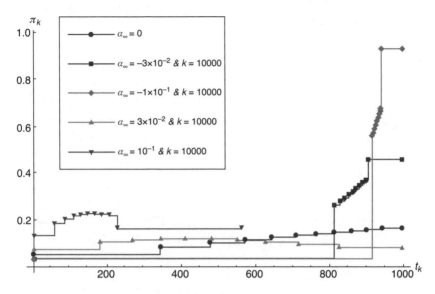

Figure 8.1 Case $\kappa \gg T_M$. The general characteristic is that the participation rate π_k increases with t_k more than a third of the time. The case ($\alpha_\infty > 0$) indicates that the price tends to rise. Therefore, it is justified to buy incrementally faster from the beginning but increasing the rate slightly with time to avoid high impact costs. After impact takes place, when t_k is closer to the end of the trade t_{N^*}, the rate should decrease slightly with time to about the initial slow rate. The case $\alpha_\infty < 0$ represents the case where prices tend to down. It is convenient to keep the rate very slow and constant more than 80 % of the time since the beginning of the trade, passing for a period of fast and constant increment until the end to more than 50 % of the original rate. Note that the starting rate π_1 is slightly higher for $\alpha_\infty > 0$, as a consequence of the expectations of higher prices, and slightly lower for $\alpha_\infty < 0$, or expectations of lower prices, than the one for $\alpha_\infty = 0$.

Table 8.1 The second column shows the cost of optimal trajectories for different values of the parameter α_∞. The third column is the cost calculated with a constant rate $\pi_i = 0.1$, $1 \leq i \leq N^* = 10$. Negative costs represent gains due to diminishing prices. Costs increase as $\alpha_\infty > 0$ increases

α_∞	Cost – Optimal ($)	Cost at 10 % ($)
0	5953.5	6266.72
-3×10^{-2}	−6082.71	721.25
-1×10^{-1}	−37608.9	−12218.
3×10^{-2}	8969.41	11812.2
10^{-1}	12982.5	24751.6

8.4.1.2 Very high urgency

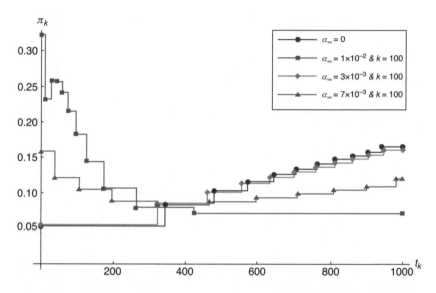

Figure 8.2 The figure shows optimal execution trajectories for very rapid alpha decay: $\kappa \ll T_M$. The two trajectories $\alpha_\infty = 0$ and $\alpha_\infty = 3 \times 10^{-3}$ coincide on this graph: an aggressive trade start is only optimal when short-term alpha is large enough to outweigh the additional impact cost. The value $\alpha_\infty = 7 \times 10^{-3}$ is the critical point for the "phase change", where the trajectory changes radically and stops behaving as $\alpha_\infty = 0$.

Table 8.2 The costs of the optimal schedule is shown in comparison to the 10 % strategy for different levels of short-term alpha in the case of very rapid alpha decay. Costs increase as $\alpha_\infty > 0$ increases; schedule optimization offers little room for profit in this case because alpha decays too rapidly in relation to the trade size: there is too little time to trade

α_∞	Cost – Optimal (\$)	Cost at 10 % (\$)
0	5953.5	6266.72
1×10^{-2}	17945.1	18325.5
3×10^{-3}	9689.93	9884.37
7×10^{-3}	14686.5	14707.9

8.4.1.3   High urgency

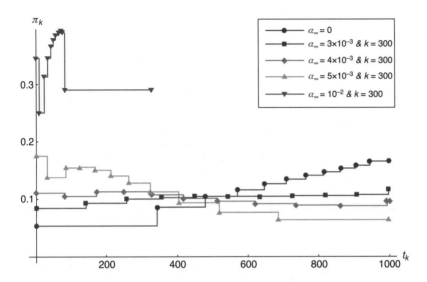

Figure 8.3   This is a case $\kappa < T_M$. For $\alpha_\infty \lesssim 3 \times 10^{-3}$, trajectories are qualitatively very similar to the one for $\alpha_\infty = 0$. The case $\alpha_\infty = 4 \times 10^{-3}$ marks the transition from back-loaded schedules to front-loaded ones when short-term alpha is larger. In the extreme case where short-term alpha is 100 bps ($\alpha_\infty = 1 \times 10^{-2}$), the high expectation of increasing prices suggests a fast start and a short trading time (about 36 % of T_M). Immediately, the optimization decreases the rate by 10 % to compensate for the impact costs. It follows a monotonous increase of more than 10 % in a lapse of $\frac{1}{6}$ of the total trading time. Finally, it reduces by 10 % to a constant rate during $\frac{5}{8}$ of the time, until the end. Those rises and falls in the participation rate are the efforts of the optimization to reach an equilibrium between impact and alpha term increments.

Table 8.3   Optimal costs are compared to the 10 % participation strategy for the case of moderately rapid alpha decay. The 10 % strategy is close to optimal for the most common alpha values, 30–50 bps. Back-loaded schedules are more economical when expectations are balanced; front-loading provides significant benefits for short-term alpha values in excess of 60 bps

α_∞	Cost – Optimal ($)	Cost at 10 % ($)
0	5953.5	6266.72
10^{-2}	14912.4	16225.3
3×10^{-3}	9248.68	9254.29
4×10^{-3}	10241.5	10250.2
5×10^{-3}	11175.6	11246
6×10^{-3}	12037.2	12241.9

8.4.1.4 Moderate urgency

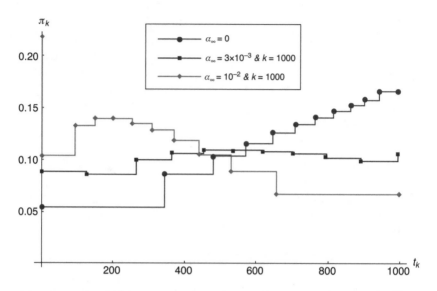

Figure 8.4 This is the case $\kappa = T_M$. Even for the high α_∞ scenario, $\alpha_\infty = 100$ bps, it is optimal to extend the execution over the entire window to minimize impact costs.

Table 8.4 The costs of optimal solutions are compared to the 10 % participation strategy for different short-term alpha expectations; the 10 % strategy is near optimal when the expected short-term alpha is 30 bps

α_∞	Cost – Optimal ($)	Cost at 10% ($)
0	5953.5	6266.72
3×10^{-3}	7987.48	8003.97
10^{-2}	11348	12057.5

8.4.1.5   Graph comparison between different time decay constants

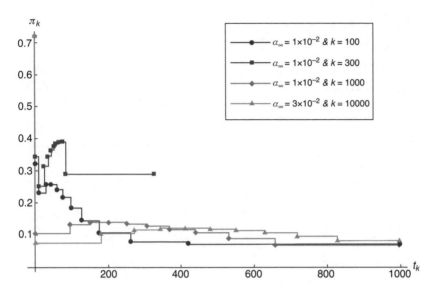

Figure 8.5   Very strong momentum.

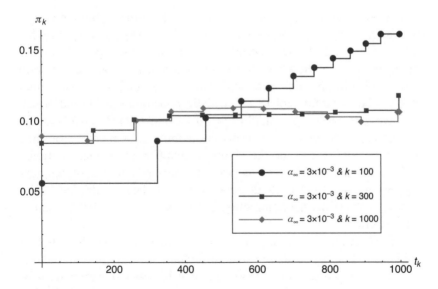

Figure 8.6   Moderate momentum.

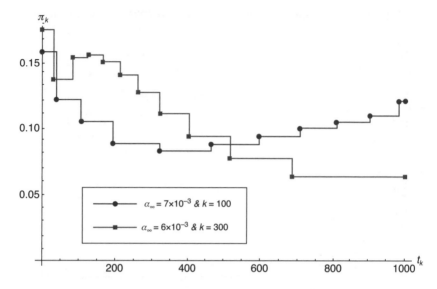

Figure 8.7 Critical momentum. It is optimal to front-load the execution schedule when the momentum is at least 60 bps or 70 bps, depending on the time decay parameter.

8.4.2   Risk-adjusted optimization

Above, we finished the analysis of the hidden order arbitrage theory for variable speed of trading with zero risk aversion ($\lambda = 0$). In what follows, we will be concentrating on finding the optimal trading trajectories for a theory with varying participation rate, alpha term zero, and arbitrary risk aversion. This means minimizing the total risk-adjusted cost function (8.16), with the constraints (8.11) and (8.12).

If we take an annual volatility of 30 %, $\sigma = 0.95\ (\$/\text{share})/\sqrt{\text{day}}$. In our case, we work with transaction units as a measure of time and $\tau = 1/\pi^2 = 100$ is the average number of a market transactions in each detectable interval. If one day consists of 6 hours and 30 minutes and each detectable interval last 15 minutes, then 1 day = 2600 market transactions. Therefore, $\sigma = 0.019(\$/\text{share})/\sqrt{\text{transaction}}$.

The shortfall of risk-adjusted cost optimal solutions is listed in Table 8.5. For this example and different risk aversion parameters, $L = \lambda\sigma^2 |n/\mu|$ is the corresponding dimensionless risk parameter.

In figure 8.8 we graph the participation rate π_k versus the detectable step k, in a continuum aproximation, for the different values of the risk constant $L = \lambda\sigma^2 |n/\mu|$ and the nule alpha term.

Table 8.5 Shortfall of risk-adjusted cost optimal solutions. We consider a mid-cap trade of 25 000 shares, in an $S_0 = \$50$ security, executed at an average participation rate of 10 % ($\pi = 0.1$). If the security's trading volume is 400 transactions/h, a detectable interval will represent 15 minutes of trading. The impact for a 15-minute interval is estimated to be 10 bps for this security, i.e. $|\mu| = 0.0315\$/$share. We take an annual volatility of 30 % or $\sigma = 0.95(\$/\text{share})/\sqrt{\text{day}}$. One day consists of 6 hours and 30 minutes or 2600 market transactions. Results are for $T_M = 1000$ transactions, $\alpha = 1.5$, $\beta = 0.3$, for the different values of the dimensionless risk constant $L = \lambda \sigma^2 |n/\mu|$. The sixth column N^* is the total number of detectable intervals realized by the hidden order. The last column indicates that the number of market transactions reaches the maximum limit T_M

α_∞	L	Risk parameter λ ($\$^{-1}$)	Shortfall per share ($\$/$share)	Shortfall E ($\$$)	Variance $\sqrt{V}$ ($\$$)	N^*	t_{N^*}
0	1×10^{-4}	3.49×10^{-5}	0.2608	6520.5	7360.83	10.99	1000
	0	0	0.2381	5953.5	9192.27	11.57	1000
	3×10^{-4}	1.05×10^{-4}	0.2917	7292.25	6290.65	13.14	1000

Because in each step the participation rate must be constant, we present a detailed graph (see Figures 8.9, 8.10, and 8.11) of the participation rate versus the transactional time, $t_k = \sum_{i=1}^{k} \pi_i^{-2}$, corresponding to each k interval, for each L. In Figure 8.12, we draw the comparative graph for the different values of the risk aversion in the quadratic approximation or continuum.

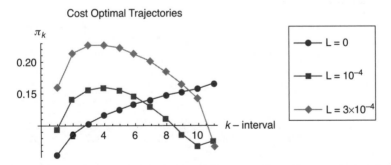

Figure 8.8 Optimal trajectories representing the participation rate in a function of the number of the detectable intervals for different values of the risk constant and $\alpha_\infty = 0$.

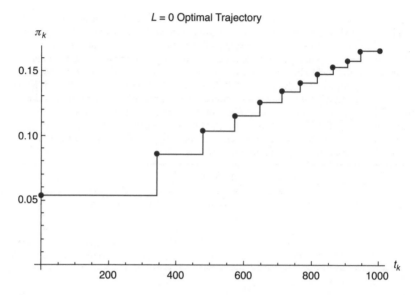

Figure 8.9 Participation rate in a function of the transactional time, $t_k = \sum_{i=1}^{k} \pi_i^{-2}$, corresponding to each k interval, considering zero risk aversion and the alpha term.

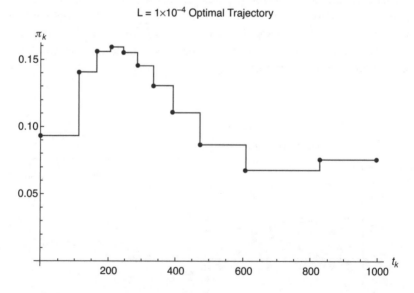

Figure 8.10 Participation rate in a function of the transactional time, $t_k = \sum_{i=1}^{k} \pi_i^{-2}$, corresponding to each k interval, considering risk aversion $L = 1 \times 10^{-4}$ and $\alpha_\infty = 0$.

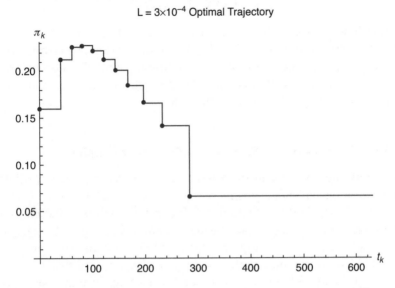

Figure 8.11 Participation rate in a function of the transactional time, $t_k = \sum_{i=1}^{k} \pi_i^{-2}$, corresponding to each k interval, considering risk aversion $L = 3 \times 10^{-4}$ and $\alpha_\infty = 0$.

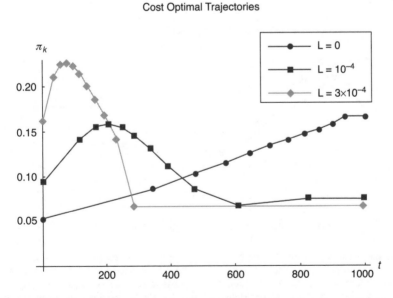

Figure 8.12 Comparative graph of optimal trajectories in a function of the transactional time for the different values of the risk aversion and $\alpha_\infty = 0$ in the quadratic approximation or continuum.

8.5   CONCLUSIONS

Using hidden order arbitrage theory, we derived execution schedules that are optimal with respect to different optimization objectives: first, minimizing implementation shortfall with short-term alpha decay profiles typical of real-world trading situations and, second, minimizing the risk-adjusted shortfall to short-term alpha.

8.5.1   Main results in the absence of short-term alpha

Shortfall minimization in the absence of alpha requires back-loading the execution schedule. This increases execution risk. Introducing risk aversion in the utility function, we found that optimal solutions for risk-averse traders move the schedule forward but avoid the aggressive trade start of the Almgren–Chriss (2000) solution. This suggests that hidden order arbitrage theory assigns a high cost to the signaling risk associated with an aggressive start of trading. In Figure 8.13 we graph the optimal risk averse trajectories for the information arbitrage theory with $L = 10^{-4}$ in comparison to Almgren and Chriss (2000).

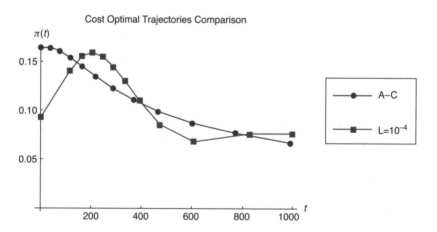

Figure 8.13 Comparative graph of the cost optimal trajectories in a function of the transactional time. The dot line is the solution predicted by the Almgren–Chriss formulation with linear impact and the risk-averse constant λ (Almgren-Chriss) $= 10^{-5}/\$$. The square line is the optimal trajectory for the nonlinear information arbitrage theory, as shown in Figure 8.10, for the risk-averse constant $L = 10^{-4}$ or $\lambda = 3.49 \times 10^{-5}/\$$.

For a buy,

$$\pi_j^{A-C} = \frac{\sinh(\kappa T)}{2X \sinh\left[(\kappa\tau)/2\right]\cosh\left(\kappa\left(j - \frac{1}{2}\right)\tau\right)}$$

$$X = 100$$

$$T = 165 \text{ minutes} = 0.423 \text{ day}$$

$$\kappa \sim \frac{3.83}{\text{day}}$$

$$\tau = 15 \text{ minutes} = 0.0384 \text{ day}$$

The shortfall calculated with the Almgren and Chriss (2000) trajectory for a risk-averse constant λ (Almgren–Chriss) $= 10^{-5}/\$$ is $E\left(\left\{\pi_j^{A-C}\right\}_{j=1}^{11}\right) = \$6879.05$. This is 5.5 % costlier than the shortfall $E(\text{optimal}) = \$6520.5$ for $\lambda = 3.49 \times 10^{-5}/\$$, and 9.8 % costlier than a constant 10 % participation rate strategy.

8.5.2 Main results with short-term alpha

Short-term alpha is the expected impact-free return given the existence of a portfolio manager's order, i.e., the expected return if the institutional order is not executed. The existence of short-term alpha is an example of semi-strong market efficiency, because it is associated with the creation of an institutional order, which in itself constitutes private information. There are several reasons why this information should be associated with short-term alpha. First, portfolio managers may act coherently, either because they are following trading styles that are currently in fashion or because they are placing orders in response to shared signals such as analyst reports. In this case, the existence of one institutional order predicts an imbalance between institutional supply and demand associated with the possibility of other orders. Second, the market may price a security away from fair value because the liquidity demand from another portfolio manager creates a risk of liquidity exhaustion. This may happen in either direction; persistent selling creates a risk that market makers will withdraw their bids or a persistent buying pressure may force liquidity providers to cover short positions. In both cases, information about the creation of an institutional order on the contra side removes the liquidity exhaustion risk and causes price to revert to fair value. The third case where short-term alpha may occur is that of news-triggered trades, either in regard to intraday news or for orders placed before the open following overnight news.

The optimal execution schedule depends on how quickly alpha decays over time. In this chapter, we considered the optimal execution problem with exponential alpha decay profiles with low, moderate, or high urgency. High urgency represents alpha decay timescales of 10–30 % of the execution horizon, in moderate urgency the decay timescale is similar to the execution horizon, while in low urgency cases the alpha decay is quasi-linear during the execution horizon.

In the moderate urgency case, we found cost-optimal strategies that are front-loaded similarly to the optimal solution from hidden order arbitrage theory with risk aversion and no alpha. In the case of high urgency, for moderate short-term alpha values there is no benefit from front-loading because there is not enough time to complete a substantial part of the trade before alpha decays, and attempting to do so would increase impact costs for the remainder of the trade. It is only profitable to front-load the execution for the strongest short-term alpha profiles (> 50 bps). In the case of negative alpha, typical of value managers, the optimal trading strategies begin slowly and increase participation near the end of the trading session.

8.5.3   Institutional trading practices

Comparing our results to the prevalent practices at institutional trading desks, we find two significant differences in the trading solutions:

1. Institutional desks tend to front-load the execution more than is suggested by our results. They adopt a front-loading profile with a monotonically decreasing participation rate, often explicitly implementing the Almgren–Chriss model. We predict that this practice increases early signaling and results in higher shortfalls.
2. Uninformed trades are generally executed using constant participation rate schedules such as VWAP algorithms, whereas our results suggest using some back-loading.

Both deviations have the effect of reducing execution risk but increasing trading costs on average. We speculate that the preference of the industry for risk aversion is motivated, in part, by imperfect communication between the portfolio manager and the trading desk. In the absence of a precise understanding of what the trading desk is executing, portfolio managers naturally respond asymmetrically, making the desk responsible for large negative results and not offering a symmetric praise for large positive results. It is worth noting that a large positive result for the trading desk (buying far below the arrival price, for example) in general occurs when the portfolio manager's decision was mistimed in the short term (a buy order preceding a large drop in the price, or vice versa). Trading desks are not usually expected to question the wisdom of the portfolio manager's decision; the institutional trader's task is to execute the trade close to the arrival price. For that reason, the desk is unlikely to hear from the manager if it executed a poorly timed trade too fast, but far more likely to hear of a good trading decision that was executed too slowly. For the same reasons, a similar economic distortion exists for broker-dealers handling institutional orders. Another cause contributing to the problem is that the broker-dealer is compensated by commissions on executed shares; this creates an additional incentive to start executions quickly to lock in the commission before the order can be canceled.

Ultimately, it is the aggregate shortfall and not execution risk that impacts the fund performance. The additional cost from excessive front-loading can contribute significantly to fund rankings. For example, a 10 bps reduction in trading costs would translate to an improvement of 10 places in Bloomberg's ranking of US mutual funds in the "balanced" category. There are 1364 funds in that category for which a one-year rate of returns is reported.

The economic distortions that cause excessive risk aversion could be rectified if institutional desks were able to measure trading costs effectively and rate execution providers accurately. Unfortunately, post-trade data analysis is complicated by the difficulty of estimating opportunity costs. Limit prices clearly bias filled orders toward lower shortfalls, but occasionally lead to incomplete executions. The opportunity cost of the unfilled shares must be accounted for to evaluate the results. However, to measure opportunity costs accurately, one would need to know how the manager reallocated the funds that were not invested in the trade. For larger trades, it is common to execute over a period of weeks or even months. The trade size is likely to be adjusted multiple times and the adjustments themselves depend on the progress in executing the trade. Finally, selection bias plays a large role in that easier trades can be sent to lower quality algorithms where order flow is used as currency for paying brokers, while difficult trades are more likely to be sent to sophisticated execution systems. Trading desks are aware of these issues and mostly ignore post-trade TCA unless it is part of their compensation, relying instead on their experience to evaluate execution quality.

It is possible to account fairly for opportunity costs for the purpose of comparing the quality of execution from different algorithms. One need only compare the number of shares filled to the number that would have been filled had the algorithm performed at the intended speed. The difference can be priced at the estimated average price that would have been incurred had the trade been allowed to continue. This may not accurately measure opportunity cost from the perspective of the portfolio manager, who has other investment options, but it accounts fairly for the failure of an algorithm to perform. A framework to measure separately the effects of trading speed, algorithm performance, and limit prices was presented in Gomes and Waelbroeck (2010), for example. Unfortunately, the implementation of this type of framework in post-trade TCA is complicated by the fact that post-trade data rarely include the limit price, intended trading speed, or type of algorithm. However, these difficulties do not lessen the value of increased portfolio returns from optimal execution.

PROVISO

Aritas Group, Inc. and its subsidiary, Aritas Securities LLC, are members of FINRA/SIPC. This chapter was prepared for general circulation and without regard to the individual financial circumstances and objectives of persons who receive or obtain access to it. The analyses discussed herein are derived from Aritas and third party data and are not meant to guarantee future results.

REFERENCES

Almgren, R. (2003) Optimal Execution with Nonlinear Impact Functions and Trading-Enhanced Risk, *Applied Mathematical Finance* **10**, 1–18.

Almgren, R. and N. Chriss (2000) Optimal Execution of Portfolio Transactions, *Journal of Risk* **3**(2), 5–39.

Almgren, R., C. Thum, E. Hauptmann and H. Li (2005) Direct Estimation of Equity Market Impact, *Risk* **18**, 57–62.

Bertismas, D. and A. Lo (1998) Optimal Control of Execution Costs, *Journal of Financial Markets* **1**, 1–50.

Bouchaud, J.-P., J.D. Farmer and F. Lillo (2008) How Markets Slowly Digest Changes in Supply and Demand, in *Handbook of Financial Markets: Dynamics and Evolution*, T. Hens and K. Schenk-Hoppe (Eds), North-Holland, Elsevier, pp. 57–156.

Chan, L.K.C. and J. Lakonishok (1993) Institutional Trades and Intraday Stock Price Behavior, *Journal of Financial Economics* **33**, 173–199.

Chan, L.K.C. and J. Lakonishok (1995) The Behavior of Stock Prices around Institutional Trades, *Journal of Finance* **50**, 1147–1174.

Criscuolo, A.M. and H. Waelbroeck (2010) Optimal Execution in Presence of Hidden Order Arbitrage, Aritas Preprint PIPE-2011-01.

Farmer, J.D., A. Gerig, F. Lillo and H. Waelbroeck (2011) How Efficiency Shapes Market Impact, arXiv: 1102.5457v2[q-fin.TR].

Gabaix, X., P. Gopikrishnan, V. Plerou and H.E. Stanley (2006) Institutional Investors and Stock Market Volatility, *Quarterly Journal of Economics* **121**, 461–504.

Gomes, C. and H. Waelbroeck (2008) Effect of Trading Velocity and Limit Prices on Implementation Shortfall, Aritas Group Preprint PIPE-2008-09-003.

Gomes, C. and H. Waelbroeck (2010) Transaction Cost Analysis to Optimize Trading Strategies, *Journal of Trading*, Fall **5**(4).

Gopikrishnan, P., V. Plerou, X. Gabaix and H.E. Stanley (2000) Statistical Properties of Share Volume Traded in Financial Markets, *Physical Review E* **62**(4), R4493–R4496.

Hora, M. (2006) The Practice of Optimal Execution. *Algorithmic Trading* **2**, 52–60.

Lillo, F., J.D. Farmer and R.N. Mantegna (2003) Econophysics–Master Curve for Price-Impact Function, *Nature* **421**(6919), 129.

Loeb, T.F. (1983) Trading Cost: The Critical Link between Investment Information and Results, *Financial Analysts Journal* **39**(3), 39–44.

Moro, E., L.G. Moyano, J. Vicente, A. Gerig, J.D. Farmer, G. Vaglica, F. Lillo and R.N. Mantegna (2009) Market Impact and Trading Protocols of Hidden Orders in Stock Markets, Technical Report.

Obizhaeva, A. and J. Wang (2006) Optimal Trading Strategy and Supply/Demand Dynamics, Technical Report, AFA 2006 Boston Meetings Paper.

Torre, N. (1997) *Market Impact Model Handbook*, Barra Inc., Berkeley.

Combined References

Abergel, F. and N. Huth (forthcoming 2012a) High Frequency Correlation Intraday Profile. Empirical Facts.

Abergel, F. and N. Huth (forthcoming 2012b) High Frequency Lead/Lag Relationships. Empirical Facts.

Abergel, F. and N. Huth (2012). The Times Change: Multivariate Subordination. Empirical Facts, *Quantitative Finance* **12**(1).

Abergel, F., A. Chakraborti, I. Muni Toke and M. Patriarca (2011a) Econophysics Review: 1. Empirical Facts, *Quantitative Finance* **11**(7), 991–1012.

Abergel, F., A. Chakraborti, I. Muni Toke and M. Patriarca (2011b) Econophysics Review: 2. Agent-Based Models, *Quantitative Finance* **11**(7) 1013–1041.

Admati, A. and P. Pfleiderer (1988) A Theory of Intraday Patterns: Volume and Price Variability. *Review of Financial Studies* **1**(1), 3–40.

Ahn, H., K. Bae and K. Chan (2001) Limit Orders, Depth and Volatility: Evidence from the Stock Exchange of Hong Kong, *Journal of Finance* **56**, 767–788.

Alfarano, S. and T. Lux (2003) A Minimal Noise Traders Model with Realistic Time Series Properties, in *Long Memory in Economics*, G. Teyssière and A.P. Kirman (Eds), Springer, Berlin.

Almgren, R. (2003) Optimal Execution with Nonlinear Impact Functions and Trading-Enhanced Risk, *Applied Mathematical Finance* **10**, 1–18.

Almgren, R.F. and N. Chriss (2000) Optimal Execution of Portfolio Transactions *Journal of Risk* **3**(2), 5–39.

Almgren, R., C. Thum, E. Hauptmann and H. Li (2005) Direct Estimation of Equity Market Impact, *Risk* **18**, 57–62.

Amihud, Y. and H. Mendelson (1980) Dealership Market: Market-Making with Inventory, *Journal of Financial Economics* **8**, 31–53.

Anand, A., S. Chakravarty and T. Martell (2005) Empirical Evidence on the Evolution of Liquidity: Choice of Market versus Limit Orders by Informed and Uninformed Traders, *Journal of Financial Markets* **8**, 289–309.

Andersen, T. and T. Bollerslev (1997) Intraday Periodicity and Volatility Persistence in Financial Markets, *Journal of Empirical Finance* **4**, 115–158

Andersen, L.B.G. and N.A. Hutchings (2009) Parameter averaging of Quadratic SDES with Stochastic Volatility, *Social Science Research Network*.

Angel, J.J., L.E. Harris and C.S. Spatt (2010) Equity Trading in the 21st Century, Working Paper, Carnegie Mellon.

Antonov, A. and T. Misirpashaev. (2009) Projection on a Quadratic Model by Asymptotic Expansion with an Application to LMM Swaption, *Social Science Research Network*.

Arthur, B.W. (1994) Inductive Reasoning and Bounded Rationality: The El Farol Problem, *American Economic Review* **84**, 406–411.

Back, K. and S. Baruch (2007) Working Orders in Limit Order Markets and Floor Exchanges, *Journal of Finance* **62**, 1589–1621.

Bacry, E., S. Delattre, M. Hoffmann and J.F. Muzy (2011) Modeling microstructure noise with mutually exciting point processes.

Bae, K., H. Jang and K.S. Park (2003) Traders' Choice between Limit and Market Orders: Evidence from NYSE Stocks, *Journal of Financial Markets* **6**, 517–538.

Bandi, F.M. and J.R. Russell (2005) Microstructure Noise, Realized Volatility, and Optimal Sampling.

Bandi, F.M., J.R. Russell and C. Yang (2008) Realized Volatility Forecasting and Option Pricing, *Journal of Econometrics* **147**, 34–46.

Barber, B.M., Y.-T. Lee, Y.-J. Liu and T. Odea (2004) Do Individual Day Traders Make Money?, evidence from Taiwan.

Barndorff-Nielsen, O. and N. Shephard (2002) Econometric Analysis of Realized Volatility and Its Use in Estimating Stochastic Volatility Models, *Journal of the Royal Statistical Society, Series B (Statistical Methodology)* **64**(2), 253–280.

Barndorff-Nielsen, O.E. and N. Shephard (2004) Power and Bipower Variation with Stochastic Volatility and Jumps, *Journal of Financial Econometrics* **2**, 1–48.

Barndorff-Nielsen, O.E., S.E. Graversen, J. Jacod, M. Podolskij and N. Shephard (2006) A Central Limit Theorem for Realised Power and Bipower Variations of Continuous Semimartingales. In *From Stochastic Calculus to Mathematical Finance*, Springer, Berlin, pp. 33–68.

Bauer, R., M. Cosemans and P. Eichholtz (2007) The Performance and Persistence of Individual Investors: Rational Agents or Tulip Maniacs?, http://papers.ssrn.com/sol3/papers.cfm?abstract_id=965810.

Bergomi, L. (2010) Correlations in Asynchronous Markets, *Social Science Research Network*, http://ssrn.com/abstract=1635866.

Bertsimas, D. and A.W. Lo (1998) Optimal Control of Execution Costs, *Journal of Financial Markets* **1**(1), 1–50.

Biais, B., T. Foucault and S. Moinas (2011) Equilibrium Algorithmic Trading, Working Paper, Université de Toulouse.

Biais, B., H. Glosten and C. Spatt (2005) Market Microstructure: A Survey of Microfoundations, Empirical Results, and Policy Implications, *Journal of Financial Markets* **8**, 217–264.

Biais, B., P. Hillion and C. Spatt (1995) An Empirical Analysis of the Limit Order Book and the Order Flow in the Paris Bourse, *Journal of Finance* **50**, 1655–1689.

Biais, B., J. Hombert and P.O. Weill (2010) Trading and Liquidity with Limited Cognition, Working Paper, Toulouse University, IDEI.

Biais, B., D. Martimort and J.-C. Rochet (2000) Competing Mechanisms in a Common Value Environment, *Econometrica* **68**, 799–837.

Bibinger, M. (2011a) Efficient Covariance Estimation for Asynchronous Noisy High-Frequency Data, *Scandinavian Journal of Statistics* **38**, 23–45. DOI: 10.1111/j.14679469.2010.00712.x.

Bibinger, M. (2011b) An Estimator for the Quadratic Covariation of Asynchronously Observed Itô Processes with Noise: Asymptotic Distribution Theory, preprint.

Black, F. (1971) Towards an Automated Exchange, Part 1, *Financial Analysts Journal*, **27**, July–August, 29–34.

Bloomfield, R., M. O'Hara and G. Saar (2005) The "Make or Take" Decision in an Electronic Market: Evidence on the Evolution of Liquidity, *Journal of Financial Economics* **75**, 165–199.

Bouchard, B., N.-M. Dang and C.-A. Lehalle (2011) Optimal Control of Trading Algorithms: A General Impulse Control Approach, *SIAM Journal of Financial Mathematics*.

Bouchaud, J.-P., Y. Gefen, M. Potters and M. Wyart (2004) Fluctuations and Response in Financial Markets: The Subtle Nature of "Random" Price Changes, *Quantitative Finance* **4**(2), 176–190.

Bouchaud, J.-P., J.D. Farmer and F. Lillo (2009) How Markets Slowly Digest Changes in Supply and Demand, in *Handbook of Financial Markets: Dynamics and Evolution*, T. Hens and K.R. Schenk-Hoppe (Eds), North-Holland, Elsevier.

Bouchaud, J.-P., I. Giardina and M. Mézard (2001) On a Universal Mechanism for Long Ranged Volatility Correlations. *Quantitative Finance* **1**, 212, cond-mat/0012156.

Bouchaud, J.-P., J. Kockelkoren and M. Potters (2006) Random Walks, Liquidity Molasses and Critical Response in Financial Markets, *Quantitative Finance* **6**(2), 115.

Bouchaud, J.-P., M. Mezard and M. Potters (2002) Statistical Properties of Stock Order Books: Empirical Results and Models, *Quantitative Finance* **2**, 251–256.

Boulatov, A. and T.J. George (2008) Securities Trading when Liquidity Providers are Informed, Working Paper.

Brennan, M.J. (1975) The Optimal Number of Securities in a Risky Asset Portfolio When There are Fixed Costs of Transacting: Theory and Some Empirical Results, *Journal of Financial and Quantitative Analysis* **10**(3), 483–496.

Brock, W.A. and C.H. Hommes (1997) A Rational Route to Randomness, *Econometrica* **65**, 1059–1095.

Brogaard, J.A. (2010) High Frequency Trading and Its Impact on Market Quality, Working Paper, Northwestern University.

Caldarelli, G., M. Marsili and Y.-C. Zhang (1997) A Prototype Model of Stock Exchange, *Europhysics Letters* **50**, 479–484.

Cao, C., O. Hansch and X. Wang (2008) The Information Content of an Open Limit-Order Book, *Journal of Futures Markets* **29**, 16–41.

Cespa, G. and T. Foucault (2011a) Sale of Price Information by Exchanges: Does It Promote Price Discovery?, Working Paper, HEC.

Cespa, G. and T. Foucault (2011b) Learning from Prices, Liquidity Spillovers, and Endogenous Market Segmentation, CEPR Working Paper 8350.

CESR (2010a) Trends, Risks and Vulnerabilities in Financial Markets, Report.

CESR (2010b) Call for Evidence: Micro-Structural Issues of the European Equity Markets.

CFTC & SEC (2010) Commodity and Futures Trading Commission and Securities and Exchange Commission, Findings Regarding the Market Events of May 6, 2010, Report of the Staffs of the CFTC and SEC to the Joint Advisory Committee on Emerging Regulatory Issues (September 30, 2010).

Chaboud, A., B. Chiquoine, E. Hjalmarsson and C. Vega (2009) Rise of the Machines: Algorithmic Trading in the Foreign Exchange Market, Working Paper, FED, New York.

Chakravarty, S. and C. Holden (1995) An Integrated Model of Market and Limit Orders, *Journal of Financial Intermediation* **4**, 213–241.

Challet, D. (2007) Inter-pattern Speculation: Beyond Minority, Majority and $-Games, *Journal of Economics, Dynamics and Control* **32**(1), 85–100.

Challet, D., A. De Martino, M. Marsili and I.P. Castillo (2005a) Minority games with finite score memory, *Journal of Experiment and Theory*, P03004, cond-mat/0407595.

Challet, D., M. Marsili and Y.-C. Zhang (2005b) *Minority Games*, Oxford University Press, Oxford.

Chan, K., Y.P. Chung and H. Johnson (1995) The Intraday Behavior of Bid-Ask Spreads for NYSE Stocks and CBOE Options, *Journal of Financial and Quantitative Analysis* **30**(3), 329–346.

Chan, L.K.C. and J. Lakonishok (1993) Institutional Trades and Intraday Stock Price Behavior, *Journal of Financial Economics* **33**, 173–199.

Chan, L.K.C. and J. Lakonishok (1995) The Behavior of Stock Prices around Institutional Trades, *Journal of Finance* **50**, 1147–1174.

Chordia, T., R. Roll and A. Subrahmanyam (2005) Evidence on the Speed of Convergence to Market Efficiency, *Journal of Financial Economics* **76**, 271–292.

Chordia, T., R. Roll and A. Subrahmanyam (2010) Recent Trends in Trading Activity, Working Paper, Anderson School, UCLA.

Christian Silva, A. (2005) Applications of Physics to Finance and Economics: Returns, Trading Activity and Income, PhD Thesis.

Chung, K., B. Van Ness and R. Van Ness (1999) Limit Orders and the Bid-Ask Spread, *Journal of Financial Economics* **53**, 255–287.

Clark, P.K. (1973) A Subordinated Stochastic Process Model with Finite Variance for Speculative Prices, *Econometrica* **41**(1), 135–155.

Cleveland, W.S. and S.J. Devlin (1988) Locally Weighted Regression: An Approach to Regression Analysis by Local Fitting, *Journal of the American Statistical Association* **83**(403), 596–610.

Cohen, K., S. Maier, R. Schwartz and D. Whitcomb (1981) Transaction Costs, Order Placement Strategy, and Existence of the Bid-Ask Spread, *Journal of Political Economy* **89**, 287–305.

Colliard, J.-E. and T. Foucault (2011) Trading Fees and Efficiency in Limit Order Markets, CEPR Discussion Paper Series 8395.

Cont, R., A. Kukanov and S. Stoikov (2011) The Price Impact of Order Book Events, SSRN eLibrary.

Copeland, T.E. and D. Galai (1983) Information Effects on the Bid-Ask Spread, *Journal of Finance* **38**, 1457–1469.

Criscuolo, A.M. and H. Waelbroeck (2010) Optimal Execution in Presence of Hidden Order Arbitrage, Pipeline Preprint PIPE-2011-01.

Dalalyan A. and N. Yoshida (2011) Second-Order Asymptotic Expansion for a Nonsynchronous Covariation Estimator, *Annales de l'Institut Henri Poincaré, Probabilités et Statistiques* **47**(3), 748–789.

De Jong, F. and T. Nijman (1997) High Frequency Analysis of Lead–Lag Relationships between Financial Markets, *Journal of Empirical Finance* **4**(2–3), 259–277.

Dea, S., N.R. Gondhib, V. Manglac and B. Pochirajud (2010) Success/Failure of Past Trades and Trading Behavior of Investors.

Demsetz, H. (1968) The Cost of Transacting, *Quarterly Journal of Economics* **82**, 33–53.

Dermoune, A. and Y. Kutoyants (1995) Expansion of Distribution of Maximum Likelihood Estimate for Misspecified Diffusion Type Observation, *Stochastics Report* **52**(1–2), 121–145.

Dohnal, G. (1987) On Estimating the Diffusion Coefficient, *Journal of Applied Probability* **24**(1), 105–114.

Dow, J. and G. Gorton (1997) Stock Market Efficiency and Economic Efficiency: Is There a Connection?, *Journal of Finance* **52**, 1087–1129.

Duffie, D. (2010) Presidential Address: Asset Price Dynamics with Slow Moving Capital, *Journal of Finance* **65**, 1237–1267.

Dufour, A. and R.F. Engle (2000) Time and the Price Impact of a Trade, *Journal of Finance* **55**(6) 2467–2498.

Easley, D., S. Hvidkjaer and M. O'Hara (2002) Is Information Risk a Determinant of Asset Returns?, *Journal of Finance* **57**, 2185–2221.

Efron, B. and R.-J. Tibshirani (1993) *An Introduction to the Bootstrap*, Chapman & Hall, New York.

Eisler, Z., J.-P. Bouchaud and J. Kockelkoren (2009) The Price Impact of Order Book Events: Market Orders, Limit Orders and Cancellations, SSRN eLibrary.

Eisler, Z., J.-P. Bouchaud and J. Kockelkoren (2010) The Price Impact of Order Book Events: Market Orders, Limit Orders and Cancellations, Working Paper.

Eisler, Z., J.-P. Bouchaud and J. Kockelkoren (2011) The Price Impact of Order Book Events: Market Orders, Limit Orders and Cancellations, arXiv:0904.0900, to appear in *Quantitative Finance*.

Ellul, A., C. Holden, P. Jain and R. Jennings (2005) Order Dynamics: Recent Evidence from the NYSE, Working Paper.

Engle, R.F. and A.J. Patton (2004) Impact of Trades in an Error-Correction Model of Quote Prices, *Journal of Financial Markets* **7**, 1–25.

Epps, T.W. (1979) Comovements in Stock Prices in the Very Short-Run., *Journal of the American Statistical Association* **74**, 291–298.

Farmer, J.D., A. Gerig, F. Lillo and S. Mike (2006) Market Efficiency and the Long-Memory of Supply and Demand: Is Price Impact Valuable and Permanent or Fixed and Temporary?, *Quantitative Finance* **6**, 107–112.

Farmer, J.D., A. Gerig, F. Lillo and H. Waelbroeck (2011) How Efficiency Shapes Market Impact, arXiv: 1102.5457v2[q-fin.TR].

Farmer, J.D., L. Gillemot, F. Lillo, S. Mike and A. Sen (2004) What Really Causes Large Price Changes?, *Quantitative Finance* **4**, 383–397.

Foucault, T. (1999) Order Flow Composition and Trading Costs in a Dynamic Limit Order Market, *Journal of Financial Markets* **2**, 99–134.

Foucault, T. and A.J. Menkveld (2008) Competition for Order Flow and Smart Order Routing Systems, *Journal of Finance* **63**, 119–158.

Foucault, T., O. Kadan and E. Kandel (2005) Limit Order Book as a Market for Liquidity. *Review of Financial Studies* **18**(4), 1171–1217.

Foucault, T., O. Kadan and E. Kandel (2010) Liquidity Cycles, and Make/Take Fees in Electronic Markets, CEPR Discussion Paper Series 7551.

Foucault, T., A. Roëll and P. Sandas (2003) Market Making with Costly Monitoring: An Analysis of SOES Trading, *Review of Financial Studies* **16**, 345–384.

Froot, K., D.S. Scharfstein and J. Stein (1992) Herd on the Street: Informational Inefficiencies in a Market with Short-Term Speculation, *Journal of Finance* **47**, 1461–1484.

Fukasawa, M. (2011) Asymptotic Analysis for Stochastic Volatility: Martingale Expansion, *Finance and Stochastics* **15**(4), 635–654.

Gabaix, X., P. Gopikrishnan, V. Plerou and H.E. Stanley (2006) Institutional Investors and Stock Market Volatility, *Quarterly Journal of Economics* **121**, 461–504.

Garman, M.B. (1976) Market Microstructure, *Journal of Financial Economics* **3**(3), 257–275.

Garvey, R. and F. Wu (2010) Speed, Distance, and Electronic Trading: New Evidence on Why Location Matters, *Journal of Financial Markets* **13**, 367–396.

Gatheral, J. (2010) No-Dynamic-Arbitrage and Market Impact, *Quantitative Finance* **10**(7), 749–759.

Genon-Catalot, V. and J. Jacod (1993) On the Estimation of the Diffusion Coefficient for Multidimensional Diffusion Processes. *Annales de l'Institut Henri Poincaré, Probabilités et Statistiques* **29**(1), 119–151.

Genon-Catalot, V. and J. Jacod (1994) Estimation of the Diffusion Coefficient for Diffusion Processes: Random Sampling, *Scandinavian Journal of Statistics* **21**(3), 193–221.

Gerig, A. (2008) A Theory for Market Impact: How Order Flow Affects Stock Price, PhD Thesis, arXiv:0804.3818.

Giardina, I. and J.-P. Bouchaud (2003) Bubbles, Crashes and Intermittency in Agent Based Market Models, *European Physics Journal Series B*, **31**(3), 421–437.

Glosten, L. (1994) Is the Electronic Open Limit Order Book Inevitable?, *Journal of Finance* **49**, 1127–1161.

Glosten, L.R. and P.R. Milgrom (1985) Bid, Ask and Transaction Prices in a Specialist Market with Heterogeneously Informed Traders, *Journal of Financial Economics* **14**(1), 71–100.

Goettler, R., C. Parlour and U. Rajan (2005) Equilibrium in a Dynamic Limit Order Market, *Journal of Finance* **60**, 2149–2192.

Goettler, R., C. Parlour and U. Rajan (2009) Informed Traders and Limit Order Markets, *Journal of Financial Economics* **93**, 67–87.

Goldstein, M. and K. Kavajecz (2000) Trading Strategies during Circuit Breakers and Extreme Market Movements, *Journal of Financial Markets* **7**, 301–333.

Gomes, C. and H. Waelbroeck (2008) Effect of Trading Velocity and Limit Prices on Implementation Shortfall, Pipeline Financial Group Preprint PIPE-2008-09-003.

Gomes, C. and H. Waelbroeck (2010) Transaction Cost Analysis to Optimize Trading Strategies, *Journal of Trading*, Fall **5**(4).

Gopikrishnan, P., V. Plerou, X. Gabaix and H.E. Stanley (2000) Statistical Properties of Share Volume Traded in Financial Markets, *Physical Review E* **62**(4), R4493–R4496.

Granado, B. and P. Garda (1997) Evaluation of the CNAPS Neuro-computer for the Simulation of MLPS with Receptive Fields, in *Biological and Artificial Computation: From Neuroscience to Technology*, J. Mira, R. Moreno-Dííz and K. Cabestany, (Eds), Vol. 1240 of *Lecture Notes in Computer Science*, Chapter 84, Springer, Berlin/Heidelberg. pp. 817–824.

Griffin, J.E. and R.C.A. Oomen (2011) Covariance Measurement in the Presence of Non-Synchronous Trading and Market Microstructure Noise, *Journal of Econometrics* **160**(1), 58–68.

Griffiths, M., B. Smith, A. Turnbull and R. White (2000) The Costs and Determinants of Order Aggressiveness, *Journal of Financial Economics* **56**, 65–88.

Grossman, S. and J. Stiglitz (1980) On the Impossibility of Informationaly Efficient Markets, *American Economic Review* **70**, 393–408.

Guéant, O., C.-A. Lehalle and J. Fernandez-Tapia (2011) Dealing with the Inventory Risk, Technical Report.

Handa, P. and R. Schwartz (1996) Limit Order Trading, *Journal of Finance* **51**, 1835–1861.

Handa, P., R. Schwartz and A. Tiwari (2003) Quote Setting and Price Formation in an Order Driven Market, *Journal of Financial Markets* **6**, 461–489.

Hansen, P.R. and A. Lunde (2006) Realized Variance and Market Microstructure Noise, *Journal of Business and Economic Statistics* **24**, 127–161.

Härdle, W.K., N. Hautsch and A. Mihoci (2009) Modelling and Forecasting Liquidity Supply Using Semiparametric Factor Dynamics, Discussion Paper 2009/18, Collaborative Research Center 649 "Economic Risk", Humboldt-Universität zu Berlin.

Härdle, W. and A. Kirman (1995) Nonclassical Demand: A Model-Free Examination of Price-Quantity Relations in the Marseille Fish Market, *Journal of Econometrics* **67**(1), 227–257.

Harris, L. (1997) Order Exposure and Parasitic Traders, Working Paper, Marshall School of Business, University of Southern California.

Harris, L. (1998) Optimal Dynamic Order Submission Strategies in Some Stylized Trading Problems, *Financial Markets, Institutions and Instruments* **7**(2).

Harris, L. and J. Hasbrouck (1996) Market versus Limit Orders: The Superdot Evidence on Order Submission Strategy, *Journal of Financial and Quantitative Analysis* **31**, 213–231.

Hasbrouck, J. (1991) Measuring the Information Content of Stock Trades, *Journal of Finance* **46**, 179–207.

Hasbrouck, J. (1995) One Security, Many Markets: Determining the Contribution to Price Discovery, *Journal of Finance* **50**, 1175–1199.

Hasbrouck, J. (2007) *Empirical Market Microstructure: The Institutions, Economics, and Econometrics of Securities Trading*, Oxford University Press.

Hasbrouck, J. and G. Saar (2009) Technology and Liquidity Provision: The Blurring of Traditional Definitions, *Journal of Financial Markets* **12**, 143–172.

Hasbrouck, J. and G. Saar (2010) Low-Latency Trading, Working Paper, New York University.

Hautsch, N. and R. Huang (2009) The Market Impact of a Limit Order, Working Paper.

Hayashi, T. and S. Kusuoka (2008) Consistent Estimation of Covariation Under Non-synchronicity, *Statistical Inference for Stochastic Processes* **11**, 93–106.

Hayashi T. and N. Yoshida (2005) On Covariance Estimation of Non-Synchronously Observed Diffusion Processes, *Bernoulli* **11**(2), 359–379.

Hayashi, T. and N. Yoshida (2008a) Asymptotic Normality of a Covariance Estimator for Nonsynchronously Observed Diffusion Processes, *Annals of the Institute of Statistical Mathematics* **60**(2), 367–406.

Hayashi, T. and N. Yoshida (2008b) Nonsynchronous Covariance Estimator and Limit Theorem II, Institute of Statistical Mathematics, Research Memorandum 1067.

Hayashi, T. and N. Yoshida (2011) Nonsynchronous Covariance Process and Limit Theorems, *Stochastic Processes and their Applications* **121**(10), 2416–2454.

Hayashi, T., J. Jacod and N. Yoshida (2008) Irregular Sampling and Central Limit Theorems for Power Variations: The Continuous Case, Preprint.

Hayek, F. (1945) The Use of Knowledge in Society, *American Economic Review* **35**, 519–530.

Hendershott, T. and R. Riordan (2009) Algorithmic Trading and Information, Working Paper, University of Berkeley.

Hendershott, T., C.M. Jones and A.J. Menkveld (2011) Does Algorithmic Trading Improve Liquidity? *Journal of Finance* **66**(1), 1–33.

Ho, T. and H.R. Stoll (1981) Optimal Dealer Pricing Under Transactions and Return Uncertainty, *Journal of Financial Economics* **9**(1), 47–73.

Hoffmann, M., M. Rosenbaum and N. Yoshida (2010) Estimation of the Lead–Lag Parameter From Non-Synchronous Data, to appear in *Bernoulli*.

Hollifield, B., R. Miller and P. Sandås (2004) Empirical Analysis of Limit Order Markets, *Review of Economic Studies* **71**, 1027–1063.

Hollifield, B., R. Miller, P. Sandås and J. Slive (2006) Estimating the Gains from Trade in Limit-Order Markets, *Journal of Finance* **61**, 2753–2804.

Hora, M. (2006) The Practice of Optimal Execution. *Algorithmic Trading* **2**, 52–60.

Hoshikawa, T., K. Nagai, T. Kanatani and Y. Nishiyama (2008) Nonparametric Estimation Methods of Integrated Multivariate Volatilities, *Econometric Reviews* **27**(1–3), 112–138.

Huang, R. and T. Polak (2011) LOBSTER: The Limit Order Book Reconstructor, Discussion Paper, School of Business and Economics, Humboldt Universität zu Berlin, http://lobster.wiwi.hu-berlin.de/Lobster/LobsterReport.pdf.

Huberman, G. and W. Stanzl (2005) Optimal Liquidity Trading, *Review of Finance* **9**, 165–200.

Jacod, J. (1996) La variation Quadratique Moyenne du Brownien en Présence d'Erreurs d'Arrondi. In *Hommage a P.A. Meyer et J. Neveu*, Vol. 236, Asterisque.

Johansen, S. (1991) Estimation and Hypothesis Testing of Cointegration Vectors in Gaussian Vector Autoregressive Models, *Econometrica* **59**, 1551–1580.

Johansen, S. and K. Juselius (1990) Maximum Likelihood Estimation and Inference on Cointegration – With Applications to the Demand for Money, *Oxford Bulletin of Economics and Statistics* **52**, 169–210.

Johnson, N.F., M. Hart, P.M. Hui and D. Zheng (2000) Trader Dynamics in a Model Market, *ITJFA* **3**, cond-mat/9910072.

Jovanovic, B. and A. Menkveld (2011) Middlemen in Limit Order Markets, Working Paper, VU University Amsterdam.

Kaniel, R. and H. Liu (2006) So What Orders Do Informed Traders Use?, *Journal of Business* **79**, 1867–1913.

Kato, H., S. Sato and N. Yoshida (2011) Analysis of Foreign Exchange Data with the Lead-Lag Estimator (in Japanese), The 2011 Japanese Joint Statistical Meeting, 4–7 September 2011, Fukuoka.

Kavajecz, K. and E. Odders-White (2004) Technical Analysis and Liquidity Provision, *Review of Financial Studies* **17**, 1043–1071.

Keim, D. and A. Madhavan (1995) Execution Costs and Investment Performance: An Empirical Analysis of Institutional Equity Trades, Working Paper.

Kessler, M. (1997) Estimation of an Ergodic Diffusion from Discrete Observations, *Scandinavian Journal of Statistics* **24**(2), 211–229.

Khandani, A. and A.W. Lo (2011) What Happened to the Quants in August 2007? Evidence from Factors and Transactions Data, *Journal of Financial Markets*, **14**(1), 1–46.

Kirilenko, A.A., A.S. Kyle, M. Samadi and T. Tuzun (2011) The Flash Crash: the Impact of High Frequency Trading on an Electronic Market, Working Paper, University of Maryland.

Kozhan, R. and W.W. Tham (2010) Arbitrage Opportunities: A Blessing or a Curse?, Working Paper, University of Warwick.

Kunitomo, N. and A. Takahashi (2001) The Asymptotic Expansion Approach to the Valuation of Interest Rate Contingent Claims, *Mathematical Finance* **11**(1), 117–151.

Kusuoka, S. and N. Yoshida (2000) Malliavin Calculus, Geometric Mixing, and Expansion of Diffusion Functionals, *Probability Theory and Related Fields* **116**(4), 457–484.

Kutoyants, Y.A. and N. Yoshida (2007) Moment estimation for ergodic diffusion processes, *Bernoulli* **13**(4), 933–951.

Kyle, A.P. (1985), Continuous Auctions and Insider Trading, *Econometrica* **53**(6), 1315–1335.

Large, J. (2009) A Market-Clearing Role for Inefficiency on a Limit Order Book, *Journal of Financial Economics* **91**, 102–117.

Laruelle, S., C.-A. Lehalle and G. Pagès (2011) Optimal Posting Distance of Limit Orders: A Stochastic Algorithm Approach.

Latza, T. and R. Payne (2011) Forecasting Returns and Trading Equities Intra-Day Using Limit Order and Market Order Flows, Working Paper.

Lewis, E. and G. Mohler (2011) A Nonparametric EM algorithm for Multiscale Hawkes Processes, Working Paper.

Li, C. (2010) Managing Volatility Risk: Innovation of Financial Derivatives, Stochastic Models and Their Analytical Implementation, Columbia University.

Lillo, F., J.D. Farmer and R.N. Mantegna (2003) Econophysics – Master Curve for Price – Impact Function, *Nature* **421**(6919), 129.

Lo, I. and S. Sapp (2005) Price Aggressiveness and Quantity: How Are They Determined in a Limit Order Market?, Working Paper.

Loeb, T.F. (1983) Trading Cost: The Critical Link between Investment Information and Results, *Financial Analysts Journal* **39**(3), 39–44.

Lütkepohl, H. (1990) Asymptotic Distributions of Impulse Response Functions and Forecast Error Variance Decompositions of Vector Autoregressive Models, *Review of Economics and Statistics* **72**, 116–125.

Lux, T. and M. Marchesi (1999) Scaling and Criticality in a Stochastic Multi-Agent Model of a Financial Market, *Nature* **397**, 498–500.

Lyons, R.K. (2006) *The Microstructure Approach to Exchange Rates,* MIT Press.

Madhavan, A. (2000) Market Microstructure: A Survey, *Journal of Financial Markets* **3**, 205–258.

Malliavin, P. and M.E. Mancino (2002) Fourier Series Method for Measurement of Multivariate Volatilities, *Finance and Stochastics* **6**(1), 49–61.

Masuda, H. (2010) Approximate Self-Weighted Lad Estimation of Discretely Observed Ergodic Ornstein-Uhlenbeck Processes, *Electronic Journal of Statistics* **4**, 525–565.

Masuda, H. and N. Yoshida (2004) An Application of the Double Edgeworth Expansion to a Filtering Model with Gaussian Limit, *Statistical Probability Letters* **70**(1), 37–48.

Masuda, H. and N. Yoshida (2005) Asymptotic Expansion for Barndorff–Nielsen and Shephard's Stochastic Volatility Model, *Stochastic Processes Application* **115**(7), 1167–1186.

Mendelson, H. (1982) Market Behavior in a Clearing House, *Econometrica* **50**(6), 1505–1524.

Menkhoff, L., C. Osler and M. Schmeling (2010) Limit-Order Submission Strategies under Asymmetric Information, *Journal of Banking and Finance* **34**, 2665–2677.

Menkveld, A. (2011) High Frequency Trading and the New-Market Makers, Working Paper, VU University, Amsterdam.

Mike, S. and J.D. Farmer (2008) An Empirical Behavioral Model of Liquidity and Volatility, *Journal of Economic Dynamics and Control* **32**, 200.

Moro, E., L.G. Moyano, J. Vicente, A. Gerig, J.D. Farmer, G. Vaglica, F. Lillo and R.N. Mantegna (2009) Market Impact and Trading Protocols of Hidden Orders in Stock Markets, Technical Report.

Morton de Lachapelle, D. and D. Challet (2010) Turnover, Account Value and Diversification of Real Traders: Evidence of Collective Portfolio Optimizing Behavior, *New Journal of Physics* **12**, 075039.

Mykland, P. (2010) A Gaussian Calculus for Inference from High Frequency Data, *Annals of Finance*.

Mykland, P.A. (1992) Asymptotic Expansions and Bootstrapping Distributions for Dependent Variables: A Martingale Approach, *Anuals of Statistics.* **20**(2), 623–654.

Mykland, P.A. (1993) Asymptotic Expansions for Martingales, *Anuals Probability* **21**(2), 800–818.

Obizhaeva, A. and J. Wang (2006) Optimal Trading Strategy and Supply/Demand Dynamics, Technical Report, AFA 2006 Boston Meetings Paper.

Ogata, Y., D. Vere-Jones and J. Zhuang (2002) Stochastic Declustering of Space–Time Earthquake Occurrences, *Journal of the American Statistical Association* **97**, 369–380.

Ogihara, T. and N. Yoshida (2011) Quasi-likelihood Analysis for the Stochastic Differential Equation with Jumps, *Statistical Inference for Stochastic Processes* **14**, 189–229.

O'Hara, M. (1995) *Market Microstructure Theory*, Blackwell.

Osajima, Y. (2006) The Asymptotic Expansion Formula of Implied Volatility for Dynamic SABR Model and FX Hybrid Model, UTMS 2006–29.

Pagès, G., S. Laruelle and C.-A. Lehalle (2009) Optimal split of orders across liquidity pools: a stochatic algorithm approach, Technical Report.

Pakes, A. and P. McGuire (2001) Stochastic Algorithms, Symmetric Markov Perfect Equilibrium, and the "Curse" of Dimensionality, *Econometrica* **69**, 1261–1281.

Parlour, C. (1998) Price Dynamics in Limit Order Markets, *Review of Financial Studies* **11**, 789–816.

Parlour, C. and D. Seppi (2008) Limit Order Markets: A Survey, in *Handbook of Financial Intermediation and Banking*, A.V. Thaker and A. Boot (Eds), Elsevier.

Podolskij, M. and M. Vetter (2009) Estimation of Volatility Functionals in the Simultaneous Presence of Microstructure Noise and Jumps, *Bernoulli Official Journal of the Bernoulli Society for Mathematical Statistics and Probability* **15**(3), 634–658.

Prakasa Rao, B.L.S. (1983) Asymptotic Theory for Nonlinear Least Squares Estimator for Diffusion Processes, *Mathematische Operationsforschung und Statistik Series Statistics* **14**(2), 195–209.

Prakasa Rao, B.L.S. (1988) Statistical Inference from Sampled Data for Stochastic Processes. In *Statistical Inference from Stochastic Processes,* Ithaca, New York, 1987, American Mathematical Society, Providence, Rhode Island; *Contemporary Mathematics* **80**, 249–284.

Ranaldo, A. (2004) Order Aggressiveness in Limit Order Book Markets, *Journal of Financial Markets* **7**, 53–74.

Robert, C.Y. and M. Rosenbaum (2010a) A New Approach for the Dynamics of Ultra-High-Frequency Data: The Model With Uncertainty Zones, *Journal of Financial Econometrics Advance Access* 1–23.

Robert, C.Y. and M. Rosenbaum (2010b) Volatility and Covariation Estimation When Microstructure Noise and Trading Times are Endogenous, *Mathematical Finance*, DOI: 10.1111/j.14679965.2010.00454.x.

Robert, C.Y. and M. Rosenbaum (2010) On the Microstructural Hedging Error, *SIAM Journal on Financial Mathematics* **1**, 427–453.

Rock, K. (1996) The Specialist's Order Book and Price Anomalies, Working Paper.

Roşu, I. (2009) A Dynamic Model of the Limit Order Book, *Review of Financial Studies* **22**, 4601–4641.

Roşu, I. (2010) Liquidity and Information in Order Driven Markets, SSRN eLibrary.

Russell, J. and T. Kim (2010) A New Model for Limit Order Book Dynamics, in *Volatility and Time Series Econometrics, Essays in Honor of Robert Engle*, T. Bollerslev, J. Russell and M. Watson (Eds), Oxford University Press.

Sérié, E. (2010) unpublished report, Capital Fund Management, Paris, France.

Sakamoto, Y. and N. Yoshida (1996) Expansion of Perturbed Random Variables Based on Generalized Wiener Functionals, *Journal of Multivariate Analysis* **59**(1), 34–59.

Sakamoto, Y. and N. Yoshida (1998a) Asymptotic Expansion of M-Estimator Over Wiener Space, *Statistical Inference of Stochastic Processes* **1**(1), 85–103.

Sakamoto, Y. and N. Yoshida (1998b) Third Order Asymptotic Expansion for Diffusion Process, *Theory of Statistical Analysis and Its Applications* **107**, 53–60.

Sakamoto, Y. and N. Yoshida (2003) Asymptotic expansion under degeneracy, *Journal of Japan Statistical Society* **33**(2), 145–156.

Sakamoto, Y. and N. Yoshida (2004) Asymptotic Expansion Formulas for Functionals of ϵ-Markov Processes with a Mixing Property, *Annals of the Institute of Statistical Mathematics* **56**(3), 545–597.

Sakamoto, Y. and N. Yoshida (2008) Asymptotic Expansion for Stochastic Processes: An Overview and Examples, *Journal of Japan Statistical Society* **38**(1), 173–185.

Sakamoto, Y. and N. Yoshida (2009) Third-Order Asymptotic Expansion of M-Estimators for Diffusion Processes, *Annals of the Institute of Statistical Mathematics* **61**(3), 629–661.

Sakamoto, Y. and N. Yoshida (2010) Asymptotic Expansion for Functionals of a Marked Point Process, *Communications in Statistics – Theory and Methods* **39**(8,9), 1449–1465.

SEC (2010) Concept Release on Equity Market Structure, Release 34-61358; File S7-02-10.

Seppi, D. (1997) Liquidity Provision with Limit Orders and a Strategic Specialist, *Review of Financial Studies* **10**, 103–150.

Sérié, E. (2010) Unpublished Report, Capital Fund Management, Paris, France.

Sharpe, W.F. (1964) Capital Asset Prices: A Theory of Market Equilibrium Under Conditions of Risk, *Journal of Finance* **19**(3), 425–442.

Silva, A.C. (2005) Applications of Physics to Finance and Economics: Returns, Trading Activity and Income. PhD Thesis.

Sorkenmaier, A. and M. Wagener (2011) Do We Need a European "National Market System"? Competition, Arbitrage, and Suboptimal Executions, Working Paper, Karlsruhe Institute of Technology.

Stoll, H.R. (2000) Friction, *Journal of Finance* **55**, 1479–1514.

Surowiecki, J. (2005) *The Wisdom of Crowds*, Anchor Books, New York.

Szabó, G. and C. Hauert (2002) Phase Transitions and Volunteering in Spatial Public Goods Games, *Physical Review Letters* **89**(11), 118101, August.

Takahashi, A. and K. Takehara (2009) Asymptotic Expansion Approaches in Finance: Applications to Currency Options, *Discussion Paper F Series*, URL http://repository. dl.itc.utokyo.ac.jp/dspace/handle/2261/26663.

Takahashi, A. and N. Yoshida (2004) An Asymptotic Expansion Scheme for Optimal Investment Problems, *Statistical Inference for Stochastic Processes* **7**, 153–188.

Takahashi, A. and N. Yoshida (2005) Monte Carlo Simulation with Asymptotic Method, *Journal of Japan Statistical Society* **35**, 171–203.

Torre, N. (1997) *Market Impact Model Handbook*, Barra Inc., Berkeley.

Tóth, B., Z. Eisler, F. Lillo, J.-P. Bouchaud, J. Kockelkoren and J.D. Farmer (2011) How Does the Market React to Your Order Flow, Working Paper.

Tóth, B. (2011) In preparation.

Tóth, B., Z. Eisler, F. Lillo, J.-P. Bouchaud, J. Kockelkoren and J. Farmer (2011) How Does the Market React to Your Order Flow?, arXiv:1104.0587.

Ubukata, M. and K. Oya (2008) A Test for Dependence and Covariance Estimator of Market Microstructure Noise. Discussion Papers In Economics and Business, 07-03, February 2007.

Uchida, M. (2010a) Adaptative Estimation of an Ergodic Diffusion Process Based on Sampled Data. In Proceedings of DYNSTOCH Meeting 2010, Angers, France, June 16–19, 2010.

Uchida, M. (2010b) Contrast-Based Information Criterion for Ergodic Diffusion Processes from Discrete Observations, *Annals of the Institute of Statistical Mathematics* **62**(1), 161–187.

Uchida, M. and N. Yoshida (2001) Information Criteria in Model Selection for Mixing Processes, *Statistical Inference for Stochastic Processes* **4**(1), 73–98.

Uchida, M. and N. Yoshida (2004a) Asymptotic Expansion for Small Diffusions Applied to Option Pricing, *Statistical Inference for Stochastic Processes* **7**(3), 189–223.

Uchida, M. and N. Yoshida (2004b) Information Criteria for Small Diffusions via the Theory of Malliavin-Watanabe, *Statistical Inference for Stochastic Processes* **7**(1), 35–67.

Uchida, M. and N. Yoshida (2006) Asymptotic Expansion and Information Criteria, *SUT Journal of Mathematics* **42**(1), 31–58.

Uchida, M. and N. Yoshida (2009) Estimation of the Volatility for Stochastic Differential Equations. In Asymptotical Statistics of Stochastic Processes VII, LeMans, March 16–19.

Uchida, M. and N. Yoshida (2010) Adaptive Estimation of an Ergodic Diffusion Process Based on Sampled Data, Preprint.

Uchida, M. and N. Yoshida (2011) Nondegeneracy of Statistical Random Field and Quasi Likelihood Analysis for Diffusion, Institute of Statistical Mathematics, Research Memorandum 1149.

Vives, X. (1995) Short-Term Investment and the Informational Efficiency of the Market, *Review of Financial Studies* **8**, 125–160.

Wald, J. and H. Horrigan (2005) Optimal Limit Order Choice, *Journal of Business* **78**, 597–619.

Watanabe, S. (1987) Analysis of Wiener Functionals (Malliavin Calculus) and Its Applications to Heat Kernels, *Annals of Probability* **15**(1), 1–39.

Weber, P. and B. Rosenow (2005) Order Book Approach to Price Impact, *Quantitative Finance* **5**, 357.

Whitt, W. (2002) Stochastic-Process Limits, *Springer*.

Yoshida, N. (1992a) Asymptotic Expansion for Statistics Related to Small Diffusions, *Journal of Japan Statistical Society* **22**(2), 139–159, URL http://www2.ms.utokyo.ac.jp/probstat/?page id=23.

Yoshida, N. (1992b) Asymptotic Expansions of Maximum Likelihood Estimators for Small Diffusions Via the Theory of Malliavin–Watanabe, *Probability Theory and Related Fields* **92**(3), 275–311.

Yoshida, N. (1992c) Estimation for Diffusion Processes from Discrete Observation, *Journal of Multivariate Analysis* **41**(2), 220–242.

Yoshida, N. (1993) Asymptotic Expansion of Bayes Estimators for Small Diffusions, *Probability Theory and Related Fields* **95**(4), 429–450.

Yoshida, N. (1997) Malliavin Calculus and Asymptotic Expansion for Martingales, *Probability Theory and Related Fields* **109**(3), 301–342.

Yoshida, N. (2001) Malliavin Calculus and Martingale Expansion, *Bulletin of Scientific Mathematics* **125**(6–7), 431–456; also *Rencontre Franco-Japonaise de Probabilités* Paris, 2000.

Yoshida, N. (2004) Partial Mixing and Conditional Edgeworth Expansion for Diffusions with Jumps, *Probability Theory and Related Fields* **129**, 559–624.

Yoshida, N. (2005) Polynomial Type Large Deviation Inequality and Its Applications, Preprint.

Yoshida, N. (2006) Polynomial Type Large Deviation Inequalities and Convergence of Statistical Random Fields, The Institute of Statistical Mathematics Research Memorandum 1021.

Yoshida, N. (2008) Expansion of Asymptotically Conditionally Normal Law. In Finace and Related Mathematical and Statistical Issues, Kyoto Research Park, Kyoto, September 3–6, 2008.

Yoshida, N. (2009) Asymptotic Expansion for the Asymptotically Conditionally Normal Law. SAPS VII, March 16–19, 2009.

Yoshida, N. (2010a) Expansion of the Asymptotically Conditionally Normal Law, The Institute of Statistical Mathematics Research Memorandum 1125.

Yoshida, N. (2010b) Quasi-likelihood Analysis and Limit Theorems for Stochastic Differential Equations. In Market Microstructure, Confronting Many Viewpoints, Institut Louis Bachelier, Paris.

Zhang, F. (2010) High Frequency Trading, Stock Volatility, and Price Discovery, Working Paper, Yale University.

Zhang, L. (2011) Estimating Covariation: Epps Effect, Microstructure Noise, *Journal of Econometrics* **160**(1), 33–47.

Zhang, L., P.A. Mykland and Y. Aät-Sahalia (2005) A Tale of Two Time Scales: Determining Integrated Volatility with Noisy High-Frequency Data, *Journal of the American Statistical Association* **100**(472), 1394–1411.

Zhou, B. (1996) High-Frequency Data and Volatility in Foreign-Exchange Rates, *Journal of Business and Economic Statistics* **14**, 45–52.

Index

Index compiled by Terry Halliday